A Mobile Fortune

Siobhán Creaton is a journalist and author. Her book *Ryanair*, the story of Europe's biggest airline, first published in 2004, is still a bestseller. She previously co-authored *Panic at the Bank*, published in 2002. Creaton is a former *Irish Times* finance correspondent. She lives in Dublin.

www.siobhancreaton.com

A Mobile Fortune
The Life and Times of **Denis O'Brien**

Siobhán Creaton

Contents

1 The Silver Chicken

The Gulfstream jet purred on the runway ready for take-off. As the taxi approached the pilot made the final checks. They would be airborne within minutes, jetting off to another South Pacific island.

It was a short enough journey to the airport. The billionaire and his colleague, his business development director, patted their pockets to find the $90 for the driver. They had little cash. It was a whistle-stop detour in the middle of a hectic schedule of meetings. Together they found just enough to pay the fare. They handed over the money and moved briskly to make their departure.

As they walked towards the runway, chatting to airport officials. Ken Mason, the business development director, mentioned that the taxi fare seemed expensive. The officials agreed: it should be about $40.

Suddenly the middle-aged Irish telecoms tycoon stopped. He wasn't happy about it. They had been ripped off. He turned back and re-entered the airport. He wanted a refund. 'Denis was raging,' Mason says. 'He said he wouldn't be leaving the airport without that money.' Fifty-two-year-old Denis O'Brien, whose fast-growing mobile phone company, Digicel, was the newest in the region, had a score to settle.

The officials and the airport police reacted promptly to the commotion and soon the taxi driver was found and guided back to meet his last passenger. He was stunned to be at the centre of this unfolding drama but wasn't immediately inclined to refund the alleged excess to the successful businessman, who had assured him he was a force to be reckoned with. He would call a lawyer if he had to, but he wasn't leaving without his $50, O'Brien told him. One of the policemen eventually intervened. 'If I were you,' he told the taxi driver, 'I would refund the money.' The driver handed back the $50, and O'Brien was ready to board his plane.

Throughout the standoff his powerful white jet, with the distinctive blue wave on the side, had been burning fuel. That was irrelevant to O'Brien; it was all about proving a point. 'Don't ever let anyone rip you off,' he told Mason. 'Denis always stands firm for fair play,' says Mason.

Denis O'Brien is a man who has to win at all costs. In 2010, the telecoms tycoon was in the eye of a perfect storm. In Ireland he was defending his reputation in light of allegations linking him with political corruption that have been the subject of a thirteen-year investigation. A High Court judge has examined whether O'Brien paid money to the government minister who in 1996 awarded his group a mobile phone licence: the foundation of his great fortune. His preliminary findings, says O'Brien, who vehemently denies any impropriety, are 'devastating' for him. He is the victim of a grave injustice, he believes, and he will be fighting the inquiry's outcome 'street by street'. He is determined to clear his name.

It had been a horrendous start to the new decade for the Irishman. The earthquake in Haiti was a blow to his Caribbean empire. O'Brien, who owns the Digicel mobile phone network that spans the Caribbean, Central America and the South Pacific, arrived swiftly in Port-au-Prince to see the devastation and help the aid efforts. He is one of the biggest international investors in the western hemisphere's poorest country and has pledged, with former US President Bill Clinton, to support international efforts to create a viable economy for the Haitian people. 'Denis O'Brien and I are going into old age fighting for Haiti's future,' Clinton said days after the disaster as they began to formulate a type of Marshall Plan for the impoverished country.

Digicel's headquarters was the only building still standing in Port-au-Prince's business district after the earthquake. A new structure built to withstand such a natural disaster, it had been home to Digicel and its staff for just six months. Their former office block had been reduced to rubble. 'They had been lucky,' O'Brien said. Even so, some of the company's staff were killed, while almost all lost family members and their homes that day. Haiti was a big market for the Digicel group, accounting for about twenty per cent of its Caribbean revenues. It will take some time to restore.

O'Brien's Digicel empire has been built in some of the world's poorest, most dangerous and corrupt countries. He has invested where others fear to tread and today his company operates in thirty-two countries worldwide, with more than ten-million customers and five-and-a-half-thousand staff. It is the 'best business' he has ever been involved with, he says.

Its success has catapulted him into the ranks of the world's super-rich with an estimated €2.5 billion fortune. He is one of the new breed of entrepreneurs who thrived during the heady days of Ireland's golden economic era, the so-called 'Celtic Tiger'. O'Brien is one of Ireland's most successful and, some would say, most controversial businessmen.

It has never been about the money, he claims. 'I've had enough money to live on since I was sixteen. I am not driven to make more and more money, it happens on the way.' It is all about beating the competition. 'I spend my time thinking of ways to create a downfall for my competitor, particularly if they are big.' Money is the scorecard, the ultimate barometer of his success.

Born into very comfortable family circumstances, O'Brien attributes his early interest in business to his father, also named Denis, a successful businessman who instilled a strong work ethic into his four children. His apprenticeship with Irish business titan Tony Ryan later showed him how to create a world-class business.

The founder of Europe's biggest low-cost airline, Ryanair, spawned more than one controversial business figure. Michael O'Leary, another of Ryan's apprentices, is the man who for the past decade has mercilessly taken the frills out of flying. O'Brien's friends like to claim there is no comparison between the two men's achievements. The Ryanair boss, in their view, is a brilliant 'manager', whereas O'Brien is an exceptional 'entrepreneur', the ultimate risk-taker.

Broad shouldered and burly, O'Brien is a mass of contradictions. He is the man who will mercilessly slash costs within his companies, but

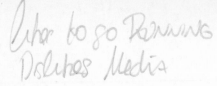

who is also known to be immensely generous and kind to friends, colleagues and even strangers.

Just as he credits his father for his induction into the business world, so his mother Iris inspired his life-long support of Amnesty International and its struggle to defend human rights and free speech. He has also established FrontLine, an international organisation for the protection of human-rights defenders. Yet while he upholds these ideals, he despises journalists and those in the media who report on his business activities in a negative light. He believes they are working to an agenda to destroy him and has shown he is willing to go to great lengths to stop them.

Some believe his more-than-€500 million failed attempt to gain control of the Independent News and Media group was about settling scores with its founder, Sir Anthony O'Reilly. O'Brien believes the newspaper group has written more negative and upsetting stories about him since the mid-1990s than any other section of the Irish media. He is said to personally blame Sir Anthony for what he believes has been a pattern of unfair coverage; something the newspaper group denies. Publicly O'Brien insists his assault on the Independent group is not motivated by his personal feelings..

He has remained reticent about his long-term intentions in relation to the group, saying he hasn't even discussed it with his wife, Catherine. According to O'Brien himself, however, his five-year-old son has raised the matter with him. 'Who is the awful man you are having a row with?' he asked, having seen his father's picture in the paper.

O'Brien has always wanted his own media empire and already owns forty radio stations throughout Europe. His close friends say his interest in the fourth estate is almost unhealthy. He reads everything that is written about him and clearly recognises the great power conferred on those who control the sector. In Ireland he owns two nationwide radio stations as well as a number of local stations, something that already makes him a powerful media figure. Should he gain control of the Independent group he would dominate the Irish media, a prospect that is viewed with some trepidation.

A long-distance runner himself, he has run marathons and triathlons and enjoys nothing more than a test of his endurance.

When he is in Ireland he loves to run in the County Wicklow Mountains around Lough Dan, a place where as a student he devised his own 'Krypton Factor' contest for his close friends, named after the television series based on an army assault course. He still likes to run and has been known to turn up for a business meeting in shorts, having jogged to it.

He values his close circle of friends, many of whom he has known since his days at university. Those who know the gang refer to them as his 'rat pack'. They include people he calls Rocky, MarsBar, Honda and Basher. Many of them have joined O'Brien in his business pursuits and have made a lot of money as a result. Among his friends he is seen as a bit of a 'folk hero', one person says, 'the archetypal bad boy'. When they talk about him, they mention his hilarious escapades, his brushes with authority and his incredible ability always to come out on top against all odds. He was the leader of the pack, the guy who set the bar for all of their pursuits. He always behaved like a millionaire, driving a flash car, meticulously groomed but still firmly 'one of the lads'.

Others say O'Brien likes to impress people he meets by playing down his very middle-class background, magnifying his achievements by portraying himself as someone who came from 'humble beginnings'. He is prone to exaggerating his many stories about his exploits and above all wants to be seen as an ordinary bloke. 'He likes to say he learned about business selling his father's horse products outside the Kentucky Derby. He likes to portray that image of a young man with nothing who has done well for himself – one person remarks 'but he is a "D4 man" [a reference to O'Brien's prestigious Dublin City postal address] into rugby and into cars,' O'Brien is described as a 'hyper-sensitive' person who prizes loyalty above everything else. If you are loyal to him, say friends, he will cherish and look after you for ever. You will find yourself within what one acquaintance describes as the 'circle of love'. His generosity and goodwill to those treasured friends is boundless.

His mercurial nature can be challenging, though, even for his closest friends. Most have experienced a cooling in their relationship at various times, due perhaps to a disagreement or to having committed the ultimate sin – behaving in a fashion he perceives to be disloyal.

His associates, who have experienced temporary exile, refer to these periods as being put 'in the freezer'. Some will eventually be allowed to thaw out again, often following an intervention from someone who has O'Brien's ear, and find their relationship restored. Others can remain in cold storage for several years or for ever. 'He is a bad enemy,' they say.

Known to friends and colleagues as Denis or D.O.B., O'Brien uses a language of his own that can be hilarious and caustic. He is as likely to greet you in his south Dublin drawl, with a friendly 'How the fuck are you?' or 'How'ya, sport?', as with the kind of formal warm welcome reserved for the prime ministers and other dignitaries he regularly meets in the course of his business.

Chasing new opportunities is just part of 'having the craic' (having fun) for O'Brien, he says. He enjoys regaling audiences with often wildly exaggerated and hilarious stories about his business exploits and is always encouraging would-be entrepreneurs to follow his lead. They shouldn't be afraid to 'go over the cliff' in his view. Risks are always worth taking.

Those who deal with O'Brien need to familiarise themselves with his lexicon of colourful phrases. If he describes a situation as 'totally SIPTU', it means it's a shambles; his damning indictment of anything associated with Ireland's biggest trade union. An invitation to join him for 'a nosebag' could be lunch or dinner and if he's 'on the blower', which he always is, it means he's on his mobile phone, an old-style Nokia model. He is famous for taking four phone calls at the same time, putting each caller on hold as he works his way through the various conversations. And he relentlessly bombards those who work for him with phone calls and text messages.

Digicel's chief technology officer, Mario Assaad, devised his own formula to get to grips with his chairman's language. The Lebanese executive started a phrasebook, meticulously writing down O'Brien's colourful remarks and asking his Irish colleagues to interpret them. If the Digicel boss tells his team something is 'shite', Assaad should interpret that as 'bad', they explained. Over many months he compiled a glossary of O'Brien-isms. When he says, 'I will in my bollix', Assaad noted that the meaning is 'no'; an instruction to 'cop on' means to use some sense in dealing with an issue; and the two greatest insults in the Digicel world are for its founder to tell someone they have become either a 'gardener' or 'too corporate'. The former means O'Brien thinks you are not working hard enough; the latter that you have become too bureaucratic. Should you fail to swiftly address either of those criticisms, you will be shown the door.

O'Brien is quick to assign a nickname to those he encounters, although he doesn't have one himself − or at least none that his colleagues will admit to. Almost everyone at Digicel has a nickname that its chairman can change depending on the situation. His right-hand man and long-time ally, Leslie Buckley, is known as 'the Sniper' for his cost-cutting ways. Lucy Gaffney, the woman colleagues describe as O'Brien's fearsome shadow, is 'Lucy Gaddafi', while another loyal lieutenant, Seamus Lynch, blessed with youthful good looks, is called 'Boyzone'. O'Brien enjoys teasing his colleagues but tends not to appreciate any reciprocation.

He likes to be seen as 'one of the lads' who enjoys going for a pint and watching rugby with his mates. When he is in Ireland he likes to go to a match with his gang of friends or to hang out at Hartigan's, known to him as 'Harto's'; his favourite bar since his college days. While he is a billionaire, he just wants to be seen as an ordinary bloke; unaffected by his great wealth and his achievements. Friends say he never invested in a big art collection because he didn't want to look like he is 'losing the run of himself to the lads', although he proudly displays paintings around his office by his sister Abigail, who is a respected artist and whose work is exhibited in Ireland's Museum of Modern Art.

His $60 million Gulfstream 550 jet is his greatest extravagance, but is something he regards as a necessity for someone with a diverse global business. It is his office and, like everything else in his midst, it too has a nickname: the 'silver chicken'. The Irishman regularly circles the globe and is said to be the second highest user of a Gulfstream jet, using it almost three times more often than the average corporate-jet owner.

People talk about his incredible work ethic. While he jets around the world he is constantly working, dealing with documents even when everyone else around him is catching a few winks. He drinks copious amounts of tea while travelling and always has teabags in his

*Loves Rugby follows
                All Sports*

briefcase; he is said to be conscious of the physical toll exacted by his jet-setting lifestyle and tries to keep fit.

O'Brien is a sports fanatic, and while his first love is rugby he has stepped in to assist the Irish soccer team's performance. He was said to be so frustrated at Ireland's failure to qualify for the Euro 2008 final he felt he should do something about it.

His friend, Eddie Jordan, the founder and former owner of the Jordan Grand Prix Formula One team, suggested someone should think about giving the Football Association of Ireland (FAI) a hand to pay for a top international manager who might make a difference to the squad. So O'Brien told the FAI to 'go and get as good as you can buy', knowing they could rely on his financial support. And when FAI boss John Delaney told him they wanted to sign up the legendary Italian coach, Giovanni Trapattoni, as manager, he was delighted. 'Jesus, Trapattoni, fantastic!' he replied and agreed to pay half of a two-year deal worth almost €3 million and has renewed it in a successive deal with the Ireland manager.

'I'm a great believer that if you hire the right people you get the right results,' O'Brien said when the news broke. A chance meeting with Samoa's Prime Minister, Tuilaepa Sailele Malielegao, prompted another magnanimous gesture. When the premier complained that New Zealand was poaching the country's top rugby players with lucrative salaries, O'Brien offered to help. Digicel would strike a sponsorship deal with the Samoa Rugby Union that included a development fund to help to retain the best players. 'This is a bit of an experiment and I may do more of this in other parts of the world,' he explained. 'I hate bullies and New Zealand bullies the islands.'

He also chaired the committee that hosted the Special Olympics World Games in Ireland in 2003, the first time the event was staged outside the USA. It was a huge undertaking that involved raising €60 million to stage it and he worked hard to achieve that goal. He continues to support Special Olympic athletes in Ireland and in the countries where Digicel operates.

O'Brien loves nothing more than building a strong brand. He believes his business should always be viewed in a positive, enthusiastic and exciting way, and today Digicel is one of the Caribbean's most visible and best-known brands. The group's bold red logo is worn by the West Indies cricket team, Samoa's national rugby team and the world's fastest man, Usain Bolt, whom Digicel has sponsored since 2005.

Digicel revelled in Bolt's triple Olympic success at the 2008 Beijing Olympics, erecting massive television screens and creating a carnival atmosphere for Bolt's Jamaican fans as they followed his success. And when he began to collect Olympic gold medals, O'Brien insisted that Bolt's father, Wellesley, should join the rest of his family in Beijing for the celebrations. The athlete's proud father later explained that Digicel had given him no choice in the matter. 'They literally put a rope around my neck,' he told reporters, 'and say, "Mr Bolt, you have to go to China".'

And the Digicel team had another surprise in store for Usain. They were going to 'pimp' his home. They organised a surprise makeover of his Jamaican house, bringing a television company along to record the five-day transformation. Top Jamaican interior designer Pat Chatman was told to capture Usain's 'exciting, flirty yet rootsy and down-to-earth personality' and the athlete's surprise and happiness at seeing his newly styled home was broadcast on live television.

Denis O'Brien is fiercely proud to be Irish but is a tax exile, resident in Malta, who flies home to his family in Dublin at weekends. He has grown disillusioned with his native land at times, particularly in light of the investigation into the awarding of the mobile phone licence more than a decade ago. The allegations sully his reputation and diminish the scale of his achievements, he believes. It is something he says his competitors will use against him. He has even said he wishes he had never won the licence.

At the same time, he likes to say there is no place like home. Addressing an international conference in 2010 he said he loves to return to Ireland, for short periods. 'Irish people are fun; they have great humour, and a good outlook. I like to go home to refill with those things, and then go off again,' he said. Despite its attractions he joked the only thing that could bring him back to Ireland to live full-time might be an 'illness'.

As he faces the challenges to his business empire and the potential damage to his reputation, some who knew O'Brien when he started out in business say he was always an enigma. They couldn't decide then whether Denis O'Brien would go on to be hugely successful or a spectacular business failure. One predicted he would 'either make a lot of money and be very successful, or shoot himself in the foot, or both'. One acquaintance who has crossed swords with O'Brien says he predicted that the telecoms boss would feature in a book at some stage. 'I always thought this day would come. I figured Denis would be the only one in the book, however, if he had it his way.'

2 The Apprentice

'As a child, all Denis wanted was a bit of fun,' says his father. 'He was never very learned. He wasn't exceptionally bright or anything like that. He was a normal child who caused the usual trouble.'

Born in Dublin on 19 April 1958, Denis John O'Brien was the second of four children born to Denis O'Brien senior and his wife Iris (née Quinn). Denis, along with sisters Abigail and Joanne and brother Kerry, enjoyed a privileged upbringing in the heart of south Dublin, one of the city's most desirable residential areas.

Denis's father, known as 'Danno', was a successful businessman and an accomplished athlete. Originally from Tipperary, he represented Ireland in international diving competitions and participated in spectacular creative diving displays at Blackrock Baths in Dublin alongside the legendary Irish diving champion Eddie Heron. Crowds would regularly gather at the gala events to watch the pair hit the water spectacularly at thirty-eight miles per hour. Blessed with boundless energy, O'Brien trained hard to be the best in his sport, showing remarkable endurance. And his fearless determination was evident when he undertook a spectacular dive, launching himself off the sheerest cliffs in Acapulco. Those who know him say he is a forceful character, a tough taskmaster with a huge appetite for work, qualities he applied to achieving success both in business and in sport.

Denis's mother is from Tandragee in Northern Ireland. The couple met while they were both studying in Dublin; a Protestant, of the Anglican faith, she was a student of modern languages at Trinity College Dublin, while he, a Catholic, was studying medicine at the Royal College of Surgeons.

When they married, O'Brien's father abandoned his studies to become a doctor in order to support his family, taking a job as a medical representative for a leading pharmaceutical business. Over the years his career progressed and he would become chief executive of Constant Laboratories.

There, his main responsibility was to develop a range of feed supplements for horses. And while the company closed some years later, in 1995 O'Brien senior founded his own company, Plusvital Ireland, to manufacture and distribute a wide range of equine healthcare products. It was a successful company in a time of economic depression and would go on to sell its products to horse owners, breeders and trainers in more than thirty countries.

While his father doesn't recall his eldest son ever taking any notice of his conversations about his business when he was young, Denis claims he was always listening closely. In radio and newspaper interviews he repeatedly mentions what he regards as the education in business he received from his successful father in his formative years. His interest in business and his own success is rooted in his father's influence, and O'Brien believes being born into a family that had a business was his biggest break: 'Your family life has a huge bearing on what you do and what your attitude is to risk-taking. If you come from a small-business background that is eating and drinking customer service, customers not paying, things falling through, that gives you a private business education. It's in the air, around the table and you are learning from that.'

From the age of eight, he says, he listened to his father talking about sales reps crashing cars, problems with employees, people not meeting their targets, customers demanding price reductions, bad debts, landing the big orders and launching new products. 'It was in the ether. It was in the air around the dinner table.'

In an interview for RTÉ radio's *Moneymakers* series in 1999, O'Brien spoke warmly about a happy home life with 'extraordinary parents' who were 'liberal, progressive and pretty open-minded'.

His father, who is careful not to praise his elder son above his other children, says the siblings are all close to one another. 'They all get on terrifically as a family,' he says. 'Their mother kept them really united.'

The O'Briens decided unusually not to buy a television for their comfortable home and encouraged their children to find other ways to occupy themselves around the house. Every weekend they set them a challenge. They each had to take their turn to make a speech after dinner on Saturday nights. 'It was to condition the children for public speaking,' Denis's father explains. 'On Saturday night one of the four had to stand up after dinner – they were very small and young at the time – and they had to speak on a subject. The girls were very good at it and the boys were too.'

The children were all 'well schooled', he says. They attended local fee-paying private schools. Their mother, who speaks fluent French, Italian and Spanish, wanted them to share her interest in languages and enrolled them at St Kilian's German kindergarten and primary school. It was a newly established school with just eight or nine pupils in each class where children were taught to learn to use a second language. Their son Denis's first day would be remembered for him coming home with the sleeve torn off his new blazer. It was to be the first of many troublesome episodes.

Conn Clissmann, who grew up close to the O'Briens, started kindergarten the same day. 'We were the two in the class who walked home in the same direction,' he says, remembering O'Brien's high spirits and propensity for mischief. 'Denis was physically strong, a big build and ebullient with it. He was getting into trouble.' His friend was quickly known as 'Denis the Menace' after the popular cartoon character. 'He was the first suspect when something happened. He just was that character.'

From there Clissmann and Denis went to High School, in Rathgar, a predominantly Protestant secondary school founded in 1870 'to prepare boys for business and the professions'. It counted poet W.B. Yeats among its past pupils. Two of only five pupils registered as Catholic who attended the school in the 1970s, they felt literally like outsiders. 'It was unusual in Ireland to be among the minority as a Catholic,' Clissmann says. 'We, together with the Jewish pupils, used to stand outside for prayers in the morning.'

Both shied away from taking any role in the annual Gilbert and Sullivan musicals. Their interest was in more vigorous activities. 'Denis was not your theatre, singing and dancing guy,' says Clissmann. 'He was more into the outdoors and sport.'

O'Brien was picked to represent his class in the boxing ring and his parents went along to watch the fight. 'He wasn't a fighter,' says his father. 'He was totally non-aggressive for a big guy like that. He didn't like boxing. He went into the ring with this chap and for the first three rounds he never hit him once. Denis just kept his hands up to his face, and we were really at the point of stopping the fight because it was silly. Then, all of a sudden, he went out and just shot at him once. He hit him once in four rounds and knocked him out.'

Had the sturdy teenager been weighing up his opponent all along, looking for his opportunity to land the knockout punch? After all, like his father, he was highly competitive and would have a fierce determination to beat his opponent.

Denis's real passion, however, was rugby. The sport was compulsory at High School, a long-established breeding ground for Ireland's rugby squad. Clissmann remembers O'Brien being 'fairly enthusiastic' about rugby, and his friend was selected for the Junior Cup team. 'He mostly moved with that set,' says Clissmann – and he still does. 'He took it seriously and trained a lot.'

The same couldn't be said for school work. Denis was a mischievous pupil who found it difficult to apply himself to learning in the classroom. And he struggled to grasp some subjects. 'I was more on the science and maths end and Denis was more on the commerce and arts end, I suppose,' remembers Clissmann. 'He was not the sort of person for whom study came easy. It was evident in primary school that he had a problem with maths. But he had great fun at school.'

The entrepreneur has often talked about his lack of application at school, saying he 'did as little as possible' and enjoyed himself. 'I was more interested in doing a bit of disruption. I would go into school and try and make as much trouble as possible.' School was an endurance for O'Brien, rather than something he viewed as a means to a successful business career. It was a way to gather a gang around him, to have a bit of fun.

His mischief wasn't always appreciated and one episode triggered a brief suspension. During this time, Denis says, he travelled on sales trips with his father. 'He told me how to sell and to present – not to put my hands in my pockets and to get a good suit,' he has recalled.

Then, a few months before his final year exams, another misdemeanour left him facing expulsion.

A rugby match between High School and the nearby Masonic School was the scene of his final act of mischief, one that he still enjoys talking about. 'I drove my mother's Renault 4 in a figure of eight in the snow on a cricket pitch,' he says. It was a deed that caused considerable annoyance to the school's headmaster.

His father still remembers the commotion. 'He borrowed Iris's small car and pushed thirteen pals in it and drove around the school grounds. He got into huge trouble. How he got all those people into the poor little car I'll never know.'

Clissmann, by now head prefect, organised a petition to save his friend from expulsion and persuaded some of the teachers to support his cause. 'They all knew Denis was a messer but he was liked,' he explains. 'It struck me as deeply unfair that, with just a few school days left, the school would expel him. This would mean he couldn't sit his Leaving Certificate exams at the school. I took the view that High School had had six years to teach him hard work and discipline and had obviously failed. But there was a feeling at the school that his messing had to be stopped.'

The campaign was successful and the school agreed merely to suspend Denis again, for a period that would last over the Easter holidays. He returned to High School for the final term but his exam results were poor. He failed to pass the crucial maths exam that he needed to pass to graduate from university. 'Maths,' he admits, 'was my killer subject.'

His was not a household where the children could idle away their time. They were expected to work hard at school and at home and encouraged to volunteer and to get jobs during the school holidays. His father, who says he has been working since the age of thirteen, believed it was important for their children to have a strong work ethic. 'We instilled in all our children the need to try to become independent as soon as they could.'

So, like his father, in his early teens Denis began working at a range of jobs. At fourteen his first job was a bellboy at Dublin's Central Hotel, where he earned about €8 a week plus tips. In later years he was a wine waiter at Dobbins restaurant in Dublin and he worked in

London, using power hoses to clean stone façades. But his most successful part-time job was as a house painter. 'He was always working. In his spare time he would paint buildings,' says his father. And Denis showed great pride in his work. 'He took me to one shop in Knightsbridge he had painted. He was so proud of it,' his father recalls. 'He was always doing odd jobs, always was a very active guy.'

While his father imbued his children with a sense of business, it was from his mother that O'Brien has said he inherited his 'astuteness' and interest in defending human rights. She is, according to her son, 'a serial protester. She protested outside the Russian embassy over the treatment of Chechens. She was also very pro the Sandinistas.' And she encouraged her family to show their support for these causes. 'Iris is very interested in anybody who has not been fairly treated,' his father explains. 'She would have the whole lot of us protesting with her. Denis and the other children would regularly go with her to protest outside the American embassy in Dublin. He probably did it more than the others, although they would all go with her. I wouldn't mind, but I was trying to do business in America at that time and to be outside the embassy protesting with a placard wasn't exactly the way to get a visa.'

His mother's influence would not only contribute to her son's lifelong interest in human rights but also instil a rebellious streak in the man who would later bitterly protest about the perceived injustices to which he would be subjected.

Having failed the crucial maths exam, Denis's parents enrolled him in Dublin's Pre-University School for the next academic year in the hope that he might progress to studying for a degree. It was a happy year for him, one in which he met a new group of friends, including Barry Maloney, who would become his best mate.

Paul Meagher got to know O'Brien, Maloney and the rest of the gang that year. 'We met through a rugby match I was organising between the two schools where we were both repeating our Leaving Cert,' he explains. 'We had grown up within half a mile of each other but I had never known or met him up until then. My first sight of him was coming through the gates in his mother's car with about eight people in it on two wheels. I knew from the off that he was one colourful character.'

O'Brien's results were disappointing again, and he failed the dreaded maths exam for the second time. He had told his parents he wanted to do a business degree but his poor maths results meant he would have to choose another course, so – along with Maloney – he applied to do an Arts degree at University College Dublin (UCD) in 1997. For the next three years, he signed up to study history, politics and logic. He would also have to resit the maths exam and was lucky enough to pass it on his third attempt. But O'Brien spent little enough time attending lectures. He and Maloney had set up their own business enterprise. Throughout the three years the pair painted houses and offices all over Dublin to make some money.

Meagher met up with O'Brien and his crew at UCD. O'Brien, always the leader, began to assemble a gang including Paddy Halpenny, Paul Connolly, Kieran O'Reilly, Aidan Phelan and John Mulcahy, who would be his closest friends for years to come. 'When he makes friendships, they tend to last for a very very long time,' Meagher says. 'He has incredible loyalty to his old friends.'

O'Brien believes one of the great benefits of going to college is the friendships forged among the pupils. He spoke about it to Ivor Kenny in his book *Leaders*, a series of conversations with Irish chief executives. 'If you go straight into work at eighteen you may make business friends but they are absolutely different from the real friendships you make in college. There's no tie-up. Business friendships are not that durable,' he said. 'Fellows get married and their wives don't like their business partner. Everything gets convoluted, particularly when there's economic rivalry – he's got a bigger car or a bigger house than we have and all that kind of stuff.'

He believes that when everyone you know has no money of their own, you make stronger friendships. 'All my friends started with nothing. None of them were lucky sperms; most had not a sausage. When you go off to Greece on a holiday and you're living on fifty quid, you see the cut of a person,' he told Kenny. His father says he never gave Denis a great deal of money as a student and encouraged him to work part-time to fund himself at university.

At UCD Denis was described as the 'life and soul' of all sorts of outings. He organised groups to go running in his favourite spot,

Lough Dan, in the Wicklow Mountains, or on camping trips – always outdoor pursuits.

At the weekends, in all kinds of weather, they would gather to run around the perimeter of Lough Dan and then dive in and swim across it before continuing their run. 'He kept that going for years,' Meagher says. His friend prefers to run in the countryside rather than in the city, he says, because he suffers from asthma. 'He likes the clean air. It was always good clean fun. He was a born leader and great fun to be with.'

While he was definitely a 'lad's lad', Denis had lots of women friends. He was dating Sally-Anne O'Donovan, whom he had met at the Pre-University School. 'Most women were very fond of him,' Meagher says. 'They liked his mischievous ways and the fact that he was always up to something and he was very warm. They knew they were playing with fire. He was no church mouse.'

Denis resolutely applied himself to sporting challenges, to hard work and to socialising, but not to academia. According to Meagher, he had an appalling attendance record at UCD. 'I had to help him through it. He doesn't like it when I say this. I gave him all of my notes. More often than not, he was involved in some off-campus activity to make a buck.' As Meagher explains, Denis was always finding odd jobs to earn some money. 'He and Barry Maloney had a contract to paint the Pre-University School in Merrion Square which they had attended the previous year. They were continuously working and that continued during the three years in college.'

Others who attended UCD at the same time mention O'Brien's propensity for causing tension among some of his fellow students, particularly late at night at their local, Hartigans. 'He was a trouble-maker,' one says, a trait that his competitors would say is still strongly in evidence.

'He could stir things up,' another of his contemporaries recalls. 'He had an uncanny knack for creating tension. Somehow at the end of the night there would be some kind of trouble.' Yet, in contrast, Denis became a member of Amnesty International at UCD.

He also continued to play rugby, though at the Wanderers Club rather than joining the college team. 'He developed a whole circle of friends at Wanderers and they are very loyal to that place,' Meagher says. 'He is mad into sport and he was very good at rugby. He would have liked to have seen himself as a dashing prop forward. He was an unbelievably strong and tough guy.'

Some who knew Denis were surprised he completed his degree, given his propensity for activities outside his college work and his struggle with academic tasks. But he graduated in 1980 and, much to his father's astonishment, was encouraged by lecturer Maurice Manning to apply for a scholarship to study for a Master's in Business Administration degree in the USA.

The student had endeared himself to Manning by canvassing for him when he ran for election to the Irish parliament, the Dáil. The lecturer saw leadership qualities in O'Brien. 'He had infectious enthusiasm,' he has said. Academically, he wouldn't have been the sharpest but he was the natural leader in his class. He was good on the doorstep. He's a born salesman.'

Denis accepted the scholarship to Boston College, intending to complete his degree – one that contained large elements of accounting and finance, surely a daunting prospect for someone who struggled with maths – as quickly as he could. First, though, he would spend a summer painting in Cape Cod.

Maria Mulcahy, a university friend of Denis's who had a summer job working as a maid at the Kennedy family's compound in Hyannis Port, met up with the UCD gang that summer. It would land her in a spot of bother with the famous Irish-American dynasty.

That weekend Eunice Kennedy Shriver's son Tim was celebrating his twenty-first birthday in Hyannis. Mulcahy and the other staff were all invited; O'Brien and a friend turned up thinking they would be allowed in, since Mulcahy was there. There was a bit of a to-do, and they made a hasty exit. Mulcahy moved on to another job shortly afterwards.

As the gang returned to Ireland O'Brien settled into Boston College, determined to complete the two-year programme in fourteen months. He struggled with the financial content from the start and missed his friends. Although fairly miserable, he showed great determination to stick at the course in order to attain this qualification.

'I remember going to see him and . . . him describing to me how hard it was and saying that he couldn't wait for it to end,' Meagher says. 'He wasn't really cut out for academia. I saw him and thought Jesus, this guy is so determined. He was really lonely in Boston. Nobody was coming to see him. He just wanted to be back to Dublin to the lads and the craic. That's the only time I saw him being really down that I can remember.'

Maloney had also moved to the USA, having secured a graduate trainee position at multinational company Becton Dickinson. Of all the gang, Maloney had the most successful career over the next few years, one that would ultimately take him to Silicon Valley to work with Xerox. He was blazing a trail in corporate America and had little interest in returning to economically depressed Ireland. His best friend, though, just wanted to go home, and had plenty of ideas about what he would do there.

The young graduate returned to Ireland having studied some of the world's most successful businesses, including the low-cost US airline Southwest. The now legendary airline, established by Herb Kelleher in Texas in 1971, revolutionised short-haul travel and was to create the template for low-cost carriers for decades to come. O'Brien was so impressed with its achievements that he harboured ambitions to start a similar airline. But until Europe opened its skies to such new ventures, there was little hope of getting the idea off the ground. Instead, he became a banker.

He joined Trinity Bank, a small merchant bank in Dublin, because his father suggested it would be a good experience to learn how banks worked. 'He felt that if I could learn how the buggers thought,' Denis has said, 'it would be easier when I went in the front door looking for money.'

Initially he worked under the guidance of veteran banker John McGilligan and was trained on the foreign exchange side of the business by a colleague, David Sykes, who would later follow him into his many business ventures.

Those who worked at the bank at the time remember O'Brien as a hilarious character. 'He was charismatic, fun, cheeky and very persuasive. Women found him particularly charming,' one remarked. Another who knew him remembers a charming, good-looking young man who paid a lot of attention to his appearance. 'He dressed like a duke and the women loved him.'

O'Brien also began a tradition of hosting suave parties for his gang, cultivating the image of a successful businessman. Every year, on the day of the so-called 'colours match', a rugby game between the rival Dublin universities, UCD and Trinity College, he invited the gang to his house, a small mews off Baggot Street. The dress code was black tie, rather grandiose for dinner with your mates at home.

'He started it a couple of years after we left UCD,' Meagher says. 'He used it as a way to have a reunion. They were black-tie bachelor parties and he would invite all his old mates from UCD and from school and bring them all together for a gigantic piss-up done with great style. He would host the whole thing. He was incredibly generous and this was when people didn't have two red cents to rub together. That continued for ten or fifteen years.'

O'Brien soon became bored with his job in banking. He has said he was 'treading water' there, just gaining experience before moving on. 'It was a little bit like what banking still is, a nice lifestyle, nine to five. There was a dining room at the top of the bank and everyone would drink wine at lunchtime,' he told Ivor Kenny. His was a sunny office and after a couple of glasses of wine at lunch, he explained, he would open the window, get on the phone to run his Wanderers 3Bs rugby team and grab a suntan at the same time.

Fresh from his stint in the USA, he now wanted to work for a dynamic company, one in the major league. Perhaps influenced by his studies at Boston College, O'Brien craved a demanding role at the heart of a fast-moving business. He wanted to learn how such companies operated and get a slice of the action. A friend made a suggestion. He should think about working for Tony Ryan, founder of Ireland-based Guinness Peat Aviation (GPA), one of the world's largest and most successful aircraft-leasing companies,.

The wealthy Irish entrepreneur had given a series of interviews in the newspapers around this time and they made interesting reading for O'Brien. 'If you were out of college in the late seventies and early eighties and you were looking to join a dynamic company, there were only a handful, such as CRH [a major building materials group] and GPA,' he says. 'Having read articles about Tony Ryan and GPA and how it got going, I said: "Jeez, he's the guy to work for".'

He wrote what he describes as a 'cheeky' letter to Ryan, saying 'I hear you are an early riser' and stating that he would meet him at GPA's headquarters in Shannon, County Clare, some morning to talk about a possible job.

'Within a week a guy called Donal Flinn, who was Ryan's accountant, met me in his office. Having passed muster with him, I met Tony a week later.' At the interview Ryan asked the young Dubliner what he ultimately would like to do. On hearing that he aspired to start up a low-cost airline, Ryan laughed and, according to O'Brien, told him he was 'bloody mad'. But O'Brien was nonetheless hired on the princely sum of about €13,000 a year.

O'Brien would be Ryan's first personal assistant, a role that was to prove varied and highly demanding. His brief was to help manage some of Ryan's investments. These included Ryan's farm in County Tipperary, Matt the Thresher's, a pub on the main road to Limerick city which O'Brien helped open, and the *Sunday Tribune* newspaper, which was being relaunched with Ryan's financial backing and for whom O'Brien acted as company secretary.

'If Tony was in Ireland, I lived at Kilboy House, his County Tipperary home,' recalls O'Brien. 'At seven o'clock in the morning I would be in the back of the car with him. Tony would take out a pad from his ostrich-skin briefcase and begin asking questions in unbelievable detail. Everything had to be done quickly. There was no time to be waiting around. That's why he was such a good deal-maker. He would just go and get it done.

'That was his philosophy. There was always a lot of urgency to get things done. Whether it was to deal with a builder, to buy something or to improve something, he would always say, "Let's do it now and get it done this week".

'So I would have lists of things and I would sit down with him and we would go through them. He was an unbelievable lateral thinker. He would say to me: "I want you to go and buy this thing", and he would think of all of the words that would be said and he would make me write it down. He would know all of the emotional things that would make a seller sell and he would nearly make you write it out. The words you wanted to use.

'He would say, "I want you to say this to the guy, then I want you to say this again and then I want you to finish up by saying XYZ." That was because he was a bit like a good jockey: he could see the jumps a half a mile down the tracks. He had a terrific brain and balls of iron. I'll say that for him, my Jesus, as a risk-taker, he was a risk-taker par excellence.'

When he wrote about his mentor after his death in 2007, O'Brien described working for Ryan as like being in an Accident and Emergency ward for business learning. 'I recall one night after he watched the movie *Ryan's Daughter*, he told me to buy the schoolhouse in Dunquin which featured those tender scenes between Robert Mitchum and Sarah Miles,' his *Sunday Business Post* tribute read. 'After three weeks of anonymous haggling with an English owner, I reported back that the purchase had been completed. I was pretty proud of having landed the schoolhouse, but he just replied: "Okay".'

City boy O'Brien laughed at being put in charge of a farm, saying he hadn't been on a farm for ten years. Within days he knew exactly what life on the farm entailed. A working dinner with his boss was interrupted when the farm manager, Paddy Ryan, burst in shouting: 'She's calving, she's calving!'

Ryan had been breeding Blonde d'Aquitaine cattle on the farm and the herd was about to increase. 'Tony jumped and ran after Paddy and within minutes we were pulling a calf in a manner akin to skiing off the back of a motor boat. All I could think of was my (new and only) FX Kelly suit, which was about to be destroyed. Swiftly and unnoticed, I positioned myself behind Tony, a man of many suits, as the calf was born.'

Some time later, Ryan decided to become involved in milk production and O'Brien was dispatched around the country with Paddy to buy eighty-two cows. They were now in the dairy business.

Denis's father says working with Ryan was a fantastic job for someone so young and it gave his son a taste of the international jet-set lifestyle. 'It was Savile Row suits and travelling around the world on private jets. It was incredible.'

His friend Paul Connolly, a trainee accountant at KPMG at the time, would see O'Brien coming in and out of the building with his boss. 'He was the bag man,' he says. 'I would see Denis bundle out of the Daimler or Jag with the briefcase, following Ryan into meetings.'

Ryan was renowned as a hard taskmaster. O'Brien says that when he met GPA colleagues they would sympathetically ask how he was getting on and throw their eyes up to heaven.

Everyone who worked for GPA and Ryan had to cope with the boss's abrasive management style. His personal assistant, who had already endured a grilling on the journey to GPA headquarters in Shannon, would often then sit in at the infamous management meetings, which became known as 'seagull meetings'. The term was used by one executive to describe how Ryan 'swoops in, shits on everyone from a height and swoops away again' as grown men cowered and paled during the tension-filled gatherings.

'It was an interesting lesson in management,' O'Brien says. 'There were guys who would fear the shite out of Tony and he would beat the crap out of them. And there were guys who would tell him to fuck off. They were too good for him to act the bollix with.'

Ryan was quick to stamp his authority on any of his business dealings and had to be in control of what was going on, something that could destroy relations with various colleagues and investors. O'Brien says he understood Ryan's dictatorial style: 'When you've got a business like that, someone has to drive the bus. Tony had put up most of the money and there can only be one driver.'

And he learned to tolerate his mentor's irritability and bad moods, accepting that it is hard to be patient and focused when you are constantly travelling around the globe. 'If you are working for somebody who spends most of their lifetime at thirty-five thousand feet, when they come down to earth they're jet-lagged, short-tempered and don't remember what they last said to you,' he explained. 'If you happened to be one hundred per cent in the right and that person thinks you're wrong – you're wrong.'

There were some perks, though, for a young car enthusiast. His boss asked him to check out the availability of a red Ferrari that was to be a gift. O'Brien recalls how much he enjoyed the experience. 'I duly flew to Heathrow, caught a taxi to the Maranello Ferrari dealership and told the salesman I wanted to buy one, but said I was unsure as to which model. That presented me with a wonderful opportunity to go for a rip on the M25 for the afternoon, testing about four models.' Laughing, he wished the 'lads' – his college mates – could have seen him driving the Ferraris.

When he reported back to Ryan, his boss had changed his mind. He wanted a DeLorean instead and sent his assistant to check out the DeLorean dealerships. 'Tony told me to conclude the purchase with an instruction to have it sprayed Ferrari red, much to the horror of the salesman who kept reminding me that this was a stainless steel car and should be left as it was.' Then, like a character in the movie *The Bourne Identity*, O'Brien says, he waited for his next instruction. He was to deliver the car at precisely 8.30 the following morning.

'I left myself two days for the trip and I did not want to miss the deadline – which for reasons not explained to me was a most important event,' he explained. 'I was driving the spanking new DeLorean on the M1 on Sunday morning – cruising at around eighty miles per hour – when suddenly there was a loud bang. I immediately pulled off the road and sought expert advice from a breakdown service only to be told that the engine had seized. Oh, Jesus!'

He practised what he would tell his boss. His heart was 'thumping', he said. 'I had only uttered four words when the volcanic verbals erupted. The grand plan was up in smoke, literally.' O'Brien avoided all contact with Ryan for the next four days to give him time to calm down. 'I never heard how the proposed recipient of the special vehicle was placated, if at all.'

Around this time Ryan was one of a number of business people considering the potential of a new generation of telecommunications satellites to deliver a lucrative global communications network. Indeed, such was his interest in the sector that a new division was established at GPA to research the business opportunities that direct broadcasting satellite systems might offer. O'Brien was the project manager.

In 1983, the Irish government would be seeking bidders for the licence to operate one such satellite broadcasting system. Consortia were already assembling to build a new high-powered satellite. Fred O'Donovan, one of Ireland's top theatre producers and the chairman of Ireland's radio and television network, Radio Telifis Éireann (RTÉ), had long been trying to persuade the government of the value of investing in a satellite that could be used to lease channels to broadcast programmes throughout Europe and to the east coast of the USA. Since it was a relatively new and expensive concept, O'Donovan even made a short film to inform the government about the potential opportunities for the country. Knowing he needed to bring others on board, he made contact with O'Brien, the young man who used to date his daughter.

O'Donovan and his wife Sally were invited to Tony Ryan's home for dinner to discuss forging an alliance to bid for the satellite. 'I had always been very impressed by Denis and I instantly liked him,' says O'Donovan. He found Ryan to be very far-seeing and says it was clear that O'Brien had learned a lot from him.

Following this meeting, a consortium comprising GPA, RTÉ, the state-owned telephone company Telecom Éireann, and Allied Irish Investment Bank, was formed and began preparing for the bid. Known as WestSat, it was chaired by O'Donovan. But the bid was unsuccessful. According to O'Brien, it failed because the government viewed the project as being too risky for Telecom Éireann and RTÉ, something that now amuses him greatly. While this particular project failed to get airborne, however, it would provide the basis for another venture into the communications sector for O'Brien and O'Donovan.

Around this time horrific scenes of people starving to death in Ethiopia were being beamed around the globe. O'Donovan, prompted by his wife, felt he should try to do something to aid their plight. He recalls that on a Bank Holiday Monday he rang O'Brien to ask when Ryan would provide a plane that could take relief to Ethiopia: 'I spoke to him at about midday and he rang back that evening to say that Tony had a plane going to Nigeria on Wednesday and he would give it to us to go on to Addis Ababa.

'I needed to get clearance from the government and fortuitously rang the Department of Foreign Affairs just as a group of aid agencies were meeting with the minister to discuss what could be done. So I was put through to them and we filled the plane.' He also brought along a camera crew.

Theirs was among the first international aid to reach Ethiopia. 'We were there before Bob Geldof,' says O'Donovan. On landing, though, they quickly realised that they had forgotten to budget for the cash they would need to transport the goods beyond the airport. 'I rang

Denis again and he said that he would be running a marathon shortly and would raise £1,000 for us. He was only a young fellow then himself but that shows what type of person he was.'

While O'Brien might have parked his ambition to launch a low-cost airline, his mentor was determined to do just that. According to O'Brien, 'Tony always wanted to have his own airline.' The fledgling airline consisted of a single Bandeirante aircraft, flown between the small airport at Waterford and London's Gatwick Airport. And it was O'Brien — who years later would feel compelled to publicly do battle with Ryanair — who was charged with organising the lease of the plane, the first to be operated by what was to become Ryanair, Europe's biggest low-cost carrier. O'Brien soon found a lawyer to organise the lease on the small turboprop plane. Paul Meagher, who was still serving his apprenticeship, explains that his friend said he should tell Ryan that he specialised in aviation.

'We all went down to Waterford to be involved in the Waterford to Gatwick service,' O'Brien says. 'We were putting hoardings up all over the place to advertise the new service. Everyone from the local Chamber of Commerce was involved.'

Despite his own earlier ambition to become an airline tycoon, O'Brien claims he was doubtful about Ryanair's success. 'I have to say that I was sceptical about Ryanair, and the single Bandeirante aircraft, but it got going and Tony then lobbied the government to get to fly from Dublin to Luton.'

By now O'Brien was considering moving on and setting up his own business. It was something his father encouraged him to do. 'I got out of GPA for the simple reason that my father overheard a conversation between me and Tony, who was burying me on the phone,' says O'Brien. 'It was difficult. I was trying to get off the phone and my father smelt it.' O'Brien senior told his son it was time to leave. 'Go before you get bought and wrapped and take on all the trappings. Get out of it and set up your own business', was his advice. 'So that's what I did.'

The pace he enjoyed in his sporting pursuits had become commonplace in his working life. Operating at Ryan's gruelling pace, he says, was to determine the way he would create his own success. 'Working with Tony was a different pace of life — it was extreme. I worked six or seven days a week for him and there was management by fear, a bit like the French Foreign Legion.'

O'Brien has often paid tribute to Ryan's mentoring skills, comparing the businessman with Manchester United's legendary manager Alex Ferguson. 'Fergie buys a few players every summer. He will say where will they play, slots them in and culls a few that are not one hundred per cent,' he says. 'Tony didn't cull but added. He trained me to write down what the objectives were each year. There would be maybe twenty objectives that would include hiring various people. He would have twenty names on a line and one of the objectives would be to bring them in. Of course it would be a different story once they came on board,' he says of his notoriously demanding boss.

And he is generous in his praise for the risk-taking culture that Ryan and his company spawned. 'I certainly walked out of the door and said: "You might be based in Ireland but what's stopping you?" He had an attitude that nothing could stop us.'

His apprenticeship served, O'Brien felt ready to emulate his mentor's success and had a few ideas as to how he might one day build his own business empire. Now he had to figure out his next move.

3 The Next Silvio Berlusconi

Denis O'Brien was looking to the future. And in seeking the next big thing, an exciting idea or product he could launch as a new business, it was to America that he returned for inspiration.

His father was also looking west, preparing to sell Plusvital's nutritional supplements for horses into the US market, having finally won approval to offer its products to the USA's enormous equine industry. It was a mammoth task for the Irish company and O'Brien was surprised when his son offered to do the groundwork and set up its US sales operation. They would conquer America together.

Working for Tony Ryan, O'Brien had enjoyed a fast-paced lifestyle. Now he was prepared to take on a relatively humble role for no salary. His father simply couldn't afford to pay him, and cautioned that it would be a difficult and often miserable task. 'I said this is a very small business in comparison. And there were no wages. We just paid his expenses,' he recalls. 'I thought Denis was fantastic to do that.'

And so O'Brien moved across the Atlantic once again to become Plusvital's US sales and distribution representative, a travelling salesman for a small company based a long way from his gang in Ireland. 'To save money we would hire a truck and Denis would collect our products at the port in New York and deliver them all over America,' his father explains. 'He didn't just deliver them, he sold them to shops and horse people and stores. He went from Kentucky to Florida to Chicago to Miami. He drove all over America for two years to help us get established.'

O'Brien proved to be a natural salesman and in the months ahead began hiring and training others to sell for the company. 'He is a terrific salesman. He was always very inventive and innovative,' his father says. 'It wasn't aggressive selling. He was great at explaining things rationally and plainly to customers.'

O'Brien has talked about driving coast to coast across America selling to horse breeders and trainers of thoroughbreds, show jumpers and eventing horses, whom he describes as 'the toughest people on earth'. The sales pitch would have to be short and snappy to hold their attention and the transactions were quickly completed: 'I'd go to Belmont Park at six in the morning, hit all the trainers, then get into the car and drive to upstate New York and hit all the dealers.'

In between sales calls he read the newspapers, scouring the business pages for ideas, collecting reports about new ventures that were doing well and might work back in Ireland. He stored them in a manilla folder.

Just as the USA had led the way in liberalising air transport, it was now preparing to open up its telecommunications industry to competition. More and more new companies were beginning to square up to the mighty AT&T, the corporation that effectively had monopoly control of US telecommunications. Plenty of ambitious business people were prepared to battle to win a share of its lucrative phone business.

Developments in other business sectors also caught his eye. Flicking through the television channels in a motel room in Kentucky, he came across the Shopping Channel. He watched as, for hours on end, its presenters sold jewellery to viewers across America. With estimated sales of around $2 billion a year, the channel was doing great business. Could it work on the other side of the Atlantic? he wondered.

Thanks to the rapid advance of technology, retailers could now sell their products directly into people's homes, and the American public seemed delighted with the concept. Its success showed the power of the medium in influencing customers' purchasing habits, a lesson that would influence the rest of O'Brien's business career. New technology and the power of the media would become his obsession.

While the satellite that O'Brien and Fred O'Donovan's consortium had unsuccessfully bid to create was never built, a Luxembourg-based company, Astra, had by now constructed the satellite that would provide the footprint for the modern European satellite broadcasting business. Its first customer was British Sky Broadcasting (BSkyB), Rupert Murdoch's Sky Television network, which in turn leased airtime on its channels to programme-makers. Murdoch had high hopes for his satellite television business. Within months, according to his forecasts, four million viewers would be watching Sky Television.

O'Brien and O'Donovan decided to get into broadcasting and launch an entertainment channel. O'Donovan, whose background was in light entertainment and who spent three months every year producing shows at Carnegie Hall and Radio City Music Hall, passionately believed such a channel could attract big audiences across Europe and America's east coast. The pair even raised money from investors in Ireland to develop the project. A group of businessmen including Paul Power, Ray McKenna, lawyer Larry Shields, Seamus Gallagher and former British and Irish Lions rugby hero Ray McLoughlin between them invested €190,000 in Éireann Satellite (Esat), the company founded by O'Brien and O'Donovan in 1986.

O'Brien's friends couldn't believe he had persuaded so many of Ireland's business elite to invest money in the new venture. 'We were in awe of him,' says Paul Meagher. 'How he got a former British and Irish Lion and other older successful Irish businessmen to back a young whippersnapper like him. We saw Denis as a bit of a chancer. A charming chancer, but they were impressed by him and he seemed to gain their confidence.' He was gaining credibility in the business world.

He was, though, a consummate networker, one acquaintance says. 'He had great contacts and he worked them really well. He also realised how much he could learn from older successful business people, even those that others might have considered to be a bit out of fashion.'

Another says that you might be forgiven for thinking O'Brien picked up everything he knew about business around the bar at Wanderers Rugby Club, but that this was a façade. In fact he is very well read and more polished than that image would suggest. 'He'd have read books like *On War* [one of the world's most successful books on military strategy], but he'd never show that side. He was always great fun, a kind of Jack the lad, but at the same time he was always deadly determined to be successful in business.' Those who knew O'Brien at the time say everything else in his life was secondary to his business. 'Business was an absolute obsession,' one said. 'Nothing else mattered in his life. He wasn't interested in anything else. He just loved the chase and was relentless in his pursuit of success.'

Some remember O'Brien's propensity for mangling his sentences, often mixing metaphors or inserting the wrong words when he was trying to explain something. But his immense charm more than compensated for any grammatical shortcomings. 'He was great with people. You would feel you were his greatest friend within five minutes of meeting him,' one person says. 'He could build an incredible rapport and quickly capture an audience.' His charm quickly endeared him to new friends and business associates. He had an energy about him and even the most savvy and ruthless business people saw something in him that made them want to give him money.

It soon became clear that the entertainment channel was doomed. An expensive feasibility study suggested that Esat would need at least €400 million to set up such a channel. It was out of their league.

A shopping channel, though, might just work. O'Brien has said he quickly believed it could be a viable business. They would set up a shopping channel for the whole of Europe and forget about going to Hollywood.

O'Donovan wasn't enthusiastic but gave his business partner the address for the Home Shopping Network's headquarters in Florida. The next day O'Brien flew to Tampa, where a senior executive was happy to show the Irishman around. He later described what he saw as being like a 'big barn' where two women sat in front of television cameras selling jewellery. In the background hundreds of people took orders from customers who liked what they saw on their televisions. 'I was staggered,' he later recalled. 'I went back to the six investors and said: "Lads, this is it".'

O'Donovan wasn't interested and told O'Brien to go it alone. 'Theatre was my first love,' he explains. So O'Donovan resigned from the company. O'Brien has nevertheless paid tribute to his role as a mentor during that period, describing him as a 'very future-focused person'. He valued this experience. 'He'd sit down and say, "This is what I think is going to happen over the next five to ten years." And invariably he was on the money.'

The other investors were more impressed by O'Brien's new idea and finally he was ready to launch his first business, the Home Shopping Television Network (HSTVN). He found a new business mentor, persuading Luke Mooney, a former colleague at Trinity Bank who had his own corporate finance company, to join him.

The biggest challenge initially was to find a partner to supply products for the channel and mail them to customers. British retailer Littlewoods, which operated the UK's biggest mail order business, was the obvious choice, but it would prove difficult to interest them in branching out into television. O'Brien spent almost a year talking to Littlewoods' executives before someone at the company helpfully suggested he should go down the road and talk to another high street retailer.

The Next clothing chain was part of the Grattan group and also had a large mail order business. It too was sceptical about going into the television business with the inexperienced Irishman. O'Brien tells how he pestered Grattan's chairman, John Whitmarsh, sitting in the company's reception area for hours, hoping to get a word with him.

Finally, O'Brien was led to Whitmarsh's office and given five minutes. He gave him the pitch he would give a horse trainer, he claims, if he didn't do it, his biggest competitor would and he might regret that. Selling on the new shopping channel could only bring in millions of new customers, he promised. Eventually they struck a deal. Grattan agreed to join Esat in the new channel and gave O'Brien a €19,000 down payment. He was in the television business.

From there he negotiated with BSkyB to lease six hours each day on the Sky Movie Channel, where the Home Shopping Channel would sell a range of products between 8 a.m. and 2 p.m. Viewers in Ireland and the UK who had a satellite dish could tune into the channel and place their orders over the phone.

Those familiar with the business at that time say O'Brien's personality was crucial in cutting the deal with Sky. He 'charmed' the senior executives into it, one said. 'His personality was hugely important; in fact, it was his biggest asset.'

Now all he had to do was assemble a television production team and raise some more money. Mooney and O'Brien trawled their contacts, of whom Irish paper and packaging magnate Michael Smurfit was top of their list.

The Jefferson Smurfit Group had made start-up funds available to businesses in Ireland for many years. Almost thirty years on, Sir Michael remembers meeting O'Brien. 'Over the years a number of young entrepreneurs called to see me looking for funds and if I liked the cut of their jib I gave them seed money,' he says. 'I remember Denis. I thought he was an outstanding individual. He was a man in a hurry.' He had many of the qualities common among entrepreneurs, says Sir Michael. 'He was mercurial, fast-talking, fast-moving, very bright and highly intelligent.' Smurfit agreed to back him. The Jefferson Smurfit Group would invest $1.5 million in the satellite television business. It was a promising start.

Dubliners Gerald and David Heffernan, who ran Frontier Films, came on board to make the programme. David Heffernan recalls the frantic rush to research and design the show before it went on air. O'Brien took them on a whistle-stop tour of home shopping channels in the US to study their formats. 'I remember we went to the US for five days. We would land, get off, go to a shopping channel, have lunch or coffee with the directors and get back on a plane. It was like a day at the races for Denis. He'd be saying, "Isn't it great craic, lads?" to his jaded colleagues.'

O'Brien's relentless pace and determination were evident to his new colleagues as they settled into an office at Sky's headquarters at Osterley in London, from where the shopping programmes would be broadcast. O'Brien, says Heffernan, was the most hard-working individual he has ever met: 'Denis was a very brave and ambitious entrepreneur and was relentless in pursuit of his objective.' Generally he was very good-humoured and good at keeping everyone focused. 'He was a good team leader. He was always one step ahead of what was going on. He was very focused in meetings, very charming on a one to one basis and could make people feel that they were central to everything. He is definitely a "big picture" man.'

By May 1989 they were ready to start selling and invited journalists and advertisers to the Home Shopping Television Network's glittering launch in London. An Irish journalist who attended still remembers the razzmatazz. Conor Lenihan, the Westminster-based political correspondent for the *Irish News* newspaper, knew O'Brien from University College Dublin, mainly through their mutual interest in rugby, but had never seen him as a captain of industry. It was a surprise therefore to see the young Dubliner emerge on stage from a haze of dry ice to launch his new business venture. 'This was the first time I had seen him appear as a businessman. He was Mr Corporate in a suit.'

According to Lenihan, the launch was a fantastic event that showed a lot of marketing flair. And O'Brien wasn't the only familiar face on stage. 'Typical Denis, all of his friends were cajoled to participate. When you looked at the advertisements on the screen lots of his friends were walking on and off.' It seemed to Lenihan at the time that O'Brien aspired to be 'another Silvio Berlusconi', aiming to replicate the Italian media mogul's success in commercial television.

The accomplished salesman didn't do any selling on television himself but his friend Peter Norton, with whom he shared a flat in west London, was happy to appear in front of the camera as the programme's anchor. In the first month, the Home Shopping Channel sold €18,000 worth of goods. But the company by now had lost almost €500,000. They needed at least one million viewers to break even, but this was never going to happen. What was more, although, according to Meagher, O'Brien would claim the channel was selling a fantastic range of products, ultimately they weren't particularly attractive. 'They had some abominable products, cheap shabby products. I think he had some American gurus guiding him on the products but it didn't work.'

Heffernan says the channel was a good concept and the programme was adequately resourced but it struggled from the start. The problem was obvious to O'Brien. 'We made one vital mistake,' he explained. 'Where were the viewers?'

Murdoch's forecasts of millions of viewers were wide of the mark. It would take another couple of years before satellite viewing figures reached close to those levels. With so few people watching the show, they could never hope to successfully sell enough of their products to make a profit.

Tensions were running high as the financial pressures began to quickly build and O'Brien struggled under the strain. Over the next eighteen months the business lurched from one crisis to the next. O'Brien's relationship with the Grattan executives virtually broke down as they lost confidence in the project and his ability to lead it.

One person remarked that while O'Brien's charming personality was a driving force, keeping everyone focused and cajoling them to work harder and harder, there were negative sides to his behaviour that could ultimately be damaging. 'The nice side of his personality was his biggest asset but the negative side is his worst attribute. There is a real decency to him but ruthlessness as well. He had tunnel vision.' There were bitter rows with colleagues and it was felt by some that he viewed criticism as disloyalty. O'Brien's paradoxical nature was already coming to the fore.

It was hard for O'Brien to admit failure, but when Grattan refused to put any more money into the business to keep it going, its days were numbered. The Irish investors who had backed the idea were also unwilling to bankroll the channel. O'Brien was forced to shut down the business. He gathered his team to break the not altogether unexpected news. As he was to explain at a later date, 'Everybody else ran for cover and it was probably one of the worst things that I have ever had to do.'

Meagher says O'Brien put his 'blood, sweat and tears' into that business and was devastated when it failed. 'He had just decided to go headlong into it. He wasn't earning a penny from it and was living in London in a flat with a couple of guys. It was all fairly basic.'

One of the investors says the deal with Sky was potentially a good one – it was just too early. O'Brien wasn't to blame for the failure, the investor said. 'He was ahead of his time.'

O'Brien himself would reach the same conclusion. 'It was a great idea but it was four or five years ahead of its time,' he has said in interviews. QVC is now a huge success on Sky. He concluded that it wasn't always best to be first; sometimes you have to be second to win. The entrepreneur's motto, he believes, should be: 'Always be second.'

It was a lesson he had learned the hard way, and he would adhere to the maxim in later ventures.

Years later, when he talked about his first business failure, O'Brien painted a picture of a disorganised, almost backroom operation, but Heffernan says it was a professionally run business. O'Brien strived for perfection throughout. 'We were more focused and organised than that. There was no lack of endeavour but if you can't get access to the service it was going to fail.'

Heffernan returned to Dublin before the Shopping Channel was axed, to work on O'Brien's next project. Before the dust had settled on one failed media business he was ready to start another.

4 Radio 2000

As his television empire teetered on the brink of collapse, Denis O'Brien was ready to move on. He still fancied himself as a media mogul and this time he would focus on radio.

In 1988 the Irish government had begun tackling the domestic radio and television sector. New laws were enacted to rein in the pirate radio stations that had proved so popular with young listeners and open up the entire sector for new competitors. For the first time RTÉ would have to compete with a range of new radio and television stations.

The media world thus offered exciting new business opportunities and O'Brien was convinced he should bid for a radio licence. The biggest prize on offer was a national licence that would allow the winner to go head to head with RTÉ throughout Ireland's twenty-six counties. Already groups of investors were coming together to form consortia to bid for the licence and O'Brien fancied himself as a contender.

His backers had lost much of their investment in the failed shopping channel, but he persuaded them that a radio licence was a sure bet and they agreed to make an application. A new company, Radio 2000, was formed to bid for the licence and O'Brien and his fellow investors identified others who would bring the valuable experience that would make it a winning consortium.

The competition was handled by the Independent Radio and Television Commission (IRTC), an independent body appointed by the government. The IRTC had set down strict rules governing the programme content and management structures that new licence-holders would have to embrace. In assessing the applications, the IRTC would consider a wide range of factors, including broadcasting experience and the ability to create a national radio station that would reflect the interests and requirements of the broad Irish audience. Anyone with ambitions to establish such a station would need up to €13 million to get it on air, and the successful applicant would have to show the IRTC that it had access to sufficient financial resources before the licence was awarded.

O'Brien quickly identified Downtown Radio, a successful independent station based in Northern Ireland, as a partner that would bring broadcasting experience to the consortium. The station's chairman, James Donnelly, agreed to become involved and O'Brien and his fellow investors brought together a diverse group reflecting various Irish cultural interests in order to meet the licence criteria. In January 1989 the Radio 2000 consortium submitted its licence application.

Weeks later the IRTC summoned four applicants – Radio 2000, Century Radio, the National Radio Franchise Consortium and Radio Nova International – to an oral presentation to make their case in front of an invited audience. Century Radio, a group led by impresario Oliver Barry, was reported to be the favourite to win the licence. Barry's high-profile consortium included BBC broadcaster Terry Wogan and pop star Chris de Burgh. O'Brien's Radio 2000, by comparison, was virtually unknown and never considered a likely contender. Nonetheless Radio 2000 meticulously prepared for the forthcoming presentation.

Each group was given forty-five minutes to convince the IRTC that it should win the licence. One person describes the hearings as being like the 'negotiations between the US and Vietnam to end the war'. The various groups were gathered at long tables, each rising when it was their turn to impress the IRTC.

O'Brien, according to the application, was Radio 2000's chairman and attended the presentations with his team, but he didn't himself make the presentation. That job fell to businessman Brendan O'Kelly, who was now part of the crew. Radio 2000, he enthused, would 'innovate, stimulate, entertain and compete' if it won the licence and would be a worthy competitor to RTÉ.

There was a great deal of public interest in the potential new radio stations and substantial media coverage of the story. When Marian Finucane invited the aspiring radio operators to make their case to the nation on her popular RTÉ 1 show, Chris Carey of Radio Nova and Kevin O'Connor of the National Radio Franchise came to the studio to talk about their ambitions. O'Brien, who was unknown in the radio business, declined the invitation, but did phone in towards the end of the programme to make a brief contribution.

Few were surprised when Barry's Century consortium won the licence. He was well known and enjoyed a good relationship with the political establishment, and had gathered an impressive crew for the licence bid. 'It was a home run for Oliver,' one person explains. Yet his victory would later be mired in controversy. In an environment where businessmen worked closely with powerful politicians who could influence who won contracts from the government and its agencies, money often changed hands. Extensive investigations later revealed that Barry had donated €44,000 to Ray Burke, the Minister for Communications who awarded the licence. The IRTC confirmed that the minister had no input into the decision, finding that the award of the licence was based on 'normal business criteria'. The controversy was a foreshadowing of events that would later overtake O'Brien himself.

The outcome was a bitter disappointment for O'Brien and his consortium. Having spent a lot of money on the application, they had come away empty-handed. According to one of the backers, O'Brien was very angry about losing. Yet, although his ambitions to become a media mogul had suffered a setback, his luck was about to change.

As Century Radio prepared to go on the air, the IRTC had other licences to award, this time for a radio station in the Dublin area. O'Brien felt his consortium should apply. Having already spent a small fortune on the national radio licence application, it wouldn't cost them much more to go after a Dublin licence that was also potentially lucrative. Radio 2000 would simply have to tweak its original application to focus on providing a radio station for younger listeners, those aged between fifteen and thirty-five. This time O'Brien would ask a young handsome television presenter to make the consortium's case to the IRTC. 'I got a frantic call on a Friday evening,' says David Heffernan. 'Denis told me to get back to Dublin by any means to prepare the licence application. He mentioned the people in his consortium were not used to losing.'

Radio 2000 began working to put together its team. As new stations began to emerge, however, there were only a few high-profile presenters they could hope to woo away from RTÉ. Mark Cagney, a popular disc jockey on the national broadcaster's station for the younger audience, RTÉ 2, recalls first learning of O'Brien's bid when a fellow radio presenter, Gerry Ryan, having heard that Radio 2000 was looking for new recruits, mentioned that this 'O'Brien fellow' might be interesting.

In the late 1980s radio presenters at RTÉ were a badly paid bunch, according to Cagney. 'We were earning buttons. We couldn't afford to go to gigs unless we were on the guest list.' Those working at RTÉ were employed on three-month contracts and were as vulnerable to internal politics as to listener preferences. 'There was no security of tenure,' he explains. 'You couldn't get a mortgage in those days on that basis. That's why everyone was doing gigs at the weekends.'

It was precarious for RTÉ stars to be associated with new rival stations. Those leaving to join Century Radio risked permanent exile from the national station, as was made clear to every employee. Nonetheless, Cagney made a few discreet enquiries about his prospective new employer.

His wife asked a friend who had known O'Brien at UCD whether or not her husband should risk his job at RTÉ and sign up with him. 'It will be a hell of a ride,' was the friend's verdict. 'O'Brien will either make £20 million or lose it.' Getting involved with O'Brien would clearly be a gamble. Reporting the conversation to her husband, Cagney's wife asked, 'How lucky are you feeling?'

O'Brien and Mooney met Cagney to talk about a possible new career. 'It was staged so that I was talking mainly to Mooney but I knew I should be talking to Denis,' he says. 'I liked both of them. Mooney was a lovely man, straight as a die, exuded probity and honesty and decency. And there was a force about Denis, an energy.'

A couple of hours later they made Cagney an offer he couldn't refuse. The details were sketched on the back of an envelope. 'I signed it,' he laughs. 'I didn't know whether I had won the Lotto or been suckered. I knew it could be a hell of a ride and that I didn't know where it would end up. But I felt that I had to do it. It was the first time in my life I was financially viable. I had a three-year contract earning three times more than I was paid at RTÉ. For the first time, I could own a home.'

Another RTÉ colleague, Jim O'Neill, was also ready to jump ship. He would be joining actor and broadcaster Bryan Murray, musician Philip Donnelly and the crew from Downtown Radio. In February 1989 they would present their bid to the IRTC.

This time there was a familiar face on the IRTC panel. Fred O'Donovan, O'Brien's former business partner in the Esat consortium, had recently been appointed to the body and had a deciding vote in awarding the new licences. O'Donovan says the presentations at those hearings were crucial for the applicants and would be the deciding factor for the IRTC. 'There were a lot of applications from people who knew nothing about radio. It seemed like every lunatic in the country had applied for a licence. One guy could be contacted through a phone box outside his house. Another guy had an office in his bedroom.'

According to O'Donovan, the presentation given by O'Brien's consortium was 'first class'. 'I voted to give a licence to them and so did the nine others.' Capital Radio, a consortium brought together by Jim Aiken, pirate radio broadcaster Mike Hogan and accountant Greg Sparks, was also successful. Dublin was about to get two new radio stations.

Some of the losing consortia were surprised at the result, claims Cagney. 'They were asking who is Denis O'Brien? What does he know about radio?' And it didn't take long before one challenged the result. Robbie Robinson, former head of pirate station Sunshine Radio, questioned the close relationship between O'Brien and O'Donovan and alleged that the licence hadn't been fairly awarded. He went to court to challenge the decision, with the result that neither licence could be awarded pending the outcome of the legal action.

When the case opened at Dublin's High Court, details of O'Brien and O'Donovan's close personal and business links would form the main plank of Robinson's claims of bias. His lawyers asserted that until recently the new radio chairman had been engaged to

O'Donovan's daughter and that they had a recent business partnership. O'Donovan had been a director of Esat, the company that was a major shareholder in the Radio 2000 consortium, they told the court, when he was appointed to the awarding body.

In the witness box O'Donovan said he had disclosed his business relationship with O'Brien when he was appointed to the IRTC. He had resigned from the company a year earlier, selling his shareholding to fellow investor Paul Power, he explained, adding that the fact that his resignation from Esat had not been properly recorded in official company records was the result of an error. There was nothing improper about their relationship and he insisted he had shown no bias in voting for Radio 2000 as the winner of the Dublin radio licence.

The matter was resolved when the judge said he didn't believe any right-minded person could have found any real likelihood of bias on the part of O'Donovan. The ruling upheld the IRTC's decision to award the licence to Radio 2000 and they could finally celebrate. O'Brien was back in business.

5 Classic Hits

'It was a touch of *Barbarians at the Gate*. Denis had a sense of being master of the universe,' Mark Cagney says of the moment when, at the stroke of midnight on 10 November 1989, Dublin's new radio station went on air.

After months of preparation Classic Hits 98FM delivered on its promise of 'better music, less talk, the music of the 60s, 70s, 80s and today', playing the Eagles' Grammy Award-winning classic, 'Hotel California', as its first song. Listeners could be in no doubt about what to expect from the new station.

Cagney and Jim O'Neill joined the station's eclectic mix at their new home on Dublin's Upper Mount Street. Dubliners could wake up to *The Morning Crew*, the early morning show presented by Elaine Geraghty and Pat Courtnay. Throughout the morning and afternoon they could tune into Cagney and O'Neill, with a late-night talk show to follow, hosted by Ireland's best-known Catholic priest, Fr Michael Cleary.

There was an air of excitement around the studios and O'Brien settled into an office in the midst of it. Colleagues commented on how pleased he seemed to bring business contacts past the studios to his office. 'He just loved being part of it all,' says one.

Having flirted with joining Century Radio, journalist Conor Lenihan moved to Classic Hits 98FM after O'Brien and Mooney offered him the news correspondent's job. 'I think I was one of the first employees,' he says. 'Denis and Luke Mooney struck me as being really professional. They were business people who didn't see radio as different to any other business. They wanted to run a profitable business and to run it in a professional way, away from the pirate radio model, properly supported by research and marketing.'

The station's line-up and content was honed using extensive research. Over many months Australian consultants Broadcast and Programming Research (BPR) interviewed thousands of listeners in the Dublin area to find out what they wanted to hear from the new station. Programme director Jeff O'Brien and BPR's Peter Benson worked with their colleagues to create playlists laced with classic hits, ensuring that the most popular songs were played at regular intervals. It would be a winning formula, they hoped.

Classic Hits 98FM was a young station in every sense. O'Brien assembled a very youthful crew to work at the station. Most were in their early twenties and eager to be part of the new force in Irish radio, though a few grey hairs were allowed in the building as Mooney, Fr Cleary and O'Brien's father, who was regularly seen around the office, raised the age profile.

Lenihan suggests that O'Brien was influenced in the way he ran the business by the founder of the Virgin group. 'He modelled himself on Richard Branson. He had read an awful lot about the Branson model, which was essentially to recruit very young people, motivate them and keep them in the company until they find other reasons to move on or not to be working for you,' he explains. 'You have them for a period and they work extremely hard, and part and parcel of that culture was to keep it so informal that the bosses never got so remote that they were unapproachable.'

Everybody who joined the company was expected to feel part of the Classic Hits 98FM team. O'Brien was their leader. 'Team was a major part of his manifesto,' says Cagney, adding that his boss was 'a strong leader'. 'All teams need a captain. You knew you were on his team and you had to play the way that he wanted you to play. He was a dictator.'

Everybody from the cleaners to the high-profile DJs was on first-name terms with O'Brien, who might in turn greet them with a nickname. You would be known by the name he conferred on you, usually based on traits or a likeness to a sports personality or someone of interest to him. Some found this endearing, while others wondered if it was a means of asserting his control. Was he to some extent creating an environment where your own name had no relevance?

A ferociously hard worker himself, O'Brien was constantly present. 'If you had been on early you would see him and when you were on late he was there or at the end of the phone,' one of the early crew recalls.

'He worked incredibly long hours. He got up at five in the morning but he loved every minute of it,' Paul Meagher says. 'He was a very serious, focused, hard-working guy. He might have been gregarious but we didn't drink midweek and would give it a serious lash at the weekends.' O'Brien insisted that everyone should be prepared to take on whatever tasks were necessary, regardless of their position at the station, dealing promptly with those he considered to be working below full capacity.

According to Meagher, his friend was always vigilant that everyone worked as hard as he did, and equally obsessed with getting value for money. 'If he sees anybody swinging the lead or using or abusing him he goes absolutely mental. He won't pay over the odds for anything and that applies to the people who work for him, the people who provide services to him, whether they are accountants, management consultants or bankers. He is a value-driven guy and he will see off any attempt to rip him off.'

O'Brien was fearless and wouldn't let anything get in his way. One former colleague remembers him climbing on to the roof with a hammer to knock some ice off the transmitter in the middle of winter. There was no job he wouldn't do himself. He regularly joined the Classic Hits gang when they put on branded T-shirts to hand out stickers to motorists at busy junctions around the city.

'We were always asked to get involved in the marketing efforts,' says Conor Lenihan. 'I don't think that you would be asked at the *Irish Times* to go and hand out stickers for the company at the weekend. Everyone regardless of their rank was expected to market the company and its commercial interests. Literally every month we had to hit various traffic points and put on T-shirts and throw out our stickers and promotional material.'

Some of the 'on-air egos' were appalled at having to get involved in these promotions and cursed management for making them do this – but 'only in private', according to Lenihan. 'It was an interesting way to build staff morale and to encourage people to make the direct connection between what they were doing and the radio station.'

O'Brien was generally charming and could be great fun, but wasn't shy about having a row with someone he felt wasn't pulling his or her weight. One former colleague puts O'Brien's view of his team members simply: 'You were either for him or against him.'

It was an early indication of what loyalty means to O'Brien. As far as he is concerned, loyalty is about compliance and willingness to constantly do what he wants. Determined to create a strong bond among his employees that would make them go that extra distance to beat their common enemies, he devised his own loyalty-building exercises. After work on Friday, the captain bought drinks for his team at the nearby Henry Grattan pub. Attendance was compulsory. They even had a team drink, tequila, shots of which they would happily down till late. They were encouraged to have fun. 'He believed in getting people drunk together and encouraged relationships within the company,' says one. 'He would often matchmake. This was all part of keeping the team together and building loyalty. If colleagues hooked up together, they had stronger links to the 98FM family and couldn't leave.'

Absences from the Friday night session were noted. 'You were obliged to be there,' says Lenihan. 'If you weren't, Denis might say to you: "You haven't been for the drinks in the last few weeks, what's going on? Are you still part of us?"'

The team had plenty to celebrate. O'Brien's competitive nature was obvious to everyone at the new radio station. Their mission was to beat their opponents at all costs. Classic Hits 98FM was a runaway success from the start, quickly wooing its target audience from RTÉ, Century Radio and its other main rival in the Dublin area, Capital Radio. 'Denis was always highly competitive and was obsessed with beating RTÉ,' says one colleague.

Ratings days, when the independently monitored listenership figures were issued, would prompt a mega party. Together the new commercial stations were eating into RTÉ's audience, up to forty-two per cent of whom were tuning into the new stations. 'They were always big days at the station. Most of the time the ratings were good,' a former employee says. 'For the first nine years we were ahead of our competitors in the ratings.'

Classic Hits 98FM's breakfast show was particularly popular with listeners, while at the end of the evening Fr Cleary's late-night talk show was another favourite. The idea to ask the media-friendly Fr Cleary to host the show had been a brave one, designed to entice older listeners to switch over to the new station. 'It was a great idea,' says Cagney. 'It got loads of publicity through the churches and pensioners' clubs. He was the highest-profile priest and the show got the type of coverage that public relations and marketing couldn't buy. And, of course, when Mick got a stage he knew how to work it.' Five nights a week callers rang in looking for advice and guidance on air, on everything from abortion and single motherhood to marital difficulties and other family problems. The listeners loved the priest who extolled the church's most conservative teachings.

'We needed a talk show host and all the good ones are locked away by RTÉ, which can offer them a TV slot as well,' O'Brien explained in an interview. 'We also needed somebody who could appeal to a wide age group, from fifteen to sixty-five, and Mick can do this. We offered to split the time with the Church of Ireland and asked them to nominate someone. They haven't as yet, but they might.' Years later, after his death, Fr Cleary gained further notoriety when it was revealed that he had fathered a son with the housekeeper he had lived with for decades.

The station's presenters were closely monitored by audio consultants who tracked their performance for O'Brien. As soon as their shows ended, Cagney, O'Neill and the other broadcasters were called to a meeting with the consultants to discuss their performance.

'The DJs would literally finish a three- or four-hour stint and they would be immediately into an appraisal session with the consultants and the programme director,' Lenihan explains. 'The consultants taped their vocal interventions and critically examined how they did. News was audited every six months and they would say "You are doing this and the listeners are saying you're not doing enough Dublin news, the story count isn't good." At one level it was a pain in the arse and people struggled with it. Eventually they saw it as being worthwhile.'

O'Brien loathed RTÉ and the feeling was probably mutual, according to Cagney. 'He hated the mentality there, that ivory tower attitude. They all had their sinecures. There was an intellectual arrogance. Some were the type of people who would have season tickets to the Concert Hall but who hated classical music. They were the establishment and had links to all parts of Irish society. They saw Denis as a jumped-up Dublin 4 gurrier [Dublin slang for a scrapper]. They would have hated him.'

Paul Meagher says O'Brien's antipathy towards state-run monopolies stems from those early days. 'When you look back then, radio was dominated by the state broadcaster. RTÉ tried to crucify him and the other commercial stations from the start. They couldn't comprehend that competition had arrived in Ireland.' Indeed, O'Brien was obsessed and appalled with what he believed were huge inefficiencies in the big Irish monopolies generally. 'He was always giving out about Cablelink and the ESB [Electricity Supply Board],' says another colleague. 'If there were six or seven of their workers on the street beside us, and there was no sign of any work going on, Denis would bring you over to the window to point it out. You were left in no uncertainty about how he felt about them.'

The thirty-three-year-old radio boss was quite the man about town by now. Featured in the business pages of the *Irish Times*, he talked about how he ran the station. 'It's a bit like having a general election a week. You have to keep people with you all the time.' Photographed sitting in the studio, O'Brien put his success down to teamwork. 'We work as a team and pull together. When the station gave away a BMW a couple of weeks ago the whole company was there to cheer the winner. That's the way we do things.'

A business associate admired O'Brien's great energy and ability to get the station up and running. 'He ran 98FM incredibly well. Nothing was ever a problem. A challenge, but not a problem. He had a short attention span but had a great ability to select good people. I would say he was a starter upper of businesses rather than a manager, and I think he recognised that fault in himself.'

Within the industry it was estimated that there was about €10 million a year in advertising revenue to be carved up between RTÉ and the independent stations. At least €4 million of this was likely to go to the new stations and Classic Hits 98FM aggressively chased that money.

Marketing executive Lucy Gaffney joined the station as its marketing manager in May 1990 after O'Brien persuaded her over lunch to leave her job at the Irish Press newspaper group and work for him. 'He was building a team around him and he had a very clear idea of what he wanted to do with the station,' Gaffney says. 'He was very engaging, had a great sense of humour. It was very exciting.'

Her first task was to find a sponsor for the 98FM Cash Call promotion that guaranteed a cash bonanza for the station's ninth caller. She was shocked to be told her job was to go out and sell the slot to an advertiser. 'I had never sold a thing in my life. I thought I was working in marketing and told Denis "I don't sell."' The consummate salesman dismissed her protest. 'We are all selling,' he told her. 'And he still says that. Denis believes everyone works in sales,' says Gaffney. Indeed, O'Brien sees himself ultimately as a salesman, a skill he primarily learned from his father. Gaffney believes he is very proud to be characterised in that way.

Together they worked on polished pitches to the advertising agencies, encouraging them to promote their clients through 98FM. O'Brien accompanied Gaffney to close a sale or to deal with a particularly difficult agency or client and he would send a clear message about how he felt if a meeting wasn't going their way. 'He walked out of a meeting with a big agency in Dublin that was bullying us,' she recalls. 'Denis would never be bullied. He was never afraid to walk out.'

98FM was an attractive station for advertisers, O'Brien claimed, because it was reaching a more mature, well-heeled audience than its rival, Capital Radio, which catered for teenagers. Its listeners had disposable income and real buying power and were a more attractive proposition for advertisers. And the advertisers seemed to agree. Within seven months the station was profitable as more and more listeners and advertisers switched to the Classic Hits formula.

Gaffney says O'Brien was always coming up with creative ideas about how to earn more money for the station. In those early years a few of 98FM's advertisers went out of business and they got 'stung', according to Gaffney, She worried about bringing the bad news to her boss: 'I remember having a fairly rough meeting with him at the time we lost money. He said, "You know a sale is not a sale until we get the money in."'

O'Brien is very 'left of field' in the way he approaches problems, she says. 'He was always trying to do something different and forcing people to think of the problem in a different way.' O'Brien devised novel ways of ensuring the station collected the money it was owed. A range of packages were offered, with early bird discounts and keen prices for a long series of advertisements, while the credit terms were strictly enforced. Lenihan is among those who mention Mick McDonnell, a colleague who doubled as a debt collector: 'He was a famous character who had a particularly awesome black leather outfit for his motorbike. Denis told him to sit in the agencies' fancy foyer area and insist in his strong Dublin accent that he had to get paid. They [the agencies] wouldn't want him to spread panic amongst any clients so they would want to get Mick out of reception and would pay up.'

By the same token, the station was happy to reward its loyal advertisers, hosting big parties every Christmas and in June to thank them for their business. Everyone at the station was expected to attend. 'It would be frowned upon if you didn't go along,' recalls one employee. 'You had to be part of the team.'

O'Brien cultivated relationships with important advertisers and political contacts who were invited on trips to see the Irish soccer team play European fixtures. In a grand gesture, the 98FM boss hired a plane to bring a group to watch Ireland play in the Italia 90 tournament. One man fondly recalled the trip to Cagliari. 'There were about forty of us, including Fr Mick,' he says. 'We played football on the beach before the match.' This was a new departure in terms of corporate entertaining. O'Brien believed in always entertaining in style and reinforcing the image of a successful businessman with a thriving empire.

By now O'Brien and his management team – Gaffney, Jeff O'Brien, Padraig Boland, Caroline Davies and Miriam Matthews – had bought out the station's early backers, who were happy to exit the business. Having initially invested in a shopping channel, they had found themselves involved in a local radio station by default. Few of them had any interest in being part of it in the longer term.

Under the new ownership structure O'Brien emerged as the biggest shareholder, with seventy per cent of the company. He borrowed heavily to raise the money, personally guaranteeing loans of more than €600,000 for his management colleagues to do the deal. And he was delighted to let everyone know that 98FM had a new owner. The station took out full-page advertisements in the Irish newspapers to proudly announce the changing of the guard.

The management team often went out for dinner together, or to elegant parties hosted by O'Brien. He was always a very generous host. 'There were great parties in his house,' says Gaffney. 'He was a great believer in working hard and playing hard but being back at the desk at eight o'clock in the morning. There was no coming in with a hangover at ten. You had your night out and that was the end of it.'

He even invited the entire management team and their spouses to Portugal for a weekend. They were looking forward to a fun break; it would prove anything but. 'It was meant to be a kind of navel-gazing weekend and he brought a couple of advisers and board members along,' Gaffney says. 'I remember my husband bought a stunning bottle of wine as a present for him, but we never gave it to him because it was such a horrific weekend. I was distraught by the end of it. Denis raked over everything and brought in people to tell us where we weren't doing well enough. It was a very, very tough weekend. We only got to see our spouses in the evening. It was a gruesome ordeal.'

The weekend was particularly gruesome for Gaffney. O'Brien was determined to take away her marketing responsibilities and put her into a sales role. She was shocked: 'We nearly fell out badly over that. I resisted it and I held on to the marketing job and we got back on track. That was an example of how hard he pushes people.' It was a pivotal moment. While the team, like O'Brien, were now shareholders in the business, he was the boss and not their equal. 'We would go on the lash but he was on a different level. We would have been unwise to ever have thought we were his peers,' Gaffney says. 'He was always one step ahead of us.'

*

Back in Dublin, business was good. After just two years in business 98FM made a €440,000 profit. O'Brien captured the sense of optimism at the company: 'If you've got a business that's making money you feel good, your confidence lifts and you begin to see things in a different light. Instead of gazing out the window and everything looking grey, you can see a sparkle of sunshine.'

By comparison, Dublin's second commercial radio station, Capital Radio, had nothing to celebrate. It was in serious financial difficulty. According to its first managing director, Mike Hogan, while Capital was well funded its market research failed to match its arch-rival: 'Denis had a good team, so did we, but he did the one thing I didn't do but should have done. He went out and thoroughly researched the market.

'We were delivering fifty-two per cent of fifteen to twenty-two-year-olds and Denis wasn't within an ass's roar of that, but nobody wanted to reach the fifteen to twenty-two-year-olds in 1989. The Irish economy was in the dumps and what money was being spent was by advertisers who wanted to be on Classic Hits 98FM.' As Hogan explains, 'He picked the right format, while we were losing money hand over fist. When we were playing Kylie Minogue he was playing the Eagles. When we were giving away Suzuki jeeps he was giving away BMWs. He absolutely wiped the floor with me.'

In a bid to stem the losses, Capital hired Peter Benson, the consultant they credited with so successfully positioning O'Brien's station, in the hope that he could find a winning formula to save Capital's business. He decided it should become a rock station and it was relaunched as Rock 104.

O'Brien and his crew were among the first to notice their rival's new brand and rapidly brought it to the public's attention. Over the coming days, Classic Hits 98FM took out full-page advertisements in the Irish newspapers featuring a picture of a mangy old leopard with a couple of tags hanging from its neck. One said 'Capital Radio', the other 'Rock 104'. 'The gist of it was that a leopard doesn't change its spots,' recalled one of the station's former crew. 'It was humiliating.'

But the name change made no difference to the station's fortunes. Within a couple of months it was once more in crisis and Hogan departed. It was a tough business environment generally for radio stations. Century Radio, which had beaten O'Brien's consortium for the national radio licence in 1989, struggled from the start and had collapsed within two years. O'Brien purchased the station's office and radio equipment and installed it at 98FM.

Following Hogan's departure from Rock 104, Dermot Hanrahan, who was running the Blockbuster video rental chain in Ireland, was brought in to run the station on an interim basis to try to keep it afloat. As he crafted a new business plan to put the station on a more secure financial footing, he quickly learned just how ruthless O'Brien and his team could be when it came to beating the opposition.

'Denis had really wrong-footed the early management team in Capital Radio, who were used to more gentlemanly behaviour,' he says. 'They were not used to people just going for the jugular.' O'Brien and his team, he says, were a 'polished act' competing with people who came from a pirate radio background. 'They didn't have the sophistication in dealing with the ad agency that would come naturally to Denis and his sidekick at that time, Lucy.'

One of Classic Hits 98FM's key selling points to the agencies, he claims, was to bad-mouth Rock 104. 'Denis had done a very good job of positioning Capital Radio and Rock 104 in the minds of the ad agencies as a downmarket station for drug-addled teenagers. He missed no opportunity to develop that image and was doing everything in his power to knock several shades of shit out of the appearance of Rock 104.'

With fresh investment, in 1992 Hanrahan and his team knew they would have to retaliate. It was clear that the switch to a rock station hadn't worked. According to Hanrahan, it might as well have been called 'Shit FM' given its poor reception with the Dublin public. The station would have to be rebranded for a third time. 'Our biggest concern was that we were going to look like an absolute joke to the ad industry,' Hanrahan says. And of course O'Brien would have a field day. 'We could just see the Classic Hits ads running again with a second leopard or an extra name tag around its neck. So we decided the only way of defending ourselves to the ad agency community was by finding some way of going on the offensive.'

The relaunch was designed to gain maximum publicity and finally reverse the station's fortunes. 'We decided we would run a teaser campaign that would herald the launch of something new and exciting without mentioning the station in the process. The real sting in the tail though would be that we would run it on Classic Hits.'

And so a large marketing campaign was devised. Enormous posters showing a big blue field that invited people to 'Catch us with our pants down' appeared across Dublin and on the side of the city's bus fleet. Hanrahan asked someone unconnected to the station to book the advertising slots at Classic Hits 98FM, he says. The sales representative who took the booking was simply told it was a teaser campaign for an international jeans brand. The details were confidential. 'We even paid up-front,' Hanrahan explains, recalling his joy when the first of the advertisements was aired. 'They ran it over and over again,' he laughs. 'We were delighted.' ·

On the launch day, the posters changed to reveal Greg Gaughren, one of the station's top presenters, with his trousers around his ankles tossing cash into the air. It was telling Dubliners that FM104 wanted to give away lots of cash to listeners.

'That morning we sent out a press release saying "Denis O'Brien has been caught with his pants down",' says Hanrahan. 'The *Evening Herald* ran the story on the front page and the 98 gang went bonkers. We heard that Denis wasn't too pleased, that he held a staff meeting where he described us as the enemy that was taxiing its aircraft to the runway. O'Brien told his troops it was their job to make sure FM104 never got airborne.' According to Hanrahan, 'Denis predicted we would be out of business by September.'

The rivalry between the two stations was well known. O'Brien publicly compared FM104's many launches and relaunches to Cape Canaveral. There was room only for one radio station in Dublin, he claimed: 'There might be two still around, but one of them won't be making money. It's dog eat dog in this business.'

Hanrahan says the enmity between the two stations was often ridiculous. The FM104 chief was nevertheless thrilled to see the station's posters attached to every railing and doorway in Dublin's Ballsbridge area where U2 were playing in 1994 as he drove past that evening. 'My staff had been busy all afternoon. Our jeeps were around and we hired about twenty kids who had put them up. When I came back from Dun Laoghaire about an hour and a half later our posters were littered on the ground. They were in shreds and had been replaced with Classic Hits 98 FM posters. So we learned a lesson there and said that would never, ever happen to us again. And it didn't.'

When Whitney Houston played the Point Depot a few weeks later, the FM104 team were prepared. 'Like the last time, we had covered all of the area in FM104 posters and, sure enough, the 98FM jeeps turned up with a bunch of kids with knives to tear them down. But what they didn't know was that we had done a deal with a bunch of little gurriers from Sheriff Street and given them each a stretch of wall to mind. They got a tenner at the beginning and would get a second tenner at the end of the day if all of the posters were still there.'

When confronted by the tough-looking group of young lads, the 98FM crew got back into their jeeps. 'They thought better of it and that was the last time that happened,' says Hanrahan.

But the rivalry was relentless. 'Our competitions always had to be better than anything the other stations were running,' says a former 98FM team member. 'We were always trying to think of new ideas. It had to be completely different. If 104 was giving away a mortgage, we would have to give away a house. We gave away Trabant cars with the release of a new U2 album that had one on the cover. We got them from Prague.'

O'Brien was equally obsessed with getting the station's journalists to ensure their 98FM-branded microphones could be seen by the television cameras at high-profile public events. According to Lucy Gaffney, it was all part of building a brand.

O'Brien had a strong vision and belief in the power of branding, learned at Boston College and reinforced by his stint working for Tony Ryan at Guinness Peat Aviation and for his father's company. His own lavish entertainment of his friends and colleagues was part of cultivating his image as their leader, the person who exuded success. And he expected his team to show the same pride and loyalty in order to constantly enhance the brand he wanted to convey to the public. 'Denis had a personalised image of what he was building,' Gaffney says. 'Everyone was part of that brand.'

O'Brien believes that if you paint your logo brightly enough and beam it out for all to see, that is what people will understand.

Everything associated with him and his empire must be exciting and bathed in a positive light, something everyone wants to be part of.

While the radio station was thriving with a large listenership, advertising revenues were on the wane. O'Brien decided it was time to take the scalpel to the station's cost base. He contacted a prominent company doctor.

Leslie Buckley, a former personal assistant to paper and packaging tycoon Michael Smurfit, was a well-known consultant who had been appointed by the government in recent years to restructure companies like Irish Steel, Irish Rail and Aer Lingus. He agreed to meet O'Brien, and over the next few weeks they discussed how the business might be transformed into a leaner and more profitable one.

O'Brien struck Buckley as a young man going places. 'And he was going in a bit of a rush. He had this incredible vision. He could see where he wanted to go and he didn't see too many obstacles in the way.' One Friday evening they met to discuss the cost-cutting plan and how they might implement it. O'Brien immediately summoned his managers. 'I am sure they were probably in various pubs around the area at the time but within fifteen minutes they were all sitting around the table in his office,' says Buckley, whose role would be to help them achieve the savings. 'I said I would give a day a week for the next six weeks and then I would be gone. I was pretty busy at the time.' Twenty years on he still works with O'Brien and is considered his right-hand man. 'I have never worked for Denis but we have done a whole load of things together,' he says.

They were ready to wield the axe in every part of the station's operations, much to the horror of everyone working at 98FM. But when O'Brien called the staff to a meeting in the newsroom to deliver the bad news, he found some opposition from his popular cleric. 'I remember there were some young recruits in the immediate firing line and Fr Mick got up and made a speech to Denis,' recalls Mark Cagney. 'He was standing up for the downtrodden.' To no avail. They would have to accept the new, leaner regime.

O'Brien had bigger ambitions and was always testing the boundaries. Keen to expand his radio empire outside the capital city where he was licensed to broadcast – according to colleagues, he was always trying to extend the signal beyond the Dublin area – he began talking about joint ventures to local radio stations in Galway and Limerick.

Thanks to concerns that O'Brien was trying to build up a national commercial radio station on the cheap, the move was blocked by the Independent Radio and Television Commission. O'Brien backed off, but not before accusing the licensing authority of having 'no coherent policy on equity participation'. He would continue to challenge the authority for years to come. For now though, having tested their mettle, he looked elsewhere for new opportunities.

New radio licences were being offered in various parts of Europe and when the Czech government put one up for tender, O'Brien decided to apply for it. As it happened, the Irish Taoiseach, Charles Haughey, was leading a trade mission to Prague. Making good use of his connections, O'Brien asked Conor Lenihan, whose father was a government minister, to enquire about joining the delegation.

The government's press secretary, P.J. Mara, told Lenihan O'Brien would be welcome. 'That was my first encounter with Denis,' says Mara, who would later become one of O'Brien's trusted lieutenants. 'He had left it too late to get a visa, but I told Conor to tell him he could come along. He could attend all of the functions and meet the Czech Prime Minister, Vaclav Havel.' And so O'Brien did. Within a few months he had won the radio licence. 'He got that directly out of that trip,' says Mara.

Having thoroughly researched the Eastern European market, the group planned to set up another adult-based station, using 98FM as its blueprint. Kiss 98FM would begin broadcasting in 1992 to a potential audience of about one and a half million. Speaking about the new licence to the media, O'Brien described it as a 'reasonably high-risk project' in terms of getting the right people and the right culture together. 'We're all learning Czech and intend to give it our best shot,' he told reporters. 'I think there are enormous opportunities for Irish people and Irish companies in Eastern Europe.' He paid tribute to Seamus Brennan, Ireland's minister with responsibility for communications, for helping his company to cut through the bureaucracy. 'Our approach has been to camp outside the appropriate door until we get what we want,' he explained. And their persistence had paid off.

A team from 98FM was despatched to set up the new station. 'Get your passport,' O'Brien told Lenihan; 'you're going to Prague.' Another colleague, Catherine Walsh, the station's sales operations head, was also transferred to Eastern Europe. O'Brien constantly issued instructions, relentlessly driving them to get the station up and running. He controlled every detail of the operation. 'He was a good man to bring pressure to bear,' Lenihan says. 'You could have a day when a decision was needed around the set-up or the management and you could have seven or nine cryptic faxes from Denis in a day. Each one would pile more pressure on you to account for what had happened or for a progress report.' He adds: 'Obviously if you weren't doing well the anger factor could increase and the word count generally got shorter, but that was part and parcel of it. He'd say, I'm not paying you guys to have fun out there.'

According to Lenihan, driving outcomes in a company was one of O'Brien's greatest strengths. 'And he wasn't afraid to roll up his own sleeves and get stuck in himself. The night before we went on air in Prague Denis was there putting up posters all over the city.'

This was the start of the international expansion. Soon O'Brien would bring his successful radio format to Sweden, where Klassica Hits was launched in October 1993. His staff would once again be expected to show enthusiasm for the new sister operation and travel to Sweden to support the brand they were building. O'Brien said he would pay their air fares to Stockholm. If they wanted to stay the night, they had to pay for their own accommodation.

Just four years after launching the Dublin station, O'Brien was head of a growing international radio group. He was on his way to achieving his ambition to become a media mogul.

6 Esat Telecom

As he conquered the radio business, Denis O'Brien was once more looking to new frontiers. Having speedily bounced back to build a successful company after the failure of his first business venture, the shopping channel which he believed had been ahead of its time, for his next venture he would follow the pioneers in another sector.

Once again he thought about the emerging trends across the Atlantic. He had closely followed the bitter battles between plucky entrepreneurs and the US telecommunications giant, AT&T, which was no longer a protected monopoly. Was it time to have a tilt at the same business in Ireland?

Entering the telecommunications sector wasn't for the faint-hearted. While it had been a struggle for O'Brien to raise the money to start his radio business, the amount of money needed to get it up and running was a drop in the ocean compared with investing in the technology and infrastructure required to compete with Ireland's state-owned phone company, Telecom Éireann. It would be a severe test of his endurance. But he was up for it.

He had learned the value of research in ensuring customers were given what they wanted and had developed his own fast-paced and demanding management style. His business education was complete. Having graduated with some distinction, it was time for him to use his winning formula to take on bigger opponents in the quest to make his fortune.

O'Brien spoke to Leslie Buckley about his plan to do battle in a bigger arena. 'I've a guy sitting over there called Mark Roden. He is working on some stuff to do with telecoms,' he explained. 'We're thinking of taking on the government and Telecom Éireann.'

Roden, an acquaintance whom Denis had recruited at a friend's wedding reception, was now working for a company called Esat Telecom, headquartered in the basement of the Classic Hits 98FM offices. O'Brien had set up the company in 1991, immediately applying to the Department of Communications for a licence to go into competition with Telecom Éireann. His first application was ignored, receiving not so much as an official acknowledgement. But that was to be expected. In the USA many of AT&T's opponents had endured bruising encounters with their mighty rival and with the authorities. Indeed O'Brien had spoken to one of them about what to expect if he entered the fray.

Jack Goeken, founder of Microwave Communications Inc., better known as MCI, had battled with and ultimately contributed to the break-up of AT&T's US monopoly. O'Brien had met Goeken briefly while he was selling his father's equine products in the USA in the 1980s. Now, as he began to build his telecommunications empire, O'Brien travelled to the USA with Roden to renew his acquaintance. Goeken advised them to visit satellite communications company PanAmSat.

There they met Doug Goldsmith, a consultant on regulatory affairs who explained the company's operations. Recognising Goldsmith's immense experience in the industry, O'Brien − in emulation of his mentor Tony Ryan, who constantly searched for the best people to join his team at GPA − asked him to come to Ireland to work at Esat Telecom. 'Probably, as only Denis knows how, he would have courted Doug Goldsmith very fast and got him into the business,' says Buckley. 'This was a very crucial point in the development of Esat Telecom.'

By now the European Commission was ushering in new directives to open up the telecommunications sector in each member state of the EU to competition. The legislation would force telephone companies to lease their lines to new operators who could then start to compete with them for customers. The measures were vociferously opposed by the giant phone companies in each country. And in Ireland Telecom Éireann was fiercely resisting the concept of competition.

The Department of Communications, which controlled Telecom Éireann, had so far dragged its feet in entertaining new licence applications. O'Brien's application was not the only one to be ignored. But by 1992 things were beginning to change. The minister now in charge, Brian Cowen, was more progressive and began issuing licences to allow new entrants to compete with Telecom Éireann for international phone calls, the most profitable part of its business.

Esat Telecom joined a number of international telecommunications companies clamouring for the new licences, including AT&T, Cable & Wireless and British Telecom. Other companies were already operating in this segment of the market, offering international phone services mainly to multinational companies based in Ireland, for which they did not need a licence.

Telecom Éireann wouldn't be making it easy for its competitors to chip away at the most lucrative part of its business. It was in no hurry to start leasing its lines to rivals. The company estimated that it could lose €250 million over the next five years to competitors, whom it claimed would 'cherry-pick' its most profitable business leaving it to maintain the loss-making local calls service that accounted for eighty per cent of phone calls on its network. But it realised it could stem the tide only for so long. It was a significant threat to a company that employed over twelve thousand staff and was being forced into competition with lean new rivals that often had just a few staff, and which, thanks to the new generation of advanced fibre-optic cables, would be able to cope with large numbers of international phone calls for a healthy profit.

A new regulatory body was to be established to make the process run more smoothly. It would decide the rates Telecom Éireann could charge competitors to use its phone lines. But the pace of change was to prove slow and frustrating, not to mention very expensive for O'Brien and his company.

By now Esat Telecom had about ten staff. Having helped to structure the business, Goldsmith returned to the USA at the end of his contract and Greg Mesch, an executive who worked in the telecommunications sector, took over the day-to-day running of the business, while Roden led the sales and marketing drive. They were supported by an expanding group that included many young college graduates eager to take up the scarce new jobs on offer in Ireland for salaries as low as €10,000.

European law graduate Jarleth Burke was hired after O'Brien rang his alma mater to find out who was the brightest and best of those about to complete their studies. Another young graduate, Sarah Carey, joined the team after imitating O'Brien's cheeky approach to Tony Ryan: she wrote a letter to the up and coming business tycoon highlighting the many reasons why she should be working for him. Accountant St John O'Gara later joined the team and became the de facto financial controller of a business with virtually no money. The engineers, who could provide essential technical back-up for the business, were among the highest paid people in the company.

They settled into the 98FM basement offices using the surplus chairs and desks purchased a few years earlier by O'Brien from the failed Century Radio. The new team quickly learned they would be expected to work seven days a week to get the business up and running. Some felt O'Brien, who rarely appeared in the office, had forgotten why he had hired them when they bumped into him. But he was always supportive, telling them they should assume responsibility for their duties rather than wait for it to be conferred on them.

And they did. 'We were working fourteen-hour days, seven days a week,' one early recruit recalls. 'We felt we had to do that to gain the respect of the older crowd. It was very demanding and none of us was being paid a lot of money.'

While they were expected to work hard, they quickly got to grips with the company's 'play hard' policy as well, frequently joining the Classic Hits 98FM parties where, at their boss's expense, they could drink the bar dry if they wanted.

Often there was a competitive element to the celebrations, and they could see for themselves O'Brien's determination always to be a winner. On one occasion, an inflatable bungee run game was set up and everyone was encouraged to see who could run the farthest before the bungee cord snapped them back to the beginning. O'Brien joined in, pitting himself against his team members. There was much amusement when one new recruit continued to beat his boss at each attempt. But O'Brien refused to give in and consistently challenged the victor to a rematch. Fourteen races on, the man operating the game offered some advice to the young participant: 'I think you're supposed to let him win.' O'Brien did win the next and final race, and everyone returned to the bar for more drink.

Back at work, Esat Telecom was still waiting for the regulatory authorities in Ireland to force Telecom Éireann to facilitate competition. So the company began looking internationally for opportunities to earn some money. It forged strategic alliances, reaching agreement with PanAmSat to acquire its satellite capacity and marketing rights in Ireland and the UK. It clinched a deal with the US and Russian joint venture satellite company, Cosmofon, to provide marketing and operations services, while US long-distance carrier Sprint allowed the company to connect to its switches in London and Washington. Esat now had something to sell.

Even when Esat Telecom was nothing more than a dream to O'Brien and Roden, the company had a shiny new logo. They were beginning to build a new brand and they wanted everyone to notice it. O'Brien insisted the logo had to be red, the most powerful and striking colour for a new brand. It would make a statement. O'Brien was so proud of it that he advertised it in the newspapers.

Over at Telecom Éireann, senior executive Cathal Magee says the logo was one of the first things he noticed. 'I thought it was vibrant. It was a brand that had ambition and dynamism. Somebody said this guy Denis O'Brien is going into telecoms and there was talk about people joining the company. We didn't take too much attention,' he adds. 'If you are a very significant player in the market, and the incumbent, you really don't have the time to be worried about these things. As far as we were concerned he had a tiny company, but it had all the ingredients of something that wouldn't be dismissed easily. There was a lot of thought behind this. He had identified this sector and wanted to make a go of it.'

Realising the importance of interfacing with politicians, O'Brien constantly sought meetings with Minister Cowen and his officials, lobbying them to speed up the process of reform. He wanted the Department to adopt immediately the European directive to force Telecom Éireann to share its network. His friend and solicitor, Paul Meagher, remembers O'Brien's frantic efforts to accelerate the process: 'He was forcing his way into the Department, battling with them trying to get licences. The licences in those days were broken up into frequencies of the radio spectrum and he had to battle for each and every licence; he was constantly meeting official resistance. The more resistance he met, the more he fought it, there was no way he was going to be beaten.'

What he saw as the civil servants' stonewalling on these issues infuriated him. 'It would just drive him around the twist,' says Meagher, 'He would write letter after letter' that plainly stated his view of the situation. His friend and lawyer would urge him to at least to 'tone down' the correspondence. 'I'd say you can't write to the Department like that. You've got to employ lobbyists, employ public relations people and build relationships with journalists. But he'd say that was bullshit. He was going to take them on head on.'

Meagher knows O'Brien to be a stubborn and tough individual who becomes fixated with winning when challenged. 'He is as tough as teak. He won't let anything stand in his way. There is no way you can say "no" to him. If you don't write the letter he will go to somebody who will. Even though he has tremendous loyalty to his friends, if you let him down, he will move on. He doesn't take any prisoners. The word "no" does not feature in his dictionary. It is not in his DNA.'

O'Brien's forceful assault on the Department had no immediate impact, yet his need for it to embrace the new regime was growing more urgent. The delays were potentially lethal for his new business. At this rate, Esat Telecom would be strangled before it got going. It would simply run out of money.

As the financial strain mounted, O'Brien enlisted the help of his 'rat pack'. Accountants Paul Connolly and Bryan and Aidan Phelan were drafted in to offer support and advice.

Based on MCI's experience in the USA, O'Brien recognised he would have to use evolving European law to force liberalisation through in Ireland. He turned for support to the European Commission. The Commission, which was leading the charge against the big telecommunications companies across Europe, was willing to facilitate meetings with small companies trying to break into the sector. Jarleth Burke was frequently dispatched to Brussels to make Esat Telecom's case and to highlight the difficulties it was encountering in the Irish market, and the company lodged a formal complaint against Telecom Éireann.

By now thirty-three-year-old O'Brien was well known in Dublin. He drove a new BMW that colleagues say was always covered in parking fines. He lived at an impressive house in one of the city's most desirable areas, Wellington Road, sharing it with his collie dog according to a profile of the aspiring telecommunications tycoon published in the business pages of the *Irish Times*.

He bought the house over the phone during a skiing trip with his gang in the plush Swiss resort of Verbier. 'I remember he bought it for a huge price. I couldn't believe it,' says Paul Meagher. 'He had taken a huge risk. I asked how he was going to finance it and he said he would figure that out when he got home.' O'Brien would remortgage that house many times over the following years to finance his emerging business. It was an asset he could leverage. He was making a bet for the future.

O'Brien has said his mortgage was €220,000, a huge amount of money at the time. He would host many stylish parties there, hiring black-tie waiters to serve his guests. 'He was always a good man to have a party. He really likes being in the company of people, has a good sense of humour and enjoys the craic,' says Leslie Buckley. 'He was always a really generous person. If he invited me and my wife to a function he would send a car to collect us. At the time I'd say his house was treble mortgaged. He probably hadn't a penny in his arse pocket.'

In fact O'Brien had borrowed more than €1 million from six banks for his business ventures. Esat Telecom was losing around €760,000 a month and the radio station in Prague was also making a loss. He would have to scrape around for cash every month to pay the wages. Months often passed by before some of the senior staff got paid.

O'Brien was increasingly in conflict with some of the other shareholders in his radio business. They fundamentally disagreed with his business strategy and had concerns about his use of the company's financial resources. Downtown Radio, a partner in the original Radio 2000 bid, was concerned that monies being invested and generated by the radio station were helping to keep Esat Telecom afloat. Its representative on the board of directors, James Donnelly, questioned loans made by the company to the Czech business and the extent to which Esat Telecom was absorbing the company's profits.

When the matter was raised at a board meeting, some sources say that 'all hell broke loose'. O'Brien wouldn't entertain anyone challenging his authority. He was the majority shareholder and things would be done his way or not at all. The relationship between O'Brien and Donnelly became what some have described as 'fragile'. In interviews O'Brien has claimed that Downtown Radio led a High Court action against him, although others familiar with the battle between them have no memory of it ever reaching the courts.

Radio 2000 and Esat Telecom had different groups of shareholders; O'Brien was one of only a few with an interest in both companies. Around this time, with war raging in the Balkans, O'Brien, ever quick to confer a nickname, began referring to Donnelly and his associates as 'the Bosnians'. Lucy Gaffney describes the struggle between Downtown Radio and O'Brien as an attempted *coup d'état* where Donnelly and his supporters tried to oust O'Brien from the company he had founded. 'There was bad blood there anyway and they wanted to unseat Denis. It was outrageous,' Gaffney says. 'But there was only going to be one winner.'

The wrangling continued for months, reaching its height just as O'Brien was about to close a deal with venture capital group Advent. The group's agreement to investment followed extensive efforts by O'Brien and Connolly to raise money. O'Brien wanted to expand into Warsaw, Moscow and Budapest. At the same time they were also courting potential investors in Esat Telecom, crossing the Atlantic every month to sell their story and find investors. 'We went every three weeks,' says Connolly. Knowing it was the only place they could potentially raise the money they would need to build a significant telecoms company, they regularly flew to the USA for just one meeting. It was a punishing schedule and they did it on a minimal budget, flying economy, or 'in the back of the bus' as Connolly describes it. They stayed at a decent hotel because their contacts wanted to know where in New York they were based, but they shared a room. In the evenings they dined casually at TGI Friday's.

Massimo Prelz Oltramonti, who oversaw Advent's investment in O'Brien's radio business, remembers his first meeting with the Irishman. He describes him as an interesting and impressive man: 'The radio business was very professionally managed and Denis was a highly motivated, bright, innovative guy who took a lot of risks. His only experience was a business failure and we took a bet that he had learned from that. I don't hold failure against anyone and felt that was a positive. I worked off the American view that if you try hard enough you will succeed.'

O'Brien likes to portray Prelz Oltramonti's investment in his fledgling telecoms business as a fluke, but that is an exaggeration. His version of the event is that Prelz Oltramonti travelled to Dublin for a look around the radio business before Advent committed to investing in it, only to stumble upon another exciting venture that its owner had never discussed with him. In interviews he has said the receptionist mistakenly took Prelz Oltramonti to the basement where Esat Telecom's bold red logo was on display. Prelz Oltramonti asked what was going on and that was the start of it.

But Prelz Oltramonti and Connolly remember things differently. Prelz Oltramonti insists he was aware of O'Brien's telecoms ambitions before he arrived that day. Connolly says that in their presentations to Advent, O'Brien and he had told Prelz Oltramonti that they were raising money for Esat Telecom.

Venture capitalists weighing up opportunities can be loath to invest in a business led by an entrepreneur with too many irons in the fire for fear he will be too distracted to deliver a return on their investment. It was a point Advent had raised several times. Indeed, according to Connolly, they were concerned about mentioning the telecoms company to Prelz Oltramonti just as Advent was about to inject some much-needed money into the radio business, but they decided to come clean. 'We told Massimo about the telecoms project and were terrified.' But the news was well received. Advent was now even more interested in what O'Brien's companies could potentially offer.

So the discussion widened. Esat Telecom wasn't making any money, but they talked about its potential. Although the small company was still in the throes of battle with Telecom Éireann, Prelz Oltramonti and O'Brien were aware that while its sights were set initially on breaking into the fixed phone line business in Ireland, there were other segments of the market that would soon also be opening up to competition.

The outlook for Esat Telecom suddenly appeared brighter when the Irish government edged closer towards embracing competition. O'Brien was relieved to hear Noel Treacy, Minister of State for Transport, Energy and Communications, announce that while Ireland didn't have to comply with the European directive and embrace competition in the sector until 2003, there was no obligation to prevent it from doing so earlier.

And in January 1994 Minister Cowen had a change of heart about the terms on which Esat Telecom's licence could be issued, perhaps in light of the complaint lodged with the European Commission. The minister effectively told Telecom Éireann to proceed with installing the facilities needed by Esat Telecom and others to compete with it for international business. Finally, they could open for business in Ireland.

And so the war began. It took Telecom Éireann just a couple of weeks to deliver some good news to its business customers. Those spending more than €2,500 a month on international calls could now enjoy discounts of between twenty and thirty per cent, depending on the size of their bills. The new deals formed part of the company's 'rebalancing' of tariffs, spokesman Gerry O'Sullivan explained. 'We welcome competition but we won't sit idly by and see our business being creamed,' he warned.

Roden publicly welcomed these developments, saying Esat Telecom customers would also get a better deal, saving thirty per cent or more on their international calls. The company would immediately recruit another fifteen people, he added, to cope with its new customers.

Despite the political impetus that was telling Telecom Éireann to make the lines available to its new rivals, there was no sign of anything happening on the ground. Roden complained to the Department about the company's initial refusal to install the leased lines, followed by lengthy delays in providing access to Telecom Éireann's network. And even where the lines were installed, they were extremely expensive. In the absence of an interconnection agreement between Telecom Éireann and its competitors, the company was charged the equivalent of thousands of euro for each line, making it difficult to create discounted packages to sell on to potential customers at a profit.

It was always going to be difficult to build a business that required technical support and access to its biggest competitor, as telecoms companies in the USA had found. O'Brien and Connolly were often joined on their fundraising expeditions across the Atlantic by the company's head of operations, Greg Mesch. During one visit they came across a piece of new technology used by a Canadian company that potentially could allow them to bypass the leased lines supplied by their rivals. If it worked, it just might save Esat Telecom.

The device that held out such promise was known as an autodialler. The matchbox-sized attachment, when connected to a telephone, would automatically divert the call from the existing Telecom Éireann line to Esat Telecom's international phone services provider, allowing the company to bypass Telecom Éireann's network. It was a potential solution that could save a lot of money and grief and they would definitely try it out, but it might prove tricky to convince the Department that by using these devices Esat Telecom was not breaching the terms of its licence. Effectively Esat was piggybacking off Telecom Éireann's network without having to pay them to lease a line.

Esat Telecom was to fight with the Department of Communications about this issue for years. Again O'Brien was testing the boundaries. He would quickly run with the autodiallers, daring the Department to rescind his licence while gambling that it wouldn't.

In the interim O'Brien had a business to launch. And a cash injection from Advent would greatly boost its prospects.

In the final negotiations, Prelz Oltramonti made it clear that Advent was prepared to invest in both the radio and telecommunications ventures, if an acceptable structure could be found. And soon they reached agreement. The money from Advent would have to be filtered through a new company and the 'Bosnians' would have to be dealt with. O'Brien would use some of Advent's money to buy them out and silence his critics. And Downtown Radio accepted the deal. It walked away with almost €1 million, a handsome return on its investment. Others whom O'Brien considered to have aligned themselves with Downtown Radio also left the company. There was no place in his organisation for disloyalty. Anyone displaying a lack of loyalty would be shown the door. 'A few people fell by the wayside,' says Lucy Gaffney. 'I stuck with Denis.'

Some viewed O'Brien's aggression towards those who challenged him as 'petulance' and say he let them know they had fallen permanently out of favour.

O'Brien has said that, as a manager, you constantly need to cull your team and bring in the skills required for the challenges ahead: 'The people you start out with aren't the people you end up with.' Decades later, some shareholders are said to still feel aggrieved about the circumstances surrounding their exit, feeling they were forced out of a business they had supported.

Now he had seen off the enemies within his ranks, O'Brien was shaking hands with Advent on a deal that would see it investing $10 million in his radio and telecoms businesses. The venture capital group would own thirty per cent of Communicorp, the parent company to the two businesses, which was now valued at €20 million.

It was a great result for O'Brien and he was able to take €1 million out of the company by selling some of his shares to Advent as part of the transaction. He had made his first million and was still very much in the driving seat, retaining sixty-five per cent of the company. He describes feeling like Red Adair, running around Dublin paying back the loans he had taken out to help him make that money and planning how he would use the new investment to make even more cash for him in the future.

Finally it was time to launch the telecoms company with the bright red logo to the public. Hundreds of companies were invited to Dublin's Shelbourne Hotel on 21 April 1994 to hear about Esat Telecom's cheaper international call packages. Minister Cowen posed with a telephone beside O'Brien for a photograph that appeared in all the newspapers. By switching to Esat Telecom, O'Brien explained, Irish customers could connect to the US telecom company Sprint's network and place calls to over 280 countries.

But they were breaking new ground and customers proved hard to convince. At the same time they had to fight a rearguard action against Telecom Éireann. Roden and his team made persuasive sales pitches to prospective customers who spent more than €2,500 a month on international calls. However, while a new customer might agree to sign up with Esat Telecom, the deal could often quickly unravel when that customer was suddenly offered a better deal by its existing provider. Not only would Telecom Éireann offer keener prices, they also issued dire warnings about the reliability of the rival phone company's services and the potential problems that might result. 'That happened all of the time,' says Buckley.

The breakthrough came when the ACT Kindle group signed an agreement to switch its international call business, extending to sixty countries, to Esat Telecom. Finally the new business had a customer. 'We broke open a bottle of champagne when we got that order,' Buckley says. And there were more celebrations when Irish Distillers, NCB Stockbrokers and accountants Deloitte and Touche followed suit.

A month later, the telecoms entrepreneur was the guest speaker at a lunch for chartered accountants in Dublin where he outlined his ambitious plans for the group. While Esat had had 'a bumpy passage' in its dealings with Telecom Éireann, O'Brien was charming and gracious when he spoke about Minister Cowen. Esat Telecom, he said, had received 'one hundred per cent support' from Cowen and his officials, a comment that amused friends and colleagues familiar with the endless rows between them and O'Brien's unflattering private comments about them. He was confident Esat would replicate Mercury's success in the UK, where the upstart telecoms group was winning major customers from British Telecom.

And it was only a matter of time, he suggested, before the company would compete in every segment of the industry, since it had plans ultimately to offer local and trunk calls to the general public in Ireland. Telecom Éireann's mobile phone subsidiary, Eircell, should also watch out for Esat, he cautioned. As mobile telephony was growing in popularity, O'Brien and his team would do everything they could to chase that emerging segment of the market.

Buckley by now was working as a consultant to the telecoms business. O'Brien christened him 'the Sniper', in recognition of his cost-cutting skills. Buckley's role extended from chairing management meetings to dealing with the day-to-day aspects of Esat Telecom's operations. He brought greater focus to the management meetings from the start. 'Denis is likely to come in and look at the agenda and go straight to the bottom item and spend most of the meeting on that,' he says. 'Hopefully I brought a bit of structure to it all.' Within a few months Buckley became the company's chief operations officer, spending three or four days a week running the fledgling business.

By the end of 1994 Esat Telecom had won over ninety customers and was earning €190,000 from its international call activities. But it continued to lose money. It was now facing a loss of about €1 million and had enough cash to survive for just one more month.

Financial controller St John O'Gara, who was working with Buckley at what O'Brien called the 'doom and gloom' department, outlined the worsening financial position at each management meeting. Esat Telecom owed millions of pounds both to Sprint, the US company that connected its customers' international calls, and to Telecom Éireann, which charged expensive rates for the line rental. And both were constantly demanding payment. Meanwhile O'Brien continued to ask investors to put money into his company, but few were willing to back such a risky venture as Esat edged closer to bankruptcy.

Buckley and Connolly pored over the figures for hours one night to see if they could avert looming disaster. At the end of the evening, Buckley decided the situation was so bad that he would loan the company the €100,000 he and his wife had accumulated in their joint bank account.

The money brought some temporary relief. And when, a few weeks later, O'Brien's father and businessman Donal Gallagher (whose late brother Seamus had been one of the original Radio 2000 investors) were among those who agreed to invest in the business in return for a shareholding, it seemed the ship had been steadied.

O'Brien's radio business was in a healthier state. Classic Hits 98FM was having another good year, making money and continuing to attract the highest listenership in Ireland's capital city. At the start of 1994 the station had scored a major coup, broadcasting the first interview with Sinn Féin leader Gerry Adams after the Irish government lifted its ban on the broadcast of comments made by members of the political party with links to the terrorist Irish Republican Army.

Political correspondent Conor Lenihan secured the interview and O'Brien and his team generated maximum publicity for the station. Television cameras were invited into the studio to film Lenihan and Adams as they prepared for the broadcast and the station took out advertisements in the national newspapers boasting about its scoop. According to one of the station's staff, O'Brien was ecstatic to have beaten the state broadcaster, RTÉ, to the interview. His company had punched way above its weight.

There were grand plans to continue to expand the radio business across Eastern Europe, but the financial pressures at Esat Telecom weighed heavily on the project, soaking up any free cash. Despite its considerable problems, however, there was an air of optimism about Esat Telecom's future. Before Doug Goldsmith, having helped launch the business, returned to the US two years earlier, he had made an interesting discovery: In Brussels the European Commission was preparing to open up the mobile phone sector to competition. Each member state would be required to issue a second mobile phone licence. And in Ireland, the government was preparing to do just that.

7 War Games

In the autumn of 1994 Denis O'Brien summoned his trusted foot soldiers and lieutenants to a bunker at a secret location.

They filed past the twenty-four-hour security guards into the secure environment from where they would launch their campaign to beat some of the world's biggest telecommunications companies in a fierce battle for Ireland's second mobile phone licence. Their conversations would be confidential. Paranoid about security, O'Brien had the room swept for listening devices, and the blacked-out windows would reveal nothing to the outside world. Only those inside knew the location, and they were sworn to secrecy.

O'Brien was directing a covert operation. Nothing would be left to chance over the coming months in his quest to win the licence. It would be his greatest achievement, the source of his great fortune.

His management team had been on a war footing since the Irish government announced it would shortly launch a competition to select a new mobile phone operator. Brian Cowen, Minister for Communications, promised to reveal the tendering process in a few weeks. It was the news O'Brien and his team had waited for more than two years to hear.

'It was militaristic,' says Lucy Gaffney, whom O'Brien enlisted to handle the marketing side of the operation. Over the phone one evening he casually mentioned his plan. 'I am going for a mobile phone licence,' he said, and asked her to join the team. The pair had fallen out more than a year before. This was a clear sign that their relationship was repaired.

As Gaffney explains, she had left 'in a fit of pique' after being passed over for the top job at the radio station company

Communicorp, and had set up her own business, the Ideas Company. Her disappointment over her failure to be promoted had been magnified by her belief that O'Brien was championing her as his successor to run Communicorp while he focused on Esat Telecom. But he had been overruled at a board meeting after Leslie Buckley and others challenged Gaffney's suitability for the job. The board agreed to hire a more experienced candidate to replace O'Brien and voted against her appointment. 'After the meeting Denis told me it didn't go through,' she says. 'Leslie said I wasn't ready for the job. I was devastated.'

Within a few months she was ready to leave and broached the tricky subject with O'Brien. The aspiring telecoms tycoon deeply resented the departure of his trusted colleagues, viewing it as disloyal. But, she says, he accepted Gaffney's decision amicably. They agreed that Gaffney, who was a shareholder in the radio business, would continue to work for Communicorp as a consultant, in much the same way as Buckley. They would both rent office space from O'Brien and run their own businesses from his headquarters.

Gaffney was surprised when O'Brien asked her to join his mobile phone licence bid. 'I said I don't know anything about mobile phones,' she recalls. 'Neither do I,' he laughed, 'but sure we'll have a bit of craic doing it.'

O'Brien's light-hearted response belied his keen interest in mobile phones. He had seen how the technology was thriving in the USA and in parts of Europe. It was transforming the way consumers used telephone services and it was growing rapidly, particularly among Europe's young population, with eighteen to twenty-five-year-olds among the biggest customers.

By the mid-1990s the European Commission estimated there were sixteen million mobile phones in Europe. By the end of the century, the figure was expected to rise to forty million, doubling to eighty million beyond the year 2000. Ultimately, it suggested, one in five people would own a mobile phone. It seemed exactly the type of business that could be a runaway success in Ireland.

Telecom Éireann's mobile phone company, Eircell, had been operating a mobile business for almost ten years. At first it offered large clunky mobile phones that cost about €1,300, an expensive item used mostly by business people. But as technology improved, the costs began to fall and over the next decade prices fell to a more affordable €300. Eircell also offered a cheaper paging system that was popular with increasingly prosperous Irish customers.

The era of the so-called 'Celtic Tiger' had begun. For the next decade Ireland would become the envy of Europe, its fastest-growing economy. Whereas so many previous generations had been forced to emigrate to find work, for the first time in its history the country's burgeoning young population could find opportunities for a career at home. It was a ripe environment to embrace the next wave of technology.

The mobile phone licences would usher in a more advanced platform, the Groupe Speciale Mobile Cellular (GSM) system offering subscribers the freedom to use their mobile phones in other countries. O'Brien was betting that if Esat Telecom could secure Ireland's second mobile phone operating licence, it would be a licence to print money. Potentially it was the most lucrative asset to be awarded by the Irish government.

It was a lofty ambition for the telecoms entrepreneur whose company was lurching from one financial crisis to the next as it struggled to stay solvent. Yet he believed they could win.

Esat Telecom's resources were meagre compared with those of the giant companies that were also limbering up for the competition, but O'Brien wouldn't see that as a disadvantage, says Gaffney. He would always find money to back his ventures. 'Denis would never let the lack of money be a deterrent to a business that he wants to grow. He knows that he will always find the backing and the investors. It would never stop a good idea. For Denis it's all about the challenge, being number one, beating competitors. Money has never been his motivation and so has never been a deterrent either.'

Gaffney, together with Esat Telecom lieutenants Mark Roden, Seamus Lynch and Frank O'Carroll, was part of the thirty-strong team summoned to 'the bunker' to hear O'Brien's battle plan. O'Brien's 'rat pack', including Paul Meagher, Aidan Phelan and Paul Connolly, were also part of the covert team, discussing tactics late into the night in their secret location.

Intermittently they were joined by new heavyweight board members O'Brien had recruited to lend gravitas to the company's efforts. Padraig OhUiginn, formerly Ireland's most senior civil servant, and John Callaghan, the former managing partner of accountant's KPMG's Irish operations, were ready to lend their expertise; also present was Massimo Prelz Oltramonti, the man who had sanctioned venture capital group Advent's $10 million investment in O'Brien's company. Beyond the boardroom O'Brien hired what he referred to as a 'bus load' of consultants to add 'a dose of expertise' for good measure.

As there was no spare cash, O'Brien had been steadily offering close friends and family the opportunity to invest in Esat Telecom. In return he offered options on the company's shares, which might some day be valuable. It was a generous gesture. 'He always decided on the amount of shares his people got,' Meagher explains. 'That was typical of the guy. He didn't have to offer share options but he wanted everybody to get the upside.' O'Brien's lieutenants, the new board members and some of the consultants were also offered share options.

Of all the business ventures he was now involved with, nothing would absorb more of O'Brien's time and energy than the bid to enter the mobile phone market. Big telecommunications companies across Europe were eyeing up the mobile phone licence. Their chances would be enhanced by including an Irish partner and the scramble to find local suitors was gaining pace. The US multinational, Motorola, a large employer in the Irish economy, was talking to Irish telecoms firm Sigma Wireless as a potential partner. The world's biggest telecommunications group, AT&T, was exploring a possible joint venture with a company associated with Tony O'Reilly. Other alliances were expected to emerge quickly.

It would take an exceptional bid to beat the big global players for the licence, so that was what O'Brien demanded. Back at the bunker he divided his army into cells, each with responsibility for key aspects of the battle plan. Lucy Gaffney was responsible for creating a brand for the new mobile phone company. Seamus Lynch was to create a network to distribute and sell phones. Mark Roden and Paul Meagher worked with the team that crucially had to figure out how to build a network that would deliver a service across Ireland. 'He was getting all the guys around him to help,' says Meagher.

Meagher remembers the first meeting at the bunker to discuss the bid. In a highly charged session, O'Brien outlined the total commitment and onerous demands he would be placing on each member of the team. Meagher, who was ready to undertake the legal tasks, was stunned to learn what O'Brien expected of him. They would need to identify locations to site mobile phone masts across Ireland and he expected Meagher to find them. 'How many sites can you get?' O'Brien asked his friend. 'I said I would come back to him,' says Meagher.

Just as his mentor, Tony Ryan, applied a mixture of fear and potentially lucrative share options to drive his team at Guinness Peat Aviation to conquer the aircraft-leasing business, so his apprentice would do with the mobile phone business. Over the following hours he doled out orders for each team, setting specific objectives to be delivered in a tight timeframe.

Some noted his constant obsession with maintaining confidentiality. He was known to tip up waste-paper baskets to check whether important documents were being carelessly discarded. Others wondered whether their phones were being monitored. However, they learned to adopt his bunker mentality. There are those who believe it is a state he continues to maintain to some extent.

O'Brien's chief task was to find a partner to join Esat Telecom's licence application. He made a list of the big global telecommunications groups and worked through the most promising leads. US group Southwestern Bell and Germany's Deutsche Telecom seemed like the most likely contenders and O'Brien meticulously prepared his pitch, with a little help from some public relations experts.

P.J. Mara, who had left politics to set up his own public relations consultancy, now renewed his acquaintance with O'Brien. He brought along Eileen Gleeson, who headed a leading public relations company in Dublin. Gleeson remembers her first meeting with the ambitious businessman: 'When I started dealing with Denis first I was completely struck by how different he was from everyone else that

I had worked with before.' He did remind her of one other client, former stockbroker and financier Dermot Desmond. O'Brien and Desmond shared many similar characteristics, she says.

'Denis was a maverick. He was well able to strategise and go out and talk, and was hugely self-confident.' And he had a unique presentation style. 'His presentations were chatty and humorous and this all comes naturally to him as opposed to being prepared. Denis just focused every day on what are we doing? How are we performing today? What's in the papers today? What's your plan? He was pushing all the time and I wasn't used to that. He was so singularly focused on his businesses and making them work, making everyone around him work.'

Their pitch was well received and it looked likely that Southwestern Bell would come on board. O'Brien flew to San Antonio, Texas, to woo the company and a group of its executives later travelled to Dublin to meet O'Brien and his team before agreeing to join the bid. It was a major breakthrough.

Meanwhile a shocking series of events led to a radical change in Ireland's political landscape. A month after Minister Cowen announced the imminent mobile phone licence competition, the Fianna Fáil-led coalition suddenly collapsed. But instead of triggering a general election, three opposing political parties came together to form a new government, sweeping the Fine Gael, Labour and Democratic Left parties into power. The biggest party, Fine Gael, led the so-called 'rainbow' government, and Ireland had a new Taoiseach, John Bruton. His party took most of the economic ministries in the new cabinet.

Those bidding for the licence would be dealing with a new Minister for Communications, Michael Lowry. They waited to see how he would continue the process started by his predecessor.

Sources familiar with the telecommunications industry in Ireland at that time suggest that some of the potential bidders had developed good relationships with the previous government as part of a lobbying exercise ahead of the competition. Indeed, O'Brien had made it his business to get to know most of the key government ministers and held meetings to discuss his telecommunications aspirations with everyone from Brian Cowen to Finance Minister

Bertie Ahern. Now the bidders would have to quickly get to grips with a new administration and its style of government.

Those eyeing the licence were pleased when in March 1995 Lowry formally invited tenders for the mobile phone competition. Licence applications were to be submitted to the Department of Transport and Communications by the end of June. A project team comprising senior civil servants would handle the competition alongside Danish consultants Andersen Management International. Applications would be compared on an 'equitable basis', the minister said. Each consortium would have to satisfy the project team that it had the financial and technical capability to build a new mobile phone service in Ireland, and each would be expected to have substantial funds on hand to meet its costs in the initial start-up phase. The battle had commenced.

Esat Telecom estimated it needed to spend up to €2.5 million to prepare a knockout bid for the licence. It would be a daily struggle to find the money to keep the project going. Buckley and O'Brien regularly disagreed about the amount of money they were spending at that time. They desperately needed its partners to share that cost. According to O'Brien, at that stage his prospective partners were refusing to contribute their share of the licence application costs. He was incensed at the way they chose to spend their own money, criticising their willingness to pay for first-class air travel and sumptuous accommodation in Dublin, rather than essential research. 'Denis just couldn't understand that,' one person said.

It was a major point of contention, but bigger problems would soon surface. Southwestern Bell intended to lead the bid, viewing Esat Telecom as a smaller shareholder that would provide the 'local' ingredient. O'Brien was having none of it. He might be the head of a small cash-strapped telecoms company but he was building a consortium and intended to be its leader. 'We felt a bit more confident than that,' he later said of that time. Having already muscled in on Telecom Éireann's patch, Esat Telecom felt it was playing in the premier league despite its size. O'Brien believed his company was entitled to a front-row seat and wouldn't settle for anything less.

As others recall, his aggressive, uncompromising stance con-tributed to the breakdown in discussions between the two sides. 'His forceful personality wasn't endearing to the Americans,' one said. 'Southwestern Bell just walked away.' It was a disaster. As the deadline edged closer, Esat Telecom needed to find a new partner.

John Callaghan, one of the new directors, joined O'Brien's efforts to woo an international suitor. After Minister Lowry mentioned to O'Brien at a telecommunications conference that France Telecom didn't have an Irish partner with whom to make an application for the new licence, the consortium set their sights on Paris. The Esat boss immediately arranged to meet some of France Telecom's senior executives for dinner, while Buckley and venture capitalist Prelz Oltramonti followed up with a trip to the French capital in the hope of striking a deal.

Negotiations focused on the strength of the financial commit-ments involved, particularly on how much money the small prospective Irish partner could bring to the consortium. It was estimated that a staggering €66 million would be needed to get the new mobile phone service up and running.

To ease any concerns about Esat's ability to meet its financial obligations, a new shareholding proposal was suggested. France Telecom and Esat each agreed to take a forty per cent share of a new company they would form to bid for the licence. They would then find a group of investors, through Ireland's largest stockbroker, Davy, to take the remaining twenty per cent. As they returned to Dublin the Esat Telecom crew were relatively optimistic. They would soon change their mind and court another partner.

The Scandinavian countries were among the first in Europe to liberalise their telecommunications sectors and had a thriving mobile phone business with more than two million subscribers. Norway had the second highest number of mobile phone users in Europe and the state-owned telecommunications company, Telenor, was among the most successful and experienced mobile phone operators in Europe.

Esat's consultants examined Telenor's impressive record in establishing and rolling out mobile phone networks. Perhaps O'Brien and his team should look northwards, they suggested. 'Myself, Denis and John Callaghan went to Oslo to meet them,' says Leslie Buckley. 'We didn't have a lot of time.'

The prospects of striking a deal looked promising from the outset.

'There was a lot of respect for both sides initially,' Buckley says. 'There was respect for what they brought to the table with their mobile phone experience and they had moved into quite a few countries. They also respected that we were very entrepreneurial and fast-moving.'

As the partnership agreement was finessed, Telenor dispatched some of its executives to Dublin to work with their new colleagues. O'Brien in turn brought Gaffney and Lynch to Norway for a tour of the mobile phone shops, where they looked at the packaging and talked to phone users and dealers to identify the most popular products and phone packages. As people chatted on mobile phones around them, they got a glimpse of how things might evolve in Ireland if they won the licence. 'We came back enthused,' says Gaffney. 'We were in no doubt but the mobile phone market could be big.'

O'Brien's war games were now in full swing. His team worked for months in the bunker to create the foundations for the business, drafting a business plan to show how they would create and deliver the new mobile phone service. The winning consortium needed to convince the group awarding the licence that it would offer Irish consumers competitive call rates and a reliable service. Each consortium was asked to provide a timetable detailing when its service would begin, guaranteed by large financial penalties to be paid to the Department of Communications if those deadlines were missed.

'We went down the road of being ready to launch even before the Norwegians were on board,' says Gaffney. 'Denis is cold in how he approaches and executes these things. He is into war-gaming. We would look at the opposition and weigh up their strengths and weaknesses. We would consider how we could negate their strengths and play against their weakness. He is very good at that. He would be good at chess if he had the attention span.'

The team had already made good progress before Telenor joined the bid in the weeks before the deadline. As O'Brien welcomed the new recruits to the bunker, he quickly made them feel part of the team. He gave them a nickname, 'The Vikings'. They were able to contribute vital technical expertise to the licence application. Gaffney says O'Brien was like a 'sponge', eagerly absorbing from his Norwegian colleagues everything he needed to know about mobile phones.

O'Brien always believed that speed would be a crucial factor in persuading the experts to award Esat the licence. The goal was to ensure that the majority of Ireland's population could access the new mobile phone service as quickly as possible. He wanted his consortium to be at least six months ahead of its rivals in terms of building and opening up its service.

As part of this process, a site acquisition team led by Frank O'Carroll travelled around Ireland for months, negotiating with landowners for small pockets of land where mobile phone masts could be erected. Each area had been carved up into counties and postal districts where suitable sites were identified, and they diligently worked to acquire each one. Then planning permission to erect a mast on each site was sought, using obscure company names to confuse the enemy.

It was a slow and frustrating process. Public concerns about the environmental impact of phone masts and the health problems caused by the radiation they emitted gave rise to numerous individual objections. These issues had already arisen in other countries and a wealth of research had been commissioned, largely by telecommunications companies, to allay public fears. But there was still considerable opposition to the construction of masts close to densely populated areas. The planning authorities also lacked clear guidelines on how to deal with these planning applications. The process was torturously slow. Acquiring the sites was an expensive gamble. O'Brien was betting that even if it failed to secure the licence, Esat could eventually sell the sites on to the winner. But it was eating more and more cash that Esat didn't have.

As well as rolling out the network, the company needed to persuade shops across the country to sell its phones. Lynch was responsible for courting shop owners to sign a legal agreement to sell its phones, which would be submitted with the bid.

The late nights continued. The team in the bunker studied Esat's enemy, dissecting every aspect of Eircell's business to see how their own new service could compete aggressively for customers. The idea, according to Gaffney, was to create a sexy, exciting brand that would appeal to Ireland's young population. And it would have to be distinctive from Eircell. Her team worked with consultants to create a name for the network, with instructions from O'Brien that it must be simple and easily understood. 'Denis didn't want anything that needed a Mensa brain to understand what it does,' says Gaffney. 'We already had Esat, from the fixed line business. Digi came from digital technology, which was very sexy at that time, as compared to analogue, and we got Esat Digifone.'

The Esat Digifone logo would be multicoloured to ensure maximum contrast with Eircell's purple brand. 'We said, "How can we be different? Let's go wild."' Esat, meanwhile, would remain in red, the colour O'Brien believed was the most powerful hue for any brand.

He was brand-building again. Now that they had a name, they could create advertisements for television, newspapers and radio. They planned to show the assessors how their new mobile phone company would offer choice and value to Irish consumers. 'We wanted to make it more tangible,' Gaffney says. 'Again these were all Denis's ideas.'

Those who know and have worked closely with O'Brien comment on his ability to compartmentalise the many different activities he is juggling at any one time. And people working on the team often wondered what the various consultants and other individuals he drafted in from time to time were up to. 'No one ever really knows his true intentions,' one former colleague says. 'He could have three sets of people tackling a problem, and none of them would know about the other group, and some would be coming at it from an entirely different angle.'

Gaffney is full of praise for O'Brien's ability to coordinate the many aspects of the bid. 'He is very good at putting people with a lot of different skills around him and he can bring ten different strands together.' She once asked him what one particular consultant was being paid to do in the run-up to the licence application, but never learned the answer. 'He just put me down,' she recalls. 'He said, "Lucy, everybody has a part to play".'

*

As the new government settled into office, the rival groups vying for the licence acquainted themselves with the cabinet and the changed political establishment. O'Brien has always claimed to have no affiliation to any party, but he understood the need to build relationships with key political players and had regularly made donations to all parties. To this end a former Fine Gael party worker, Dan Egan, had joined Esat Digifone's team of consultants. Hired to raise O'Brien's profile generally and within the main government political party, Egan advised his client to start attending Fine Gael fundraising events as a means to meet cabinet ministers in an informal setting. Soon O'Brien and Esat Digifone were making contributions to the party and the ambitious businessman began mingling with the party faithful.

The same month in which Minister Lowry launched the licence competition, Denis O'Brien/Esat Digifone made a €1,300 donation to the party's Carlow-Kilkenny constituency. The payment was recorded in the Communications Minister's diary. Just weeks before the application deadline, O'Brien left the bunker to attend a fundraising event for the Wicklow by-election, at which Taoiseach John Bruton and Minister Lowry were also present, where he contributed €6,000. He says the donation, made once again in the joint names of O'Brien himself and Esat Digifone, followed a letter from the cash-strapped Wicklow branch seeking donations.

As well as attending fundraising events, Egan claims to have set up meetings with ministers, in Government Buildings, in order for O'Brien to outline his interest in the licence. Meanwhile over the following weeks and months O'Brien/Esat Digifone became an increasingly generous donor, handing to party officials bank drafts amounting to €13,000.

Lowry was a controversial minister and was increasingly in conflict with the chairmen and directors of the big state-owned bodies, including the national rail company, as he stamped his authority on the sector he now governed. In the media he was portrayed as a dynamic 'can do' minister, a future party leader even.

Political journalist Sam Smyth, who was following Lowry's high-profile spats for the *Irish Independent*, explains how his interest in the minister brought O'Brien into focus: 'Denis just kept hopping into the picture when I was writing about Lowry and I began to follow him.' Soon Smyth learned of the donation made by O'Brien and Esat Digifone to Fine Gael in Wicklow and wrote about it. 'It struck me as odd,' he says. 'It wasn't a great deal of money, but it struck me why would somebody pay by banker's draft? Usually you would only do this so everyone could see who was paying.'

Meanwhile it looked as if Esat Telecom had finally found a partner. Its discussions with Telenor had progressed well and a formal partnership agreement between the Norwegian group and Communicorp, Esat's parent company, was signed on 2 June 1995. They would be equal partners in the licence bid.

It was agreed that they would use the funding model proposed during the France Telecom negotiations. If they won the bid, they would each take a forty per cent shareholding in the new company, to be called Esat Digifone; the remaining twenty per cent would be held by a syndicate of investors gathered by Davy Stockbrokers.

Throughout the negotiations, however, Telenor remained concerned about its partner's ability to fund the deal. O'Brien's side would be expected to cough up its share of the licence fee. The amount still had to be decided, but based on similar competitions, it might be anything between €6 million and €25 million.

To ease its concerns, Telenor asked O'Brien's group to provide a financial guarantee to show it could get its hands on the millions needed, in order to supply the officials with evidence that the company had sufficient equity to launch the new network. That guarantee would never materialise.

In fact, Communicorp, and Esat Telecom in particular, was still lurching from one financial crisis to the next. As the end of June deadline for the licence applications drew closer, there was little confidence that O'Brien's team would be able to meet its share of the costs.

Telenor started to contribute money towards the application, but refused to pick up the tab for any work done before its arrival and agreed to pay only half of the money incurred in those final weeks. Having essentially carried almost the entire cost of the application, Esat had run out of cash. And apart from the money it was spending on the licence bid, there were also problems in the radio business. The stations in Ireland and in Prague were doing well but Klassika Hits in Stockholm was in trouble, losing up to €130,000 a month. All they could do now was make a last-ditch effort to raise even more funds to keep their hopes of winning the licence alive.

Connolly and O'Brien travelled to London to persuade Advent to give them more money. It would be a test of O'Brien's brinkmanship.

O'Brien, who enjoyed a good relationship with Massimo Prelz Oltramonti, opened the meeting by telling him how well the licence application was coming along. But there was some bad news, he explained. They had run out of money. Not only had they spent the $10 million Advent had already given them, they needed another $5 million. Prelz Oltramonti was shocked.

This desperate plea for more cash undermined Advent's confidence in O'Brien's ability to lead a serious licence application. 'There were a number of discussions that weren't easy,' Prelz Oltramonti says, recalling the weeks of tough negotiations that followed. It was a high-wire act. Esat desperately needed the money but O'Brien and his fellow shareholders didn't want to dilute their stake in the company, thus ceding control to Advent. They wanted Prelz Oltramonti to agree to loan the company the $5 million in a straight deal. As Prelz Oltramonti observes, 'Denis was very focused on his own share-holding and his own success as well as the company's.'

O'Brien has admitted that he resisted giving any further shareholding to Advent because he wanted to retain the sixty-five per cent stake in Esat Telecom that kept him firmly in the driving seat. As he explained to Ivor Kenny in his interview for the book *Leaders*, he couldn't contemplate losing control. 'Maybe it was a stupid thing but I always felt I had to have more than fifty-one per cent and be in control. That was ingrained in me for a long time. I could never get over that.'

But Prelz Oltramonti had the upper hand and was determined to maintain Advent's position during the lengthy negotiations. O'Brien has claimed the venture capital firm even demanded his resignation at this meeting, although Prelz Oltramonti denies trying to oust him: 'I never asked Denis to resign. I wouldn't still have the relationship with him if I had done that. At that time I would have believed that a significant value of the company would have gone if Denis had left.'

As O'Brien negotiated the $5 million cash injection, his personal finances became healthier, thanks to a substantial property deal. Years earlier he had bought a building at Dublin's fledgling International Financial Services Centre and he was now able to sell it for over €2 million – or, in his own words, 'two bar'. Willing to stake everything on the licence bid, he was ready to use this windfall to save the company he had founded, but others urged caution. As he later recalled, his father and his legal adviser, Owen O'Connell from solicitors William Fry, told him he was out of his 'bloody tree'. They warned that if the licence bid failed, he would need that cash to start again.

Taking their advice, O'Brien went back to talking with Prelz Oltramonti and tried a new tack. He would ask Advent to lend him the money instead of taking a greater share of Esat Telecom. And he would make it interesting for them. Prelz Oltramonti would expect a thirty per cent return on his investment, he said, so O'Brien asked him to lend him the $5 million at that rate of interest. It was an expensive deal for Esat Telecom but it would ensure the company's survival for a while longer. It was the final roll of the dice, but O'Brien had bought some time. They shook hands on it and returned to Dublin to continue their work.

O'Brien's belief was that Prelz Oltramonti viewed the arrangment as a temporary financial solution and that Advent would ultimately end up taking control of the company in the months ahead. 'He had calculated that I'd be bollixed another six months down the road and that he'd be converting his $5 million anyway, so he saw me as only putting off tomorrow,' O'Brien told Kenny. 'What he didn't realise was that if I won the licence I'd never have any problems about finance. I'd have other options at a higher price. At the end of the day he had all of the twine.'

Impending financial disaster had been averted. But the more crucial issue, of where Esat would find the multi-millions for its share of the licence fee and the rollout of a new mobile phone network, was threatening the credibility of its application. It was relying once again on Advent to step into the financial breach and provide the financial guarantees demanded by Telenor, and this still had to be secured.

*

There was some respite for the team in the bunker when Minister Lowry extended the deadline for applications by five weeks to allow more time for the government and the European Commission to decide on the scale of the fee it would demand for the new licence. It had initially favoured holding an auction to ensure it got the maximum possible price for such a valuable asset, but this was about to change.

As O'Brien had considered, an auction would favour the consortia with the deepest pockets. Although most of the applicants lobbied on this crucial issue, to advance the most favourable scenario for their success, O'Brien claims Esat didn't. Board member Padraig OhUiginn had all the connections and influence in Europe to advance the company's case, but O'Brien insisted that one of Ireland's most influential former civil servants hadn't been asked to intervene for fear it would backfire.

They were relieved, therefore, when the Irish government decided to abandon the auction and cap the licence fee at €19 million, at the lower end of the potential price range. The decision had been influenced by a recent ruling in Italy following a similar competition there, the Minister explained. The outcome was ideal for Esat Telecom. It meant O'Brien would have to find less money to contribute towards the consortium's initial costs.

Back at the bunker O'Brien was piling on the pressure. Under extreme pressure himself, he revealed a tough, unforgiving, volatile side that some of his friends had never seen before. 'He would drive people. Everyone had to contribute. That was part of the loyalty he expected,' says Eileen Gleeson, who was consulting on the media side of the application. 'This meant that you did your work as best you could and always gave an extra ten per cent. If you did just one hundred per cent nothing, was said. If you were below the one hundred per cent, there was plenty said. One hundred per cent was just normal. It was not the best you could do.'

They had to contend with the chairman's tirades and often bruising comments as he forcefully drove them to achieve perfection. Some of the team were shocked that they continued to accept such treatment.

O'Brien expected a full-time commitment even from the consultants, who also had a responsibility to their other clients. 'You were on crisis mode operation all the time with Denis,' Gleeson says. 'Working long hours became part of your life rather than part of the spike of the normal working life. It was quite an unusual way to work as a consultant. You felt as though he was around you all the time, not with a hard stick, but nearly challenging you. You felt it was in your own self-interest but something was driving you. The loyalty thing got into people. There was nearly a feeling of pleasing the master about it,' she adds. 'Because the targets were always so high you felt it would be better for yourself to beat it all the time. He imbued that in people.'

No one was immune from O'Brien's relentless demands. Even board members were expected to diligently execute whatever tasks the chairman demanded and to report on their progress. 'They were given lists of people to phone to get business in and they had to come back and report on that. Denis would be asking "Where's your list? What did he say? Bring so and so with you? What did he say? Go back to him," ' says Gleeson. 'Nobody got away with playing on a day when they were supposed to be working.' It was a far cry from the Denis O'Brien who laid on parties for his friends and enjoyed the craic of a business deal.

Everyone was feeling the pressure. Meagher remembers endless crisis meetings. 'The entire site acquisition team was hauled in and we were all dressed down and told we weren't performing. Denis said we had failed to deliver our targets, that we were all monumental failures. We were acquiring sites at the rate of one a week and he said we needed to acquire about ten a week and that if we didn't all up our game we would all be out of work, and we would lose our contracts and retainers.'

Those meetings were stormy affairs, leaving team members visibly shaken. As they tried to compose themselves after the ordeal, Meagher says, 'People were coming out and just going, "Christ". This is the unglamorous end of the business that nobody saw. We had to do weekly printouts of the sites and everyone had to give an account of themselves.' By early August 1995 the consortium had amassed 140 sites but had permission to build just twenty masts. O'Brien was determined to have permission to build fifty by the application deadline and forcefully told his team to deliver their target.

He continually referred to the licence competition as the 'exam paper', dissecting each section of the application to gauge how the assessors might mark it. All the applicants broadly knew the criteria and the importance of each one to the assessors. But Esat Digifone discovered some additional information to help it figure out which sections might attract the most marks.

The company's legal expert, Jarleth Burke, got his hands on a letter about the competition that had been sent to Minister Lowry in July by European Union Commissioner Karel Van Miert. The letter, a copy of which was received by Burke just ten days later, stated that the section of the application concerning the licence fee payment should be given a weighting of less than fifteen per cent of the overall marks assigned by the assessors.

That important piece of information allowed the consortium to figure out how the rest of the application might be marked, enabling them to focus on the sections carrying most marks. Esat Digifone, which was the only bidder that had that information, has said the letter was available to anyone who knew where in Brussels to look for it. It had just been diligent.

Sections of the bunker were regularly blocked off to let the hired consultants calculate the dummy scores on each part of the application, based on their best assessment of how each part of the 'exam paper' would be marked. 'He is big into that stuff,' remarked one insider of O'Brien. 'Most people who worked on the licence application had other day jobs and would be drafted in to work on specific sections. If you were drafting a section of the licence application and you stayed late in the evening you would find that someone else was rewriting the same thing.'

O'Brien paid most attention to the marketing and sales side of the pitch and displayed a challenging level of attention to detail. Gaffney, the leader of this cell, says they were focused on conveying Esat Digifone's proposition in the most concise and effective way to those advising the minister on the award of the licence.

'The Norwegians were great technically but they weren't great marketers,' she explains. 'I think they were fairly shocked at some of the things we were doing and they probably thought we were a bit mad. We had some great meetings. We were always coming up with new things. And Denis would put people in to fill the gaps. We came up with the phrase "Marry me because . . ." and we still use it in all of our businesses. If you can't say "Give me this licence because . . ." in a few sentences and with a few slides then you have lost your audience.'

The board members then gathered to assess how the application was developing. O'Brien, as chairman, was at the forefront, voicing fierce criticism expressed in his usual colourful language. He would regularly declare, 'That is shite,' ordering those presenting to return with a new version within a few hours. The bid proposal was further refined over the following month and a fresh team of consultants brought in to evaluate it. And the late nights continued.

O'Brien slipped away to Portugal for a break in July, holidaying with his girlfriend Catherine Walsh, head of commercial operations in Prague, but he constantly phoned the team in the bunker. They faxed repeated new drafts to him, hundreds of pages, and he pored over every word.

By now the site acquisition team had delivered. Esat Digifone owned 153 sites and had filed planning applications to build phone masts on all but two of them. It planned to impress the assessors by showing them written agreements with 100 shop owners around Ireland who would sell Esat Digifone products if it won the licence. The consortium advertised for tenders to supply services to its mobile phone network for equipment, billing systems and mobile phone cards, and had letters from 150 Esat Telecom customers vouching for the efficiency of its operations. All these components, they hoped, would win high marks.

All the while they were playing to their strengths in terms of presentation and detail. However, they knew that Esat Telecom's precarious financial position was the consortium's weakness and could potentially scupper its chances. O'Brien's team still had to convince Telenor and the officials judging the competition that it could access the more than €32 million needed to get the new mobile phone service up and running.

O'Brien maintained that he would once again turn to Advent to potentially provide the money. But Telenor demanded that Advent should put it in writing. Two days before the bid deadline it still hadn't received the assurance it sought. When Telenor executive Knut Haga phoned Prelz Oltramonti to enquire about the delay, he was shocked to hear that Advent had never agreed to give any such commitment.

Over the next twenty-four hours, O'Brien and Telenor held lengthy meetings, before at the last minute the Esat boss reluctantly agreed to accept Advent's offer of financial support. Telenor's legal adviser, Amund Bugge, who attended those meetings, said a compromise was eventually reached when O'Brien agreed in a letter to Telenor to accept the offer. Bugge's Norwegian partners were not given the details of its terms and he formed the impression that O'Brien had believed he might get a better deal elsewhere.

It was a lesser assurance than Telenor had sought, but at the eleventh hour it was forced to accept that Advent had pledged the money. Although nothing had been put on paper, Esat Digifone was able to state in its application that it had received an 'irrevocable undertaking' from Advent to underwrite its share of the consortium's financial commitments.

The fraught discussions between O'Brien and Telenor ended ten minutes before it was due to submit its carefully crafted application to the Department of Communications. O'Brien rushed through Dublin's busy streets to meet his team, who had planned to make a spectacular entrance.

On 4 August Esat Digifone created a Viking invasion in Dublin's city centre. A forty-foot juggernaut was transformed into a Viking ship with twenty-four warriors on board carrying the twelve glass boxes that contained its bid documents. Through a haze of dry ice the Vikings stormed through Dublin's streets towards the Department where Norway's Eurovision winner, Irish violinist Fionnuala Sherry, played the winning entry, 'Nocturne'. The Department officials were stunned. 'People were hanging out the windows to watch what was going on,' one of the crew says. Photographers and journalists recorded the dramatic street theatre event and that evening O'Brien threw a party.

After a mammoth effort their application for the mobile phone licence had been submitted. O'Brien had staked everything on its success. Only time would tell whether or not he would end up as the head of Ireland's second mobile phone company.

8 'The Kaiser'

The aspiring telecoms tycoon was now looking forward to a few days of downtime. He was going to Scotland the following weekend to watch Celtic play Liverpool as a guest of the Scottish club's major shareholder, Dermot Desmond.

Desmond, one of Ireland's richest men, was a controversial figure who had made his fortune as a swashbuckling stockbroker. He and O'Brien were business acquaintances. The younger entrepreneur had tried in vain to persuade the man known as 'the Kaiser' — due to his luxuriant moustache — to invest some of his wealth in Esat Telecom when he was scrambling around trying to raise money for his business. O'Brien was nonetheless delighted to help Desmond out when he asked if he could arrange for his friend's son to do a two-week work placement at his radio stations. The invitation to watch Celtic was a 'thank you', Desmond has said. He and O'Brien spoke about the licence competition on the flight to Glasgow.

Six groups were bidding for the licence and O'Brien believed the Esat Digifone consortium had a good shot at winning. While it wasn't viewed as the odds-on favourite, O'Brien has said, he believed the competition would be professionally run and free of political interference, giving all the applicants a fair hearing. He has described the competition as the first sign of the 'new Ireland'. The 'old Ireland', he claimed, would 'all be chicory with politicians becoming involved, nudge nudge, wink wink'. The mobile phone licence competition was the first example of a 'transparent process', independently assessed. It didn't matter whether you were Fianna Fáil, Fine Gael or Labour, he believed. 'It must have been the first time in the history of the State where there was no agenda.'

According to Desmond, O'Brien told him Esat Digifone had submitted a good application. The only aspect where it was weak was on the financial side, and it had been a struggle to find backers. Esat Telecom had received what O'Brien described to Desmond as 'waffly' commitments from the other investors assembled by his old rival Davy Stockbrokers to join the consortium if it won the licence. Many of the investors approached had told O'Brien to come back when he won the licence and then they could talk about putting some money into the company. But that was no good to him; Esat needed to be able to show the assessors it could meet its financial obligations.

While many wealthy Irish business figures were involved in the six consortia hoping to win the licence, Desmond, it seemed, hadn't given the prospect of investing in this emerging sector any consideration until his conversation with O'Brien that day. A few months earlier, Tony Boyle, the chairman of another bidding consortium, later claimed to have discussed the competition with Desmond at the Aintree Grand National in May. Both men were guests of Desmond's close friend J.P. McManus and watched the races from his private box. According to Boyle, whose Persona consortium included Motorola and was viewed as the favourite to win, Desmond said that O'Brien had asked him to become chairman of the Esat Digifone consortium but that he declined, saying he wasn't interested.

Speaking under oath some years later, Boyle claimed that Desmond then asked him to explain the process involved in winning the licence, including who would make the final decisions. It would be the Minister for Communications, 'Michael Lowry', Boyle replied, to which he claims Desmond said that O'Brien would know exactly 'who to use to get to Lowry'. Desmond has denied ever saying this and has no recollection of meeting Boyle that day.

Desmond, who had just established a new private equity firm, International Investment and Underwriting (IIU), was nevertheless always on the lookout for investment opportunities. As he listened to O'Brien, the man, who describes himself as an 'eclectic investor' with no rules to guide his investment decisions, appeared to be weighing up an investment in Esat Digifone, even at this late stage.

Eileen Gleeson, who has worked with Desmond for many years, says he is attracted to complex deals that will keep him engaged:

'Dermot likes nothing better than a clever game. If it's just a boring business he has no interest, but if there are twists and turns and you will have to fight with this guy or that, then he is in with you.'

Investing in Esat Digifone was one of a number of deals IIU was getting involved in. As well as talking to O'Brien, IIU had begun to negotiate with British building group Mowlem to buy its loss-making City Airport in London. Those who know Desmond suggest his decision to invest in Esat Digifone was probably based on Telenor's involvement. 'Telenor at the time were among the leading people in Europe in mobile phones,' one person says. 'If IIU was getting in on the same terms as Telenor he would have probably felt this was a good potential investment.' Desmond himself explained his interest in Esat Digifone by saying he likes to back the underdog. 'Denis may be a Goliath now,' he told an inquiry, 'but he was a David then, and I like helping the Davids of this world.'

Whatever Desmond's motivation, over the following weeks IIU made a proposal to strengthen the Esat Digifone consortium's bid for the licence by addressing its main weakness compared to the other applicants, even though under the rules of the competition applicants were not allowed to improve their submission once the bids were being assessed. Michael Walsh, who ran Desmond's company, has said his boss handed over the execution of his entry into the Esat Digifone consortium to him. Desmond, he said, was 'probably on a golf course' as he hammered out a deal with O'Brien.

As part of the arrangement, IIU potentially committed to provide €74 million, the money to be contributed by IIU and Esat for its share of the cost of building the new mobile phone network and to launch the company. It would either invest this money directly itself or raise the funds from investors. In addition IIU was proposing to pay for its share of the bid costs even if the application was unsuccessful, although it had only joined the consortium after the application was submitted. According to Desmond, this showed his company was prepared to take a 'considerable financial risk'. 'Unlike the conditional interest expressed by the proposed institutional investors, I was prepared to take the downside as well as the up,' he explained. IIU's involvement, Desmond suggested, would also help to improve the Irishness of the bid.

Advent's Massimo Prelz Oltramonti says his group was happy to make way for Desmond's proposed involvement, as all the partners wanted to ensure that the consortium included the highest possible number of Irish shareholders compared to the other applicants. 'We all agreed that it would have been better to have a local investor so it would not look like a foreign investor was coming in to make money out of this licence in Ireland. The big international companies didn't have a clue about Ireland. They had a model they would apply to any new market for a licence application where they would find a local partner, but none of the others had a serious local context.'

As the deal took shape, however, Desmond's company insisted that it wanted a bigger slice of Esat Digifone – twenty-five per cent – than O'Brien and Telenor were making available to the investors assembled by Davy. This was five per cent more than had been agreed between the consortium's two biggest shareholders when they submitted the bid. The new structure would radically alter the make-up of the group. Not only would it include a new shareholder, IIU, but Esat and Telenor would both have to agree to reduce their forty per cent stakes to make way for Desmond.

The competition was overseen as part of a sealed process by a project team led by senior civil servant Martin Brennan, while Minister Lowry had overall responsibility. It was organised so the project officials, including Fintan Towey, who would play a key role in the assessment, had control of the entire competition, including contact with the applicants and the minister. In addition to Andersen Management International, the team was assisted by a number of working groups, each of which temporarily evaluated aspects of the applications. They assessed the bids under ten headings, including marketing, technical, management and financial aspects, ascribing marks to each section.

In early September, Brennan told the Department's Assistant Secretary, Sean Fitzgerald, that three bids qualified for the licence with three others subject to reservations. There was 'clear water' between the first two and the third. And while the project team had more work to do, he said, Esat Digifone was the likely front runner at this stage.

Fitzgerald was surprised by this early assessment. He told Brennan such a result was going to be controversial and would have to be well founded or it would be open to attack. Minister Lowry, according to Brennan, was informed of the preliminary result and had not expressed any view. The minister did however ask if he thought they would get a 'good operator' from the applicants and Brennan said that at this stage it was akin to six people with differing strengths and weaknesses applying for the same job.

Fitzgerald was aware of the financial pressures O'Brien's radio and telecoms company, Communicorp, was facing given its battle with Telecom Éireann. Esat Telecom would need huge financial resources to continue to compete against the State-owned telecoms company and it was clearly finding the going tough. He mentioned to Brennan the prospect that O'Brien's company might even go out of business before the competition winner was announced. The project team was aware of Esat's financial weakness, Brennan explained, adding that its partner, Telenor, a company owned by the Norwegian state, would ensure Esat Digifone would be financially viable if it won the licence.

O'Brien, while still struggling to keep Esat Telecom afloat, remained totally focused on winning the licence. And, as the project team continued to appraise the applications, he decided to raise the stakes. 'Let's put an ad in the paper looking for employees for Esat Digifone,' he suggested to Leslie Buckley. 'I'd never have thought of that,' Buckley says. 'It was a real pressure point. Denis had such faith in what he was going to do, and if he was going to be beaten, then it was going to be bloody good.' And so, just weeks after its application had been submitted, Esat Digifone's colourful new logo appeared in newspaper advertisements seeking to recruit staff to work at Ireland's new mobile phone company.

Back at the bunker his team were rehearsing for a presentation on 12 September to the officials assessing the bids. This phase of the 'beauty contest' was crucial, giving each applicant an opportunity to answer specific questions and to highlight the winning aspects of their bid.

They resumed the war games, teasing out any advantage they could gain over their rivals, going through the presentation line by line. O'Brien would lead a team that included executives from

Telenor, Lucy Gaffney, financial controller Peter O'Donoghue, Esat's human resources head John Hennessy, and O'Brien's best friend from his schooldays, Barry Maloney, who was planning to return to Ireland from the USA to run the new mobile phone company if it won the licence. Knowing the assessors would identify the weaknesses in each bid, they concentrated on scrutinising their rivals' weaknesses, seeking ways to make Esat look stronger in comparison. After another late night of rehearsals they were ready to face the officials.

O'Brien led his team into a presentation that would last exactly three hours. They answered questions and played television and radio commercials advertising their new service. Their objective was to show that, if they won the licence, they would be ready to open quickly for business.

As expected, the project team focused on Esat's perceived financial weakness. O'Brien at once gave the reassuring answer he had so meticulously rehearsed. All of the necessary finance was in place, he explained, highlighting the importance of having a group of blue-chip Irish financial institutions, as he referred to Davy's clients, that was ready to invest in the project if it won the licence. And O'Brien claimed that Advent had pledged to make $30 million available to his company to meet its share of the required upfront investment.

His consortium was also the most 'Irish' of all the applicants, he said, a tactic intended to highlight the dominance of multinationals in the rival bids. O'Brien later described the session as 'brutal', but felt they had done well. Now they would just have to wait for the result, expected by the end of November 1995.

The following Sunday, 17 September, was the biggest day in the sporting calendar in Irish amateur Gaelic football, when the All Ireland final was held at Croke Park. Huge crowds descended upon the capital city and government ministers were among those who attended to cheer on the teams from Dublin and Galway. O'Brien went along to support his home county, together with Esat Telecom director Padraig OhUiginn, and was seated close to Michael Lowry. Dermot Desmond was also in Croke Park that day and O'Brien had arranged to meet him at 6 p.m.

At half-time O'Brien bumped into Lowry in the hospitality area and they arranged to meet for a drink in Dublin's city centre at 6.45 p.m. Their first meeting point was too crowded so they went to Hartigan's, or Harto's, O'Brien's favourite watering hole since his college days. Both men say they didn't discuss the licence, although O'Brien says he did use the opportunity to talk about Esat Telecom's ongoing problems with his department.

O'Brien was dealing with the minister and his officials on two levels. He wanted to persuade them to award the mobile phone licence to his consortium. And he was still in conflict with the Department about using autodiallers, the technology that allowed Esat Telecom to bypass Telecom Éireann in providing international and long-distance calls within Ireland.

Telecom Éireann had marshalled fierce opposition to Esat's use of the devices, complaining to the Department that by so doing its competitor was acting beyond the terms of its licence. It wanted the Department to apply sanctions to stop Esat misusing its public phone network. Esat had responded by making a formal complaint to the European Commission claiming that the Department's refusal to allow it to use the autodiallers was in breach of European law. And the saga continued.

Meanwhile Esat Telecom was struggling on a daily basis to survive. Leslie Buckley, who was now running the business, was trying to hold its biggest creditors at bay while finding enough money to pay the staff salaries and avoid going bust. 'We had spent a lot on the licence,' Buckley says. 'The licence became very important. We were going to run out of cash. We didn't want to dilute the business any more to Massimo [Prelz Oltramonti of Advent] or it wouldn't be worthwhile. We were really on a knife edge and it was a lot of pressure. Every time you did the cash flow it became worse and not better.'

By now Esat Telecom owed millions to its two biggest creditors, Telecom Éireann, which was providing the phone lines it used to offer its services, and Sprint International, the US company handling Esat's international calls. They had a plan to deal with Telecom Éireann that had worked so far. Every time they got a phone bill, Buckley and his young financial controller, St John O'Gara, pored over it to find something they could turn into an official complaint. 'We owed them millions but we weren't too upset about them. They were trying to put us out of business,' Buckley says. 'When we looked at every bill we would bang in a letter of complaint because while you had a complaint against the company they couldn't cut you off. St John O'Gara went through some training. Jesus, he learned everything there is to know about cash flow in those twelve months.'

They enjoyed a better relationship with Sprint, and O'Brien and Buckley had got to know Vince Gregaro, the company's London general manager, very well. As Esat's debts mounted, Gregaro was anxious to meet them and to get some of the money they owed. 'During those months Sprint was our banker. It was providing the traffic and we weren't paying them,' says Buckley, who travelled to London with O'Brien in September. 'On the way over, Denis said to me, "We'll talk to him about everything apart from paying the bill".'

O'Brien kicked off the London meeting with an impressive presentation of the company's prospects, telling Gregaro how Esat Digifone had applied for the mobile phone licence and that it considered it had made a good application. 'Eventually I could see the guy looking at us wondering when we would talk about the money,' Buckley says. 'I decided at that stage to say that we didn't have a cheque for him. I remember he was sitting on a seat behind a desk and he just slid down into the seat. He slid so far while I was talking that all you could see was his two eyes up over the desk. In his mind he must have been saying; "These two f'ing Paddies have taken me for the biggest ride and I am probably now going to lose my job." We were sorry for him because we had got to know him very well, but we had no money.'

O'Brien's radio empire was also experiencing mixed fortunes. Its flagship station, Classic Hits 98FM, continued to thrive and was the main source of funds for the group, while the station in Prague was also performing well. But the group's Swedish expansion was a disaster. O'Brien's father, who always kept a watchful eye on his son's businesses, spoke to Buckley about the problems in Stockholm and the pair decided to confront the younger entrepreneur about the situation. 'Denis is a builder and he had to think about selling it even though it was chewing cash,' says Buckley. O'Brien reluctantly agreed and the station was put on the market.

O'Brien has admitted the pressure on him and the business was 'immense' at the time. 'Everything was riding on winning the licence,' he said. 'This was putting all your money on one horse. We could not make a mistake.' There were rumours that various banks from which O'Brien had borrowed money were preparing to foreclose on the loans and other creditors were growing concerned about ever getting paid. His friend Paul Meagher sums up the situation: 'Denis knew he was snookered if he didn't get the licence.'

In the background, however, the discussions with IIU were progressing and in the days after the oral presentation it looked as if O'Brien had found a solution to his weak financial position. He was ready to tell Telenor about their new partner.

The Norwegians very much respected O'Brien's credibility in understanding the Irish scene but thought he exaggerated the extent of his political contacts and his official knowledge of what was going on in relation to the licence. In their view, O'Brien was always trying to create the impression that he was a 'very influential person' who had good sources of information; however, according to Telenor's Arve Johansen, he never referred to any 'concrete channels' and was 'vague' as to the source of his information. And they did not believe this meant he had access to information from official sources or from people who were privy to such information. They understood his sources were the advisers or consultants he hired. Knut Haga has said he thought O'Brien liked to emphasise his usefulness as the leader of the consortium, perhaps to deflect from his company's lack of financial muscle.

Telenor's Per Simonsen claims O'Brien boasted he talked about the licence with Minister Lowry over a drink in the pub in September. Simonsen in turn told Haga O'Brien's 'colourful story' and, he has explained, the pair had 'a little laugh about it'. According to Haga, they dismissed the episode as O'Brien doing a bit of 'name-dropping' to impress them. As part of that story, their Irish partner is also said to have mentioned the minister's suggestion that Desmond's company, IIU, should get involved with Esat Digifone. O'Brien and Lowry have both denied that such a suggestion was ever made.

By now, however, IIU had laid out its terms for getting involved in the bid. O'Brien introduced the deal to Telenor, presenting it as a solution to Esat Digifone's perceived financial weakness, with the added bonus that Desmond's involvement would help to distinguish its bid as containing the most Irish elements of all the applicants. There was a catch though – the twenty-five per cent stake in the consortium demanded by Desmond as the price for his company's involvement.

Haga recalls that Telenor was 'favourably impressed' when it first learned that Desmond was prepared to support Esat Digifone. It had long harboured concerns that Esat would struggle to find its share of the money, particularly after its failure to provide a letter guaranteeing that it could raise similar funds in the future. As well as committing to provide the finance for the bid, Haga said, Telenor was told that Desmond's company would bring 'political contacts in Ireland'; he did not, he said, associate this comment with O'Brien's story of his conversation with Minister Lowry in Hartigan's.

Telenor was aware that Desmond had been 'in some sort of difficulty with the Irish authorities' in the past, its lawyer Amund Bugge recalled. This referred to an investigation in 1993 by a High Court inspector into the purchase of a site in Dublin, which had resulted in criticism of Desmond and his apparent association with two companies connected with the purchase of the property. According to Bugge, however, Telenor didn't know any further details and believed the matter had been resolved, and that by 1995 Desmond had been 'rehabilitated'. His impression was that Telenor was not concerned about Desmond's involvement in this regard and accepted that O'Brien had brought him on board at this late stage because it would be helpful for the bid.

OhUiginn too was very supportive of IIU's involvement in the consortium and has said he felt Desmond's company would be a far better partner than the financial institutions Davy had brought together. His opinion was that it would be better to have a single investor whose bona fides he knew. Desmond had been a close friend of former Taoiseach Charles Haughey and it had been at his prompting that Haughey's government created the international

Financial Services Centre in Dublin in the early 1990s. OhUiginn, as secretary-general to the government, had worked closely with Desmond on the project and knew his style of doing business. 'I knew Dermot Desmond's commitment. He was the kind of person you would like to have on our side where we were launching a new system and there was a lot of work to be done and decisions to be taken, rather than finance houses whose legitimate interest would be what return they could get out of their money.' Desmond had many investments in Ireland and OhUiginn suggested he would be concerned to ensure that the project was a success: 'It was the difference between one man and anonymous financial institutions who would not have the same commitment.'

But the most contentious part of IIU's arrival was always going to be its demand for an increased shareholding. This would trigger a fresh series of difficult negotiations between O'Brien and Telenor and mark the beginning of the breakdown of their business relationship.

From the start, O'Brien had wanted a majority shareholding in the Esat Digifone consortium. Telenor had insisted on an equal shareholding, refusing to cede control to its Irish partner. Now, after the bid had been submitted, O'Brien was proposing that Telenor should reduce its shareholding from forty to thirty-five per cent to make way for Desmond's company. Esat, he suggested, would continue to hold forty per cent.

Telenor's executives viewed this as a brazen attempt by O'Brien to reduce its influence in the consortium and were suspicious he would ultimately gain control of the company by acquiring IIU's shares. During the delicate discussions between O'Brien and Telenor's Arve Johansen, O'Brien hung up mid-conversation on at least one occasion. Johansen has said the relationship between the two partners was so bad in September 1995 that he feared for the future of the Digifone project.

Throughout the discussions O'Brien forcefully tried to influence Telenor to agree to his demands, while Telenor stood firm in its belief that the two main partners in the bid should maintain an equal shareholding. And so the terse exchanges continued.

Eventually, at the end of September, they reached agreement. O'Brien was reluctantly forced to agree to the Norwegians' demands:

IIU would get twenty-five per cent of the company and Esat and Telenor would each hold thirty-seven-and-a-half per cent. Although O'Brien had told the bid assessors that he had a binding commitment from Advent, the consortium's partners decided to urgently fax it to the Department to show that the Irish-owned part of the consortium, which together accounted for sixty per cent of the company, had access to €74 million to meet its share of the estimated €150 million that would be needed to pay for the licence and roll out the new service.

The letter was addressed to Martin Brennan, leader of the team assessing the bid. It was returned by Fintan Towey, who explained that additional information would not be accepted outside the application deadlines. Brennan later sent another letter to O'Brien to emphasise this point. The contents of the original letter were not revealed to the other members of the assessment team.

Esat Digifone waited until 29 September, the day IIU officially joined the consortium, before telling Davy it no longer needed its clients as investors. On that day, Esat director John Callaghan asked Davy's joint managing director, Kyran McLaughlin, if the firm's clients would stand aside to make room for a new investor with stronger financial backing, although the backer was not named.

When he subsequently found out that Davy's clients had been replaced by IIU, McLaughlin was incensed. He sought a meeting with O'Brien and eventually managed to sit down with him and Callaghan for an explanation. He suggested that IIU wasn't as financially strong as the three banks – AIB, Bank of Ireland and Standard Life – that had indicated they would collectively invest €11 million in the consortium subject to certain conditions. He was also annoyed, he said, that the moves to exclude his clients from the bid had taken place after the licence fee was capped at €19 million instead of holding an auction, something that improved Esat Digifone's chance of winning.

O'Brien and Callaghan insisted that the consortium needed a firm financial commitment for the twenty per cent stake to be held by Davy's clients and for Esat's forty per cent shareholding. O'Brien said he knew that no 'normal' institution would have given it that kind of financial support, but that IIU had agreed to do so.

McLaughlin wondered if IIU had some 'inside knowledge' of the consortium's likely success in winning the licence when it pledged its investment, and made a note of his question in a written account of the meeting. O'Brien and Callaghan flatly rejected this suggestion, but told him that the civil servants involved in the bid had informed Esat Digifone that its written submission was the best received. They mentioned that O'Brien's other telecoms venture, Esat Telecom, might use Davy's services if there was any Irish interest in providing private funding to the company in the future. But the likelihood of that happening was remote.

By October, Esat Telecom was broke. O'Brien and his lieutenants met to consider the dire prospect of winding up the company. It could only stall the debts owing to its creditors for so long. Dermot Desmond was not interested in putting money into O'Brien's fixed-line phone business, so he would once again have to look to Advent to step into the breach. And in return for saving the company from financial ruin, it would now be demanding a bigger stake in Esat Telecom. O'Brien stood to lose everything. Everyone knew the Department was unlikely to award the mobile phone licence to a consortium that included a failed business.

'A week before we got the licence I remember sitting down to lunch with Denis and Paul Connolly and we were pretty down and out. Telecom Éireann was threatening to cut off the phone lines and effectively put us out of business for not paying the bills. The pressure was really coming at us. We could see the end of the runway and could see danger there. If Advent was to take any more of the business it would hardly be worth it for us,' says Buckley.

O'Brien mentioned he was due to make a speech to business students in Trinity College Dublin on how to succeed in business. Contemplating the irony of the situation, he told Buckley he could already see the headlines when the media reported his business failure. He wanted to cancel the engagement. 'I think you should just hang in and give it a few more days,' Buckley advised.

Despite his company's financial distress, Esat Digifone continued to make donations to Fine Gael after the bid was submitted. In October 1995, it sent a cheque for €5,000 – co-signed by O'Brien and Telenor's

Hans Myhre — to the party to sponsor the seventeenth hole of a golf classic at the K Club in County Kildare. The funds came out of the consortium's joint expense account. In a note written by O'Brien to go with the donation, he insisted — like other bidders for the licence, who had also given money towards the tournament and made similar requests — that Fine Gael shouldn't put up any signs to say that Esat Digifone was sponsoring the hole.

The donation was organised by Sarah Carey, who was part of Esat Telecom's site acquisition team and a member of Fine Gael. For many months now she had been attending party fundraisers on behalf of her employer. Carey told her new boss that some of the party's senior members did not have a positive view of him, while others knew nothing about him or his business and advised him to raise his profile.

The reason O'Brien asked the party not to publicly acknowledge the company's sponsorship of the event, she says, was in case it might be misrepresented by the media or other bidders. Esat also didn't want its rivals to know the size of its contribution to the party in government. When asked about it, Carey said: 'We wanted everything to be higher' than the other bidders. She was under orders to ensure Fine Gael complied with O'Brien's wishes in relation to the sponsorship. Her boss was 'a very strict employer', she explained, and she wanted to ensure that his instructions were not 'disobeyed' in any way.

Myhre would later claim he didn't know the cheque was being used for a political donation and would not have signed it for that purpose. 'It would have been inappropriate to give a political donation in the phase of the competition before we got the licence because it might have a political influence and an impact,' he explained.

O'Brien was also lunching with Fine Gael members and met auctioneer and party activist Mark FitzGerald the week after the golf classic. FitzGerald has said that at an earlier meeting in August, O'Brien explained he was facing an uphill struggle for the phone licence and wanted to 'keep up his profile with Fine Gael'. At that stage FitzGerald introduced him to David Austin, another influential activist within the party. At their lunch that October, FitzGerald says the pair were joined by two other Fine Gael stalwarts, Phil Hogan and

Jim Mitchell, but Hogan has insisted he has no recollection of that meeting.

That day, O'Brien asked FitzGerald if he had heard anything about the mobile phone competition. He told him about a conversation with Minister Lowry at the fundraising event at the K Club where he was told O'Brien had 'made a good impression'. The Esat Digifone consortium had good sites to build its network and a good marketing plan, he said. Later, FitzGerald said he was annoyed at having relayed this news to O'Brien as he believed it was 'gratuitous' and 'unimportant'. After the lunch he rang some of Minister Lowry's advisers who told him the licence award would be a matter for the government, not the minister alone.

The project team and the consultants advised Lowry against meeting with any of the bidders during the selection process to safeguard its confidentiality. As well as meeting O'Brien, though, Lowry met Persona's chairman, Tony Boyle, for a drink. He also raised the ongoing competition with another applicant.

At the opening of the Arcon zinc mine, the minister spoke to the mining company's chairman, Tony O'Reilly, another of the applicants for the licence. The former Irish international rugby star, who had gone on to become chief executive of the H.J. Heinz Company, owned various prominent businesses in Ireland. As well as Arcon, he was a major shareholder in the country's famous glass manufacturer, Waterford Crystal, and was chief executive and chairman of the Independent News and Media group that owned newspapers in Ireland, Australia, India, New Zealand, South Africa and the UK as well as 130 international radio stations.

O'Reilly claims the minister said, 'Your fellas didn't do too well'. He believed the comment referred to his consortium's oral presentation the previous day, although Lowry has denied this.

Meanwhile, at the Department, the project team was moving ahead with its final report and had picked the top three contenders for the licence. Esat Digifone had gained top marks from the assessors, moving ahead of its competitors. It had overtaken the favourite, Persona, with MobiCall in third place.

However, the terms of the competition specified that all those who applied for the licence were expected to have substantial funds available to meet their start-up costs. The project team still harboured concerns about Esat's frail financial resources. Once they won the licence, they would of course be in a strong position to raise finance from investors to support the next phase of building the new network. But their initial equity would be vigorously examined during the assessment process, and there were questions over the strength of Advent's pledge to O'Brien to provide the many millions his company required. The project team made a recommendation to Minister Lowry that if Esat Digifone could not satisfactorily cover these financial risks the Department should enter into licence negotiations with the second highest scoring applicant, Persona.

The Department's most senior civil servant, John Loughrey, reviewed this assessment and did his own calculations to evaluate Esat's financial strength if it won the licence. He concluded that O'Brien's group did not have the funds required to pay for his company's part of the €19 million fee for the licence. His desktop calculation, he said, showed that its parent company, Communicorp, had no money to contribute. This did not however mean the company wouldn't be able to raise it if it won the licence. In his view, it was a bankable project: 'The minute Denis O'Brien had a licence in his hip pocket, it was not a matter of whether he had access to the capital markets or whether he would get funding, it was only a matter of when and on what terms.' Anyway, if it did win the licence, in his view the company had enough money to cover the first critical year of the new business. According to its application, the consortium had lodged €6.4 million and had another €6.4 million 'locked in'. It also had €25 million in cash in its bank account. This assessment seemed to alleviate any concerns about how Esat's dire financial situation might impact on Esat Digifone's ability to launch a new network if it won the licence.

Michael Lowry was now keen to deliver the good news. The dynamic minister felt he had sufficient information to make the decision and consulted with the Labour Party Minister for Finance, Ruairi Quinn, on the winner. The project team never produced a final report on the competition for minister Lowry and wasn't asked to reach a consensus or to take a vote on the winner. And so, two weeks earlier than expected, Minister Lowry convened a press conference to make the announcement.

From 5 p.m. on 25 October journalists from the Irish and international media made their way across the city to hear the news. O'Brien sent Andrew Hanlon, head of news at 98FM, to the press conference. In fact, O'Brien already knew he had won. He had taken a call conveying the good news to him an hour or so earlier, although he was asked not to disclose the result before the official announcement.

Unable to contain his delight he went to find Buckley, who recalls, 'I was in a meeting with Greg Mesch when I got the word. The news was going to come out at 5 p.m. and Denis got a call beforehand. He rushed into the meeting, pulls me out into another room and said "We've got it".'

Now, without betraying the outcome, O'Brien summoned his troops into the tiny 98FM newsroom for the announcement. Hanlon would officially convey the news. As they gathered, O'Brien delivered a pep talk. He was worried, he said, that the young staff would be crestfallen if the bid failed: 'I told them if we didn't win it we'd just move on to other things.' Winning the licence meant more to them than it would for many of the large international companies involved, he continued. It was 'crucial' for Esat as it only employed seventy people, thirty of whom had worked directly on the bid.

Just after 5.15 p.m. the result was announced. 'We've won,' Hanlon said when he rang from the press conference and the place erupted in what one person described as a 'huge boxing stadium cheer'. In the midst of the excitement O'Brien jumped for joy and punched the air, only to put his fist through the suspended ceiling. 'We just did a dance,' he said. 'Half the people were crying, half were shouting and roaring. That was it. We knew we were saved. We had moved from the fourth to the third division. Winning the GSM licence would bring us to the second division and we'd a great chance of getting up to the premier league.'

Just days after contemplating the failure of his business dream, O'Brien was looking forward to a bright future at the head of Ireland's second mobile phone company. The victory, he told journalists, was like winning the Jules Rimet (the original World Cup trophy).

'Everybody said we would get trounced but we've been planning for this for three years.' The decision, he said, proved that an Irish company, in tandem with a strong foreign partner, could take on the best in the world and win. The quality of Esat's partners, Telenor, and the network of sites it had created to build phone masts around the country, he believed, were the reasons it had beaten its rivals.

Eileen Gleeson says she was as surprised as anyone when they won. She had worried about assembling everyone in the newsroom in case it was bad news. Conor Lenihan, who was being groomed as an executive in an expanding radio empire, was also shocked by the announcement. 'Nobody would have expected it. The general view within Esat before it won the licence was that we weren't going to win it. And Denis himself, I would have expected, would have felt that too.'

Almost everyone else was equally surprised by Esat Digifone's victory. For weeks the media had been reporting Persona as the favourite. Esat Digifone had made a lot of noise and was cheekily talking up its chances, but few believed it would emerge with the licence. It was a great achievement by the underdog.

O'Brien brought the team to nearby Scruffy Murphy's pub for 'a rake of pints' but wanted to put off the main celebrations until their Norwegian partners came to Dublin the following day. After the pub, he walked home and went for a burger. 'I stopped in Burger King in Baggot Street for a Whopper and chips and stuffed myself,' he said.

He was wide awake early the next morning and went into the office at about 4 a.m. There he found a letter on the fax machine from NatWest Capital Markets. It read: 'Dear Mr O'Brien, congratulations on winning the licence. We are very happy to provide you with £70 million towards your capital costs.'

Within twenty-four hours his concerns about finding enough money to keep his businesses going had evaporated. Now everybody wanted to give him money. 'That was a good example of the difference between the low and the high and the inch that separates success from failure,' he has said. 'Sometimes businesses don't get the lucky break. Half the time, people just collapse. Business is fifty per cent luck and fifty per cent preparation.'

As the drinks flowed that evening O'Brien and his team gave a warm welcome to the Vikings. Seamus Lynch, who had played a crucial part in the bid effort, danced an Irish jig for the visitors and the party continued into the early hours.

It was the result O'Brien had worked so hard to achieve. This time he was truly on his way.

9 Upwardly Mobile

Esat Digifone had won the war, but its bloodied opponents were refusing to accept defeat. Some were even crying 'foul'. Had the competition been a fair one, they wondered. Had Denis O'Brien used some means to influence Minister Michael Lowry and his officials to favour his consortium? His victory was now mired in controversy and associated with corruption. The allegations would haunt him for the next decade.

Seeing a brief window during which they might be able to reverse the result, the losing consortia used all their firepower in an effort to derail the process. As O'Brien's consortium had so far only earned the right to enter into exclusive negotiations with Ireland's Department of Communications for the new licence there was a slim chance that they could scupper those discussions and stop Esat Digifone in its tracks.

Six months on, allegations of interference and underhand tactics continued to swirl. The powerful American corporations in particular raised their concerns at the highest political levels. And the level of disquiet heightened further when newspaper reports outed Dermot Desmond, who had played no part in the group that applied for the licence, as a shareholder in the up and coming mobile phone company that some estimated was already worth about €120 million. The Motorola-led consortium, Persona, said it was considering legal action against the minister and his department to challenge the selection process, while Comcast and Southwestern Bell, Esat Telecom's original partner in the licence bid, were also disgruntled.

In the Irish parliament, the Dáil, Minister Lowry was already under fire for interfering in some of the big state-owned transport companies under his department's control. Now his selection of the consortium to be awarded the new mobile phone licence was under scrutiny. Opposition politicians attacked Lowry, saying the controversy was damaging Ireland's reputation internationally as a place to do business. Others had more specific questions. Did Esat Digifone have enough money to build Ireland's new mobile phone network, they enquired. And were there other factors that helped the group to win the competition?

The minister repeatedly denied any wrongdoing. 'I was acutely aware of my duty not to interfere with the selection process,' he explained. The 'exhaustive and fair process', he said, could serve as a model for future decisions in other areas. 'It is an example of the standard of decision-making that I wish to see become the norm across the spectrum of Irish public life.'

The controversy was such that Lowry and his high-ranking associates held a press conference to reassure the public about the competition's integrity. The Department's senior civil servant, John Loughrey, was present to support the beleaguered minister and firmly rebut all allegations of wrongdoing. 'There was nothing dodgy about this competition whatsoever and I believe it will stand up to any scrutiny,' he told the assembled journalists. The only conclusion that could be drawn was that Esat Digifone was 'the best performer. This is as squeaky clean a competition as you can imagine being run by any public sector in the European Union. There was no outside or political interference in the decision-making process.' The minister, he insisted, had 'no hand, act or part in the process. The sole determinant was finding a consortium that would give the Irish business sector and the Irish telephone user the best service.'

Not everyone was unhappy with the result, however, and one partner in a losing consortium was prepared to be magnanimous in defeat. Tony O'Reilly, the Irish newspaper baron, penned a personal letter to the younger businessman congratulating him on his great achievement. 'My dear Denis,' he wrote. 'Many years ago at Blackrock Baths I watched your father in the national championships I think against a certain Eddie Heron. The multitude of the Kavanagh brothers were there flexing their pectoral muscles and I was sure your father would win an Olympic Gold. In fact, he didn't and you did, and

I think your achievement in securing the second digital network is your equivalent.'

O'Brien was annoyed by the continuing questions and allegations of corruption. They were 'an insult to the many Irish staff who worked on the bid for Esat, not to speak of the experts who assessed all of the bids', he said. 'It was an open competition. We met the six criteria and we made a better bid.'

The discussions between O'Brien, his Telenor colleagues, Dermot Desmond's representatives and the Department before the final awarding of the licence were nevertheless said to be tense. The officials still had to ensure the company had enough money to actually build a network and there were now concerns about the legality of issuing the licence to a group differing from the one that had originally applied.

Telenor of course had huge financial resources at its disposal. Desmond's arrival had strengthened O'Brien's company's financial position, as the financier had pledged to underwrite the money it needed to contribute for its share of the start-up costs. But the Department had to be certain that Desmond had enough money to meet these commitments. His company, IIU, was a new entity that didn't publicly disclose its financial details. And as the integrity of the licence competition was still being publicly challenged, IIU might find it difficult to raise from other investors all or part of the €74 million it had committed. Before issuing the licence the Department wanted to ensure that Desmond's privately owned company could raise that money. 'Telenor was undoubted as it was essentially the Norwegian government, so the only area of discomfort was over Denis's funding,' one source explains. 'With all the debate about the licence it would have been very difficult to place shares with investors. Nobody wants to be associated with something that's tainted.'

Desmond's covert arrival also posed another problem for the Department. Not only had Esat Digifone's composition changed from the group that applied for the licence, so had the size of the investors' shareholdings. The Department had originally been told that O'Brien and Telenor would each own forty per cent of Esat Digifone and that a group of investors, made up of four financial institutions, would hold the remaining twenty per cent. But Desmond's insistence on receiving twenty-five per cent had meant a reduction in his two partners' stakes to just over thirty-seven per cent each. The Department insisted that the original shareholding structure would have to be restored before it could award the new licence. Officials told O'Brien and his colleagues to sort it out among themselves.

All parties wanted to get the licence as quickly as possible and Desmond broke the logjam. He agreed to sell five per cent of his shares equally to Telenor and Esat for a non-negotiable price of €3.5 million, reducing his stake to twenty per cent and restoring Esat and Telenor's each to forty. 'The Kaiser' had already made a return on his investment.

With the final hurdle cleared, Esat Digifone paid the €19 million licence fee to the Irish government and in May 1996 it was awarded the new licence. Finally it was in the mobile phone business. Relieved and delighted, O'Brien promised that Irish people using Esat Digifone's network could expect a twenty-five per cent reduction in the price of calls made on its network when it launched, it was hoped, before Christmas.

As the new company's chairman, O'Brien would preside over many heated board meetings in the months and years ahead. Almost immediately there was an almighty battle in which he insisted that his best friend Barry Maloney should be given the role of chief executive, something that Telenor refused to entertain. As Leslie Buckley, O'Brien's senior lieutenant, observes, 'I know Denis put his neck on the line with Telenor at a very early stage because he wanted Barry Maloney to be the chief executive. We had to fight to get him in place. Denis thought that highly of him.' The Norwegians had already fought off O'Brien's previous challenges to dominate the company's operations and had no intention of letting his candidate take the reins now. As a compromise it was eventually agreed to appoint joint chief executives, Maloney and Telenor's Knut Digerud. It was a cumbersome structure that reflected the deep distrust between the two major shareholders.

With a thriving career as a senior executive at the Xerox Corporation in California, Maloney had so far been the most successful of O'Brien's gang. 'Barry had the home, the pool, and all the rest and had gone on to this other life as a corporate soldier in Xerox while Denis was knocking around radio stations,' says Paul Connolly. 'There was an element of "you should have left when I left".' Now O'Brien, who had been the groom at Maloney's wedding, wanted his best friend to return to Dublin with his family to run his new mobile phone company. Maloney had been wooed by O'Brien and the 'rat pack' to come home to Ireland. O'Brien flew to San Francisco to recruit him and Connolly dropped in to see him shortly afterwards to urge him to take the role. 'I was part of the lobby team to bring Barry to Ireland, to land the big fish so to speak,' Connolly says.

O'Brien and his associates were keen to have Maloney on board such an exciting venture. 'Of all his friends this was the biggest compliment of all,' Paul Meagher says. 'A lot of his other friends had done other things but Barry was the standout candidate for Denis. He would have had huge loyalty to him and was very fond of him and thought he was the right man for the job.'

Maloney was offered what was described as an extremely generous contract with locked-in guarantees and entitlements to potentially lucrative share options. If the company was successful he would be a very wealthy man. It was too lucrative to dismiss. Maloney was happy to sign.

With the Esat Digifone team expanding rapidly, O'Brien insisted on meeting everyone who came to work at the company. Intent on getting the measure of everyone who worked for him, he got angry if he found someone had slipped in under his radar. 'If he saw somebody that he didn't know he would say, "I didn't interview that person over there,"' says Leslie Buckley. 'He might only spend five minutes with them but it was to see if they had the culture within them. You have got to recognise pretty fast whether they are on the button or not.'

O'Brien himself continually hired new people, something that brought its own challenges for his colleagues. Conor Lenihan had now moved from working as a political correspondent at 98FM to a senior executive role at Esat Digifone. O'Brien had simply walked up to him and told him he was transferred, saying, 'You're to report down there on Monday.' As Lenihan explains, 'Before you would get a chance to talk about the job or your salary you weren't presented with options. Then you would get fevered calls afterwards from him asking, "How's it working out down there? What are you doing?"'

A bevy of O'Brien's new recruits continually reported for duty. 'One of the issues that Denis had and that would have frustrated the board was that his natural inclination was to hire people, often on a whim,' Lenihan says. It was a demonstration of the impulsiveness that contrasted so strikingly with his attention to detail in other matters. 'You could find yourself in the situation where someone would walk in and say "I've been hired. I met Mr O'Brien last Friday night and he said I would be working with you" and that would be the first you'd heard of it. You got used to it. That was his style.'

The chairman's hands-on style certainly irked his Norwegian colleagues, to whom he continued to refer openly as 'the Vikings'. There was a feeling among some of the Esat Digifone team that Telenor would prefer O'Brien to be a mere figurehead for the mobile phone business, but they knew that would never happen.

Lenihan settled into his new desk next to Maloney's fellow chief executive, Knut Digerud, and had a ringside seat to all the comings and goings between the opposing shareholders. 'We were literally back-to-back with each other. He believed that I was Denis's man and I believed he was a seriously important man,' he laughs. 'We were both in a state of mutual wonderment for about six months about what we were supposed to be doing. There was a lot of chaos.'

Lenihan joined the team charged with rolling out the network. They had mapped out the optimum locations for the 170-plus masts they needed to erect to ensure maximum coverage for mobile phone users, but the project was beset by problems. Esat Digifone had acquired most of the sites before the licence application but was finding it difficult to get permission from the planning authorities to erect masts. By July the company had permission for just over sixty masts and the outstanding applications were moving slowly. Thanks to these delays it was way behind schedule for building its network. It would soon have to pay hefty penalties to the Department for the delay and it was already under pressure to raise its share of the network's mounting cost.

Meanwhile, its competitor, Eircell, was busy expanding its own network. As a subsidiary of Telecom Éireann, it didn't need permission to erect masts and its steel structures were rising all over Ireland. Under the direction of Stephen Brewer, it was executing its own battle plan to take on the competition.

The former France Telecom executive had been headhunted to lead Eircell's offensive. 'We knew we were going to be playing Manchester United whoever won the licence,' Brewer says. 'I knew Denis was very much in the running for the licence. He had done very well in the radio stations. We knew he was going to make his name and mobile was the place to do it.' Eircell, Brewer says, just got out there selling its mobile phones, trying to capture as much of the market as it could before Esat Digifone was launched. The new mobile phone company had a network of dealers with over 100 shops ready to sell its mobile phones as soon as the network was switched on. It had almost 150 staff in place to work at its customer care offices, but it could do nothing until the phone network was ready.

Lenihan had a suggestion. There was another way to quickly roll out a mobile phone network, he said. They should talk to the Irish police force, the Garda Síochána, about piggybacking off its communications network, which extended across the length and breath of Ireland. Esat was one of a number of bidders to explore this option when they were preparing their licence applications, but all had been rebuffed. Lenihan thought it was time to reopen the discussions, an idea that wasn't universally supported by the rest of the team. But Maloney liked it.

'When Maloney came in he sorted out a lot of the problems in the company,' says Lenihan. 'I had become involved in the Garda deal and wasn't really getting any traction internally with my own crowd who were quite hostile to the idea. When Maloney came in I was given a free hand to go off and work on that full time.'

And so 'Project Blue' was born. Lenihan and Maloney met with the Garda authorities and within a month they had carved out a deal. Esat Digifone proposed that it would rent space on 450 Garda masts, agreeing to upgrade them to carry mobile phone transmitters. The digital network would also allow the Garda to install a new radio network that had been sanctioned by the government. The total cost to Esat was estimated at €40 million.

It would take a few more months for the agreement to be signed off by the government, but the new mobile operator had overcome a major obstacle. It finally had a nationwide mobile phone network. 'That famous deal effectively saved the company from becoming a basket case with no coverage,' says Lenihan.

Following this success, Lenihan was elevated to number three at Esat Digifone, reporting directly to the two chief executives, a situation that was often bizarre. 'It was quite comical for me,' he recalls. 'I would have to time my run to Maloney's office so that the other man wouldn't see me. Both would become jealous if they thought I was paying attention to one more than the other.'

As the company grew, there was a sense among some of the staff of how little O'Brien actually knew about the telecommunications business. 'A lot of people criticised him when he started the telecommunications companies because he knew nothing about it,' says Lenihan. 'This was a frequent complaint of some of the people that joined the company in the beginning. You would pick it up on the corridors, that he knew nothing. But he learned pretty fast and pretty much soaked anyone that worked for him for their knowledge.'

And he wasn't afraid to get involved in the technical side of the business. 'He's not a slow learner. When it's not his own area he learns everything about it. He's not lazy-minded,' continues Lenihan. 'If he's in a business he wants to know everything about it. Even though he hires brilliant people in various areas, he doesn't depend on them to tell him. He'll learn it himself.'

Esat's network could be tested only when all the masts were in place, a process that was taking longer than anticipated. By now it had missed the lucrative Christmas period and was struggling to stay on target. Two months later O'Brien and the other directors were reluctantly forced to agree to push the launch date back until March. This meant the company would have to pay a IR£1 million penalty to the Minister. And this was the least of O'Brien's company's financial worries.

By now Esat Telecom had a growing customer base but it was still struggling to make ends meet, largely owing to the high cost of using Telecom Éireann's network. In 1996, the company celebrated its one thousandth business customer, including US computer chip manufacturer Intel, but made a €500,000 loss.

The telecommunications sector was being slowly dismantled across Europe to allow for new competitors. The issuing of new licences was an early phase of the liberalisation programme, to be followed by the introduction of new systems of regulation, paving the way for competitors to build their own telephone networks. The European Commission wanted telecommunications infrastructure to be liberalised by the middle of 1997, but the Irish government wasn't rushing to facilitate the change.

Esat Telecom was still battling with the Department over the use of autodiallers to allow it to bypass the Telecom Éireann network. Relations between the company and the Department officials had become strained. For O'Brien, his colleague Mark Roden and those trying to force the changes through, their biggest concern was that the company's systems couldn't cope with the new business it was winning. O'Brien's goal was to get the European Commission on side to act as a barrier between the company and the Department. Esat Telecom's in-house lawyer, Jarleth Burke, was practically living in Brussels, according to Buckley, as the company lobbied for support and relentlessly fought its case.

The routers would deliver huge savings, enabling Esat Telecom to avoid the exorbitant rates its rival charged for using its phone network. They could be temperamental; some who used them described the devices as 'early technology', a 'leaky bucket' that could result in dropped calls from time to time. And once the market was fully liberalised, Esat and its rivals would have arrangements to interconnect with other networks, with alarms and backups if the circuits failed. But in the prevailing circumstances, the devices were the best they could offer. And Esat now found some support for its position.

Although, O'Brien and his colleagues believed, Telecom Éireann was wielding its influence with officials behind the scenes to restrict the scope of Esat's business, Humbert Drabbe, a senior Commission official, believed the company should be allowed to use the call routers and expressed his opinion in a letter. It would prove to be a valuable piece of correspondence for Esat Telecom, enabling it to stop the Department from pulling its licence while it continued to install the devices.

By now the company had offices in other Irish cities outside Dublin and was about to expand its services to include domestic as well as international phone calls. As the Department and Telecom Éireann were flexing their muscles in Brussels in order to effectively kill the Drabbe letter, O'Brien was getting ready to announce the move into domestic calls at a lavish event at Dublin's Shelbourne Hotel. Comedian Dermot Morgan, the star of comedy series *Father Ted*, entertained potential customers as O'Brien arrived straight from lengthy discussions with the company's lawyers, William Fry, about how to react if the Department sought an injunction blocking its entry into the domestic market. Again he was pushing the boundaries and testing how far he could roll out the business. And it worked. The Department wasn't pleased but made no official moves to block the expansion.

As the company expanded its business around Ireland, however, Telecom Éireann was doing everything it could to thwart its ambition. 'Suddenly our customers started to get calls from Telecom Éireann trying to win back their business,' Buckley says. In Cork, one customer told him the Telecom Éireann caller had enquired why his business had decided to go with a company that was operating 'illegally'. He told Buckley he hadn't had a call from Telecom Éireann in the past twenty years. Other customers were offered new cheaper phone packages by its rival, tailored to their business, and some received dire warnings about the unreliability of Esat's phone services.

Conn Clissman, O'Brien's former school mate, switched his company's business to Esat and was immediately cautioned about the move by Telecom Éireann. 'It did everything possible to dissuade us,' he recalls. 'As a consumer, it warned me the autodiallers would cause problems with our exchange and wanted to come to my office to discuss it. They really jumped up and down on this little upstart.'

As the flow of sales calls from Telecom Éireann to Esat's customers increased, O'Brien wondered whether its phones were bugged. 'All they [Telecom Éireann] were probably doing was getting printouts of numbers being dialled. When the dialler redirected the call, their exchange would see where the call was coming from and going to,' one former employee suggests. 'They would then turn up to a customer with a tailored package that would suit them.'

Telecom Éireann senior executive Cathal Magee acknowledges that there was a war of attrition between the two competitors: 'Denis would push the boundaries of everything he could and we would try to be defensive about it. I think he was in a much stronger position because people wanted the market opened up. They wanted competition. He was seen as the good guy and he played that extremely well.'

O'Brien was the aggressor, according to Magee. 'He was the attacker, the attacker brand. In many ways he came into the market before the regulatory model was fully developed and mature. It just shows how early he was. He was the early mover. That was really impressive.' Esat Telecom, says Magee, led the market in introducing discounted packages and bundling services to attract the most lucrative type of business. 'He was a very dynamic force in the market and he was always in our face. He got close to customers while we were one step removed. We were tracking where Denis was and where his team was. They were going face-to-face with customers. They were going in doors. They were winning market share a customer at a time and that was their model.'

Magee suggests O'Brien and his team forced its rival to change the way it carried out its business. 'Maybe they taught us in many ways that you build market share one customer at a time and you lose market share one customer at a time. And unless you actually come to terms with that in how you function in business, you are going to be in trouble. So we had to transform our whole sales operations and pricing to respond to these challenges.'

Yet O'Brien still struggled to find enough money to keep Esat Telecom going. He juggled money from the radio station, played banks off against each other and constantly travelled to meet investors who might commit some of their money to his projects. And now the mobile phone company was an added financial strain.

Lenihan says it was O'Brien's obstinacy and determination, coupled with his ability to travel anywhere 'at the drop of a hat, if it involved raising investment or loans for the company', that kept it afloat. 'Denis had huge energy for all of that. He'd never give in to tiredness or jet lag after a long flight. Of course he was always a good sleeper. He always went to bed early at night. He was a great man to sleep while the rest of us were out late. He always had his head together in that regard.'

And O'Brien meticulously prepared the presentations he would use to convince investors to back his ventures. According to Lenihan, he was 'almost nerd-like' and 'even obsessive' when it came to preparing his pitch. Just as his mentor Tony Ryan had issued his apprentice with clear instructions about what he was to say when he sent him to complete a task, forcing him to write down every word and phrase he should use, O'Brien exercised similar control over his own team. 'He would run through the pre-planning to an obsessive extent, before a sales call or a presentation,' Lenihan says. 'He always insisted that people had to have their presentations right. Nothing unexpected occurred and we didn't overachieve or underachieve the expected outcome.' Every last word and sentence would be meticulously pored over and considered and O'Brien would insist that everyone stick to the final script. 'I had a huge row with him because I chose to innovate on a sales call as opposed to sticking to the scripted conversation we were meant to have,' he recalls of a dressing-down from the chairman. 'I had to walk out of the room.'

Others talk about O'Brien's attention to detail, his expectation that everyone around him should be fully in command of their brief. 'Not knowing a detail, even a small one, would be very bad,' says one member of his team. In other words, the offender might well receive a monstrous tirade of criticism. 'He is a perfectionist and the master of presentation,' remarks another.

Lenihan says that if O'Brien believes in a project he will go to 'hell and back' to assist you, whether you need his input or not: 'he will sit on your case and give you unsolicited advice whether you want it or not because it's his money and his reputation that's on the line. The time when he was most volatile, with myself and other staff, is when we were not behaving professionally.'

According to Lucy Gaffney, O'Brien always insisted the company should be managed as if it was a public company. It should hit its quarterly targets, have good management disciplines and constantly sell its story to investors. 'He would gather a good board of directors and expect to see an action plan as to how to resolve any problems.'

The autodiallers were a temporary remedy for Esat's networking difficulties, as well as a contentious one. Ultimately Esat wanted to build its own fibre-optic network, an item O'Brien added to the list of projects he needed to raise finance for. The US market was ahead of Europe in terms of liberalisation and numerous US telecommunications companies were managing to raise money from investors to invest in such networks. US investors understood the concept and were interested in backing such projects. Esat Telecom badly needed to get a share of that cash.

Having researched their market, they began in their presentations to adopt language and terms familiar to US investors. They would 'talk American', according to one former employee. 'Fundraising in the US was the biggest lesson in psychology. It's all a confidence game.' Many of the investors, others say, liked O'Brien's casualness and his bluntness and enjoyed the story he told about the company's ongoing battles with the Department of Communications and its arch-rival. O'Brien and Paul Connolly worked their way through a list of US venture capital companies that had invested in telecommunications and radio and travelled from the east coast to the west with their presentation. Next they went to Europe.

Again it was a high-stakes game. Esat Telecom desperately needed to raise enough money to meet its commitments in the radio and telecommunications businesses, while the delay in launching the new mobile phone service was leading to rumours about Esat Digifone's ability to deliver the network. There were suggestions that Esat Telecom might go bust. Now, in the middle of O'Brien's discussions with potential investors, the *Sunday Times* reported that the company had lost €9.5 million in the preceding nine months and was in imminent danger of collapse. It was a devastating development that might undermine investor confidence in O'Brien and the company he hoped to persuade them to invest in.

'We're in trouble, deep trouble', was O'Brien's response to the story as he and Connolly flew to New York to soothe the concerns of investors who had pledged funds for the company. It took a couple of days of meetings before they finally managed to sign a deal for $85 million from some of the biggest US investment houses. He announced the successful deal on his return to Dublin.

And there was more good news. Finally the mobile phone network was up and running. It was all systems go. Esat Digifone would open for business on 20 March 1997 in spectacular style.

That night O'Brien beamed as he welcomed 750 invited guests to Dublin's Point Theatre for the official launch. He borrowed a line from the Sex Pistols to sum up how he was feeling: 'We done what we done, because there wasn't anything else we could do.' Government ministers, civil servants and business people mingled and marvelled at the show. Outside, fireworks cascaded over the River Liffey in a display shown on national television, where the new mobile phone company took over the advertising slot in the middle of the main news bulletin to herald its arrival.

Banks of video screens filled the stage with links to similar events in Cork, Limerick and Galway. Singers Brian Kennedy, Mary and Francis Black and Eleanor McEvoy came on stage, as the support acts to O'Brien and his crew.

It was hard to be oblivious to Esat Digifone. For weeks its colourful advertisements had been everywhere, promoting an offer for a free family holiday every year for twenty years to each of the twenty countries where customers could use their Esat Digifone phones. The winner, the first person to make a call on Esat's network, was announced that night. It was quite an occasion.

And O'Brien wanted to praise all those who had helped him along this epic journey. Michael Lowry was there as sort of a 'fifth Beatle', he said, and was very proud of the part he had played in bringing competition into the mobile phone market. O'Brien took the opportunity to publicly thank Lowry and also paid tribute to the man who had stepped in at the last minute to provide him with the financial strength to launch the company. 'Nobody epitomises the "get up and go" attitude of the new Ireland, the Celtic Tiger, if I may, better than that bravest of brave Irish investors Dermot Desmond,' he declared. Telenor's chairman, Terje Thon, said it was a 'great thing for Ireland' to have competition in the mobile phone market.

It was a bittersweet moment for Lowry as it was left to the new Minister for Communications, Alan Dukes, to launch the network officially that night. Just two months after Esat Digifone won the licence, Lowry had been forced to resign from government and his membership of the Fine Gael party, following damaging revelations about tax evasion through his business dealings with wealthy Irish businessman Ben Dunne. The man once tipped as a possible future leader was out on his own, fighting for his seat in the forthcoming general election. Referring to the mobile phone competition that night, he said ruefully: 'I started this before I left office and I would have loved to have seen it through to the end, so it is with a touch of sadness for me personally that I am here.'

So the new Digifone service was up and running, offering those who signed up for its phones much cheaper calls. It was a runaway success from the start. Within a few months it captured more than forty per cent of Ireland's mobile phone market. But in that regard it was a victim of its own success. The network struggled to cope with the surge in traffic. Parts of Ireland had patchy coverage and there were problems making and receiving calls to such an extent that Ireland's second mobile phone network quickly earned the nickname 'Dodgyfone'.

10 Blowing the Whistle

In August 1997 Denis O'Brien gathered friends and family for another celebration. The thirty-nine-year-old businessman was marrying his colleague Catherine Walsh at a lavish reception at Luttrelstown Castle in County Dublin, the scene two years later of David and Victoria Beckham's wedding. It was a stylish and joyous affair at which O'Brien's family and his 'rat pack' mixed with business acquaintances and members of his radio and telecommunications businesses.

Some were surprised that the groom's best friend wasn't at the wedding. Paul Meagher stood beside O'Brien as his best man that day, a role some felt Barry Maloney might have assumed. But Maloney hadn't been invited. Many wondered why.

Those aligned to O'Brien's mobile phone business knew the reason. The pair had fallen out spectacularly. While they continued to work together they were barely speaking. As the wedding approached, Meagher had tried to resolve their dispute, pleading with the two long-time close friends to resolve their differences, but he was unable to repair that bond and so Maloney was off the guest list.

The cooling of their relationship, some say, began almost from the day Maloney arrived. 'It's difficult to work for someone when you have a very close personal friendship, and Denis can be a very demanding guy and commands fierce loyalty,' Meagher says. 'And I don't think Barry wanted to kowtow to Denis.' Paul Connolly believes the relationship fractured because of their competing ambitions: 'Barry wanted to be his own man, the entrepreneur, but he was the hired gun.'

Everyone acknowledges Maloney's was a difficult role given the conflicts and deep distrust between the shareholders who owned Esat Digifone. From the start, those working at Esat say, he set out to run it as an independent company and not as part of O'Brien's business empire. This, most believe, is what enraged his friend.

'It was a bad fallout,' Conor Lenihan says. 'I heard both sides and still had to work and report to Maloney. It was a difficult situation to manage myself. I had respect for both of them. Maloney was a great manager and brought great international expertise. He and Denis are very different people.'

The row grew out of the competing interests of Esat Digifone's shareholders, he believes. 'Pressures and problems developed from the shifting sands of shareholder interests who had rival and competing ambitions for Esat Digifone. There was pressure from Denis to amalgamate the mobile business with Esat Telecom and to cross-sell their services. This was resisted by the Norwegians, who wanted to keep the mobile business separate.' As far as O'Brien was concerned, Esat Telecom's fortunes were intrinsically linked to Esat Digifone's success, which he saw as an opportunity for Esat Telecom to generate new business.

According to Lenihan, there were logical arguments on both sides but the divergent views about the relationship between the two companies made for a difficult working environment. By now, he says, the chairman and chief executive weren't speaking to each other and not speaking well about each other. 'And they weren't too quiet about it either.'

Public relations consultant Eileen Gleeson also witnessed the deterioration in the relationship between Esat Digifone's chief executive and chairman. 'Barry was a great operator but once the relationship soured there was suspicion on both sides,' she says. 'One of them would be saying "I can't tell you that because you will tell him", or asking what the other said about something. I don't know of any one incident that happened between them. Barry was strong and he was resisting any of Denis's efforts to help Esat Telecom to leverage off Esat Digifone. Barry saw his role as heading Esat Digifone and he had other shareholders to consider. He was the chief executive, but that attitude doesn't work in Denis's world, where everyone is part of the family.'

Gleeson suggests that O'Brien's attitude is that everyone should pull together. 'He would think if you could help him, even if it takes up your time and effort and resources, that doesn't matter. Just do it. But Barry didn't see it that way and that is where the belligerence and the separation of the two started.' Paul Connolly suggests that Maloney adopted a very American-style 'business school' approach to running the company that didn't work with O'Brien.

Whatever the reasons for the falling out, it was a tricky situation for everyone who worked for the company. O'Brien eventually forced the consultants working for both the mobile and fixed-line businesses to choose where their loyalties lay – with him or Maloney. 'A lot of consultants had to make a decision,' Gleeson recalls. 'They were told they could only work for one company or the other. Digifone was where the money and fees were and we were asked by both companies to continue to work for them. We had to make a decision and opted to stay with Denis. I knew he would do that in the same situation.'

Until the launch of Esat Digifone, she says, everyone had worked for O'Brien. 'We all saw one person as the leader. Then Barry saw himself as separate and was establishing his own fiefdom, whereas Denis would take the view that he was taking that too seriously.'

Maloney's friends were sympathetic to his situation and many concluded that O'Brien was simply an impossible person to work for. 'It was a tough situation for Barry,' one said. Meagher believes Maloney felt he didn't owe great loyalty to O'Brien for giving him the top job at the new mobile phone company. 'Barry would say he got the job on merit; he was right for the job and that he was going to be independent. It didn't matter what pressure he was going to come under as chief executive.'

O'Brien didn't share that view, says Meagher. 'Denis saw it as a breach of the loyalty that Barry owed to him personally. The bottom line is that Denis was the person who had been driving Esat Digifone. He was the guy who had the vision and when it settled down into a company he was no longer involved in the day-to-day aspects and didn't exercise as much control over the business as perhaps he wanted to. Entrepreneurs like to be in control. When they sense a loss of control they can be very difficult to deal with.'

*

While O'Brien would continue to battle for control of Esat Digifone, he was very much leading the charge at Esat Telecom. He strengthened its team by hiring experienced executives to manage the rapidly expanding business, and was now hoping it would shortly trade on the stock market.

Accountant Neil Parkinson and multinational executive Seán Corkery joined Esat Telecom's two hundred staff, heading the finance and operations side of the business respectively. Parkinson, who would soon earn the nickname 'Doom', says he was given an unenviable task: 'There aren't too many people who would go in and say "no" to Denis but as chief financial officer that was my job. He was like a child who wanted all of the sweets in the shop. Denis would come in with five or ten new ideas every day. My job wasn't to say, "No, Denis, you can't do those ten things." I'd have to say these eight are great ideas and hope he would forget about the other two. He wants to do it all.'

That is what you expect when you are dealing with entrepreneurs, Parkinson says. But he realised he would need to be able to cope with that kind of energy. 'When I joined Esat I would have asked myself, could I live with someone like Denis? Strong individuals require a certain persistence and that was part of the challenge,' he says. 'When you meet Denis his sense of energy comes through. He doesn't have blood. He has adrenaline running through his veins. You know fairly quickly that you will have good and bad days, which was true. He gets a lot of work out of you. Denis is driven and drives everyone around him but he leads from the front and does more than anyone.'

Seán Corkery remembers arriving at Esat Telecom's new headquarters at Grand Canal Quay. 'If you stood in the lobby, the place would be abuzz at six on a Friday evening. There was an energy in the company that reminded me of Apple in the early days.' O'Brien likes managing businesses, Corkery says, and is good at it — but more as a builder than running the day-to-day operations. He testifies to O'Brien's tendency to micro-manage when under pressure, in contrast with his willingness on other occasions to entrust individuals with high levels of responsibility: 'He is smart enough to know that and to delegate the operations. On a bad day, though, he would think he could run the operations better than any of us.'

It was O'Brien's incredible sales skills that impressed Corkery most. 'He is a front of house person with great ability to bring customers around in terms of sales. It was unbelievable how impressive he was, how people wanted to do business with him. He would give them very strong commitments and was simple around price. And he would give them his personal number and say "Call me anytime", which was a bit eerie from an operations point of view.'

O'Brien loved meeting people who had ideas about starting a new business or getting involved with his ventures and always agreed to meet them. Colleagues say his diary was constantly filled with meetings with various contacts and even strangers who had something they wanted to run past him, making it difficult for them to discuss urgent matters within the business. 'He had so many contacts and so many irons in the fire all of the time,' Corkery says. 'People were always turning up bringing him ideas and you would be asking whether they were worth it. There would be no business case analysis done. They didn't all come to fruition but invariably a lot of them would be good. But you wanted your time as well.'

O'Brien, like his mentor, Tony Ryan, was relentless when it came to hiring someone he had set his sights on. He identified the best people in the global telecommunications business and launched a charm offensive to persuade them to join his company. He had plans to establish a call centre to deal with Esat Telecom's customers and his enquiries about who he should get to run it led him to Cedar Rapids in Iowa to meet Dan Rogers, a well-regarded figure in the telecommunications sector, particularly in the area of customer service. Rogers had pioneered a number of techniques, including the two-ring response, where customers were guaranteed their call would be answered by an operator by the second ring.

O'Brien was sufficiently impressed by Rogers that he had already made three or four offers to him to entice him to work for Esat Telecom. Rogers didn't want to uproot his family. Refusing to take 'no' for an answer, O'Brien flew to Iowa for dinner with the family as part of what Rogers says was his 'love-bombing' campaign.

He was flattered by the Irish entrepreneur's persistent overtures and came to regard O'Brien as 'the most innovative businessman in this area in the world'. At a personal level, he said he found him to be 'one of the nicest, most open people' he had ever met. And he was an entertaining and engaging dinner guest. That night O'Brien told the Rogers family he would 'make them rich' and he made a particularly big impression on Rogers' two teenage sons. In a note to O'Brien after the meal, Rogers said one of his sons had the opportunity to leave the table but stayed to hear more. 'Quite a compliment from a teenager,' he wrote. His other son told his father that all through dinner he felt O'Brien was talking directly to him.

Rogers was persuaded to come to Dublin for a week to look around Esat and the family were invited to the city for Christmas. Rogers himself was unable to travel over the holiday period because of work commitments but O'Brien flew his wife and sons to Ireland for a break and showed them around.

Eventually Rogers was made an offer he couldn't refuse and returned to Dublin to discuss it. O'Brien wanted him to establish the call centre and offered him a potentially lucrative shareholding in the company as part of a very generous remuneration package. He then left Rogers alone in the boardroom to mull it over. A few minutes later, Leslie Buckley rang through to offer some helpful advice. 'Denis has made a lot of people rich,' he said. 'If he says he will make you rich, he will.' Rogers was won over and accepted the astonishing offer. He and his family were moving to Dublin. What happened once he joined the company illustrates one of the more unfathomable aspects of O'Brien's character – his impulsive unpredictability.

Around the office O'Brien would amiably talk to everyone, greeting them either by name or by the nickname he had given them. But he was a mercurial character, one day cheery and full of conversation, another moody and aloof. One person recalls O'Brien getting into the lift and ignoring him, the only other occupant. The unsettling encounter left him wondering if he had done something to annoy the chairman. Worried about the consequences, he unburdened himself to a colleague, who offered some advice: 'Just go up and apologise.' 'For what?' he asked. 'It doesn't matter, just do it.' It worked. A friendly relationship with O'Brien was swiftly restored.

This kind of experience was far from being an isolated example.

Colleagues developed a code for assessing the boss's mood as they prepared to approach him. Over the years his personal assistant, Nicola Prendergast, grew used to describing the 'weather conditions' round the chairman's office. News that it was 'sunny', for instance, signalled a good time to think about dropping in. Days when the outlook was 'stormy' suggested it might be better to reschedule or prepare for a hostile reception.

Unsurprisingly, it took new recruits a while to figure out how to deal with O'Brien. More experienced colleagues would watch in horror as newcomers needlessly vied for the chairman's attention. 'It was a difficult working environment,' one said. 'You had to learn how to survive.' Some of the longer-serving crew concluded that the best way to have a good working relationship with O'Brien was to draw on his time only when it was essential and always to be responsive to him. 'We would see new managers trying to maximise their face time with Denis and we would joke about never flying too close to the sun. We saw some real clowns who would be constantly asking Denis's PA for time with him. That wasn't the way to go. You should just get on with it.'

And Dan Rogers was among those who found it difficult to adjust to working for the man who had so persistently and charmingly pursued him to join the company. Only a few weeks after Rogers' arrival there were signs that things weren't going to work out. Rogers would later claim in a court action for wrongful dismissal that O'Brien and his lieutenants spent the next six months trying to 'drum him out' of the company. They found it difficult to adjust to his American style. Thanks to O'Brien's enthusiasm to hire Rogers, the contract between them was a difficult one for the company to deal with. According to Corkery it contained too many guarantees. 'As the company got bigger we would try to make sure that Denis wasn't the only person involved when new people were being hired.'

Rogers was not the only one to suffer such a fate, having been won over by O'Brien's charm and persistent courting only to quickly fall foul of him. 'It was often a very different story when you joined,' explained one recruit.

As Conor Lenihan says. 'I would have some sympathy with people who ended up in a difficult relationship with Denis, and I would still be friendly with some of them. He put such a huge premium on loyalty that if he even sensed that criticism had moved from honest and constructive to what he perceived to be disloyal he became hugely difficult to deal with. If he perceived that anyone was being disloyal he became utterly unforgiving, and that was basically the end of you and the company.' Others also attest to this, saying that once you lose O'Brien's respect your only option is to leave. 'It would be impossible to survive,' one suggests.

Seán Corkery, who found himself in the role of 'executioner' where Rogers was concerned, believes O'Brien had the best of intentions when he hired the American and felt guilty about the impact on his family now that he felt he wasn't the right person for the job. 'His bias is to like people. Denis really wants to engage them. It takes others to say the references are bad or to ask if they're looking for too much money. If something wasn't working it could be Leslie or Lucy who would flag that to him.'

Some of the disagreements with various staff members are due to the phenomenal pace at which O'Brien operates, Corkery suggests. 'When you get a person who has achieved as much as him, there are going to be fallouts if things are not going fast enough for him. Denis is different from everybody in terms of pace. He demands loyalty. He needs to be able to trust you that if you were to do something it would be similar to what he or Leslie might have done. He is a man of definite opinions. That can make it difficult. He can form an opinion of people that can be unfair. He calls that stuff early whereas most operations guys would give the benefit of the doubt. I'd say most of the calls were about right. Maybe he called a few too early but that was because he is moving at speed.'

Lucy Gaffney, who was viewed by colleagues as O'Brien's 'shadow', says the telecoms tycoon constantly challenges those who work for him to put in an incredible performance. 'Denis stretches people like elastic bands.' Working at Esat, she explains, is like a hectic journey on a fast-moving train. 'Some people can hack the pace and others can't. If you were lazy or disloyal you were pushed off but if you couldn't stay on board through no fault of your own Denis would be very loyal.' Nobody gets to be as successful as her friend and colleague, says

Gaffney, without falling out with people along the way. 'Some people have stayed with him for the entire journey but it's not a huge list.'

The pressure was rarely released even when O'Brien was away from the office. Although he still travelled extensively raising money for the company, he was always in touch by phone and text message. Only when on aeroplanes was he forced to remain out of touch. New satellite phones would eventually puncture even those peaceful episodes, allowing their boss to call even from thirty-five thousand feet, but for now everyone at Esat Telecom could breathe a sigh of relief while the chairman was airborne and his phone was off.

Management meetings were a source of further tension. According to Lenihan, O'Brien had a professional approach to such meetings, putting people under pressure in order to see what they were actually doing and making sure they were able to account for themselves. Others, though, describe the meetings as awful.

'He wasn't a saint or anything like that,' admits Lenihan. 'I remember telling him that I couldn't be bothered to work for him any more and I resigned. I had a temper tantrum and we both shouted and screamed at each other. I walked out and went down the street and he came running after me and pinned me up against a Georgian railing. He pleaded with me not to leave him now and invoked loyalty and friendship and a hundred different things if I'd stay. I said I would stay if his behaviour changed. In fairness to Denis he was always ready and willing to entertain a behaviour change if that was what was required to keep you in the company.'

Others say there were days, particularly at the beginning, when two or three people might be ready to resign in exasperation at the demands and the tongue-lashing O'Brien subjected them to. 'There was one week when a group of people were all prepared to jump ship. They had had enough,' recalls one employee. 'Unbeknownst to each other he managed to talk them down and hold on to them. He was a very good manager. He knew how to keep people together.'

Colleagues felt he resented it when people left the company. 'He was the one person who didn't like people leaving him,' Lenihan says. 'He was very strong on the loyalty thing and in fairness to him he repaid that loyalty to staff. It wasn't one-way traffic.'

He could also show an extremely caring and compassionate side that often took people by surprise. O'Brien visited staff in hospital and could be paternalistic, offering support to people going through a difficult patch in their personal lives. 'There were many human situations where he helped people out and it was always kept discreet,' Lenihan says. 'If he ever sensed there was anything wrong in that area he would cut through the management structures and privately go to those people and sort them out and not make it a source of leverage, or a source of embarrassment or something that was talked about. He was very gentlemanly to all sorts of people in the company. He would feel for people in those situations.'

By now Esat Telecom was working with its advisers to float part of the company on New York's Nasdaq index, a move that would bring fresh investors and give O'Brien and the other early shareholders an opportunity to realise some cash. Indeed, almost everyone who worked at the company received share options as part of their remuneration. O'Brien believed in sharing the spoils as a means to incentivise people and drive them to work harder to create a more valuable company. According to Neil Parkinson, the company-wide share option scheme fed the 'win-win culture' among the staff.

Even consultants like Eileen Gleeson got share options. 'Denis was very generous. When we got options the company was losing a fortune and we never had a discussion about what they might be worth. Options were quite new for people other than a close group around a management team. Few understood what that could mean. It really wasn't until we started on the process of the flotation that people began to understand what having share options could mean for them individually. And by that stage we had all well earned them and were sucked into it.'

Those working at Esat Digifone could only look on enviously as colleagues at the parent company began to speculate about how much they might soon be worth. Buckley says O'Brien wanted a similar scheme at the mobile phone company but Telenor resisted. 'We had very strong and hard discussions to get share options for the Esat Digifone employees and Telenor wouldn't move. God, I thought that was awful. You had people on one side of the house who went on to make quite an amount of money and the Esat Digifone staff didn't.'

Some observers suggest Telenor's resistance to granting share options was part of its determination to maintain the company as a separate entity. 'The Telenor executives weren't happy about it. They were worried it would create an allegiance to Esat Telecom,' one insider said.

The imminent stock market flotation was perceived to have added further tension to O'Brien's fragile relationship with Barry Maloney. Maloney didn't have share options in Esat Telecom and wouldn't benefit from the flotation, although he had generous options in the mobile phone company. Some suggest he wanted O'Brien to float Esat Digifone on the stock market ahead of Esat Telecom, although he has denied this. Leslie Buckley says that, although O'Brien and Maloney didn't disagree over shareholdings or the terms of his contract, there were 'various disappointments' for Maloney at that time that might have annoyed him. Whatever the reason, O'Brien and Maloney's fragile relationship was about to implode. For the telecoms tycoon, the consequences were ultimately to prove devastating.

Despite their strained relationship, O'Brien and Maloney continued to go for gruelling runs in the mountains, together and with the rest of the 'rat pack'. O'Brien has explained that he found it easier to deal with Maloney in this setting and used it as a means to restore a working relationship: 'In the running context I found it was easier to get him to do things, rather than in the context of his office, in an environment which was much more heated and pressurised.' One Sunday morning in November 1996, soon after Maloney joined Digifone, the pair set off running, chatting about business issues along the way. What they discussed that day would haunt them for years.

O'Brien was pressurising Maloney that morning to make what he called 'success fees' to some of the consultants and advisers who had helped Esat Digifone win the licence. There was no paperwork for some of the payments and Maloney wanted more details before making them.

Maloney had already dealt with a vague request for $50,000 that turned out to be a political donation. Just weeks before Esat Digifone won the mobile phone licence competition, the money had been paid by Telenor, at O'Brien's request, to Fine Gael activist David Austin, towards a fundraising event in New York. Esat later reimbursed the

$50,000 to Telenor and Maloney reclassified the payment as a donation.

Another 'success fee' had been paid after Maloney re-negotiated the payment down from an option to buy shares in the company to a financial sum. But there was no paperwork for two other payments, one of which was due to P.J. Mara for his public relations consultancy work. Maloney has said he felt 'caught' between the two issues. In response, he claims, O'Brien said: 'You think you've got problems. I've had to make two payments of £100,000 each, one of which was to Michael Lowry.'

Recounting the conversation under oath years later, Maloney said he told his jogging partner he 'didn't want to know' about any such payment. From the conversation, he said, he believed the payments had been made through an intermediary and had nothing to do with Esat Digifone. They had continued running.

Twice over the following months they revisited a subject that was becoming potentially more lethal. The government had recently established a Tribunal of Inquiry to investigate payments to politicians. It began by investigating payments made by wealthy business figures, including Dunnes Stores former boss, Ben Dunne, and Dermot Desmond, to Ireland's former Taoiseach, Charles Haughey. It was now looking at payments Michael Lowry had also received from Dunne.

Now the spotlight was shifting on to Lowry. The Tribunal would be examining the decisions he had made as a minister and looking for any evidence that might link a bribe with a corrupt decision that favoured the donor. Maloney was growing ever more concerned about what he claims O'Brien had told him.

When they next spoke about it O'Brien attempted to allay his concerns. He claims to have told Maloney, 'I didn't actually do it. Thank God.'

Maloney has recounted that one of these discussions continued as they walked down the stairs to the street. Suddenly, according to Maloney, O'Brien turned and looked him in the eye. 'You're not buying this, are you?' Maloney claims O'Brien asked, and waited for the reply. Maloney said he was having difficulty accepting his former best friend's word as they continued to walk, turning into a laneway. 'What I haven't told you,' Maloney claims O'Brien continued, 'is that

I was going to make the payment but it got stuck with an intermediary.' When they parted Maloney drifted back to his office. He believed O'Brien hadn't given money to Lowry but he was now concerned that a third party knew of his intention to make a payment.

Meanwhile O'Brien had become openly hostile to Maloney and his Norwegian colleagues. The atmosphere was tense. 'Maloney wanted to build an independent empire, Denis wanted to control as much as possible of that, then you had Telenor as well,' one insider says. 'You had three groups trying to control the organisation, which made for a lot of tension.'

Eileen Gleeson was among those who witnessed O'Brien's growing disdain for his Norwegian colleagues: 'The Telenor people were nice fellows, civil servant types who were serious about their business and knew exactly what was going on, but Denis ran rings around them.' O'Brien would often entertain the troops with sarcastic comments about the fact that some of the executives commuted each week between Dublin and Telenor's Oslo headquarters. Gleeson recalls that he would look at his watch and loudly say: 'What time is it? Three o'clock on Thursday, sure they're on the fucking plane back to Norway by now. Ah sure, they'll be going for a bit of skiing and they won't be back till next week.'

O'Brien's relationship with Digifone's joint chief executive Knut Digerud was particularly strained. According to Gleeson, once she suggested consulting Digerud about something they were working on for the company: O'Brien laughed and said, 'Are you mad? Sure he won't care. He'll be on the slopes.' The Telenor staff were often sitting at their desks listening to such tirades, she says. 'He didn't care.' Some of the Irish staff wondered just what their Telenor colleagues might be saying about O'Brien, but because none of them spoke Norwegian they could only speculate.

It was no secret that the Telenor executives too were fighting their corner. 'Neither side were angels,' one person observed, saying the Telenor executives could be equally combative. 'They played Mr Nice Guy to Denis through an interpreter but this was far from the truth.' Both sides were seasoned warriors with different combat styles. And then there was Dermot Desmond. He would do anything to protect his investment and would be nimble to spot an opportunity to strengthen his position.

The Telenor executives saw Desmond as closely aligned to O'Brien. While O'Brien could depend on Desmond's support, however, he and the rest of the Esat camp were constantly looking over their shoulders and trying to ensure they didn't hand Desmond the opportunity to take over their share of the business. Desmond was a wily corporate warrior, who in ruthlessness and determination was more than a match for O'Brien.

There were fundamental disagreements on virtually all aspects of the mobile phone business. Telenor had the experience of operating a mobile phone network, while Esat saw itself as having the edge in building a business in Ireland and in the branding and marketing of its service. 'There wasn't necessarily one hundred per cent agreement between them on each of these areas,' according to one insider. Leslie Buckley refers to the 'cultural' differences that existed between the two shareholders from the start: 'That got progressively worse as time went on.'

The two sides frequently squabbled about which name should be used in the company's branding and marketing. Telenor had always been uncomfortable with using Esat in the mobile phone company's brand, and preferred it to be known as Digifone. Trademarks for Esat Digifone and Digifone were separately registered and Telenor saw the use of the Esat name as another attempt by O'Brien to align the two companies as he tried to create opportunities for Esat Telecom from the mobile business.

Just weeks after the mobile phone network had finally launched, O'Brien angered his Norwegian partners by writing a letter to Esat Telecom's shareholders highlighting the links between the two companies. At the next board meeting Digerud and his colleagues took the opportunity to launch their attack. Referring to the letter, they accused the chairman of 'misrepresenting' the relationship between the two companies and demanded he rectify the situation. They had even drafted a letter to shareholders clarifying Esat Digifone's independence from Esat Telecom and were insisting he sign it. O'Brien was furious and refused to comply. Digerud then shocked everyone by calling for O'Brien's resignation as chairman.

It was a clumsy attempt, but it showed the depth of the deep distrust and personal animosity between Esat Digifone's main shareholders. In fact no one other than the three Telenor executives supported the motion calling for O'Brien's resignation, with Michael Walsh, Dermot Desmond's representative, supporting the other Esat directors. The meeting continued as normal after the challenge. Telenor had lost the battle. But the internecine war continued.

At Esat Telecom, meanwhile, preparations continued for the company's launch on the stock market. Its advisers prepared documents for shareholders, outlining the potential risks associated with investing money in the company's shares. The company's forty per cent shareholding in Esat Digifone added to its potential stock market value and was an attractive element of its business, but O'Brien and Maloney clashed over the information it could disclose about the mobile phone operation.

The company would also have to disclose fully to potential investors any information relating to the mobile phone business, including the fact that the minister who awarded its licence to operate was under investigation for corruption. The documents would be filed with the New York Stock Exchange and had to be signed both by Esat Digifone's directors and by Maloney. They were aware the company could face legal action from investors in the future if it turned out they had been misled in any way when they purchased shares in Esat Telecom.

Maloney therefore confronted O'Brien once more about whether or not he had made a payment to Lowry to influence the awarding of the licence. 'Absolutely not,' O'Brien assured him. But Maloney wouldn't let the matter rest. Later he went to his friend's house to privately confront him yet again about the payment and was promptly dismissed. O'Brien said he was frustrated to find Maloney waiting outside his home on returning from a night out with his wife and gave him 'short shrift'; Maloney, he believed, just wanted to delay the flotation.

Given the potentially serious consequences for the company and the directors personally, Maloney now made them aware that O'Brien had told him he made payments to Lowry. It was a shocking allegation, the last thing they wanted to hear as they steered ever closer to the stock market. But it was one they could not ignore.

According to Leslie Buckley, everyone was concerned: it came at a very sensitive time for the company. Not only could evidence of a corrupt payment potentially derail Esat Telecom's flotation bid, it could put the mobile phone licence in jeopardy. What was more, the directors knew that if there was any evidence of a payment to Lowry, it should be reported to the Payments to Politicians Tribunal.

They were also acutely aware of the bad blood between Maloney and O'Brien. Some were suspicious of Maloney's motive in reporting the conversation to them now, a year after he claimed it had taken place. They asked the company's solicitor, Owen O'Connell, to establish the truth.

O'Brien has never denied the conversation with Maloney but claims what was said was part of his 'spoofing' of Maloney, 'part of a wind-up' to encourage his friend to make the 'success' payments O'Brien had promised to various consultants. He never paid any money to Lowry, he insisted.

As Michael Walsh, Dermot Desmond's right-hand man and his representative on the Esat Digifone board, has pointed out, however, O'Brien's explanation that it was a 'wind-up' didn't make the directors feel any more comfortable: 'People felt it was plausible – it is Denis's nature to cajole people into doing whatever he wants them to do. But it did not remove the concerns.' Desmond, it seems, took the allegation very seriously and was threatening to sue O'Brien and anyone else involved for any resulting damage if he had been misled in relation to a payment to Lowry. Others were equally troubled. Paul Connolly describes the allegation as 'horrific' and says it created an astonishing degree of concern and alarm within the company's boardroom.

Over the next few days Esat Digifone's directors met at IIU's offices in Dublin's International Financial Services Centre. It was the first time that Desmond had attended a meeting of the board.

As part of his investigation into Maloney's accusations, O'Connell, helped by O'Brien's close friend and accountant Aidan Phelan, had examined O'Brien's bank accounts for evidence of any alleged payment to Lowry. They found nothing. They also investigated the $50,000 Esat/Telenor donation to David Austin for Fine Gael shortly after the licence award. The board asked Austin, who was gravely ill, to write a letter to say the money had been passed to the Fine Gael party, which he did. A simpler course would have been to ask the political party for a receipt for the donation, but this wasn't done.

Desmond said that if nothing suspicious was found, he would accept O'Brien's word that he had not given money to the former minister and that would be the end of the matter, but he would still seek a written assurance from everyone involved, stating they had nothing to do with such a payment.

By now IIU had sold another ten per cent of its holding equally to the two other shareholders for €7.4 million. Some observers interpreted the sale as Desmond bailing out of the troubled company amid the infighting and the company's huge demands for cash. Others say IIU was merely acting in accordance with the shareholder agreement, responding to the pressure from both share-holders to gain a larger share of the company, while steadily realising a profit.

At Desmond's insistence, though, he would continue to hold two seats on the board regardless of the size of his shareholding. To the further infuriation of the Telenor executives, he would thus continue to wield considerable influence at the fledgling company, despite the fact that he was gradually exiting it with a handsome profit.

While Desmond and the other board members met to consider Maloney's allegation, O'Brien and Connolly were travelling in the USA and Europe presenting Esat Telecom's story to investors to gauge their appetite ahead of the flotation. O'Brien joined the board meeting on a conference call. After some questioning, his boardroom colleagues quickly accepted his version of events. As far as they were concerned there was nothing to suggest he had made a payment to Lowry. That was the end of the matter.

Maloney's allegation had been investigated and firmly dismissed.

But Maloney hadn't been silenced. He would go on to repeat the allegations under oath in a more public setting. It was O'Brien's old school friend who would blow the whistle on him.

11 Selling Out

By the end of 1997 Denis O'Brien was one of Ireland's wealthiest citizens, joining Dermot Desmond and Tony O'Reilly on the rich lists. Esat Telecom was trading on the New York Stock Exchange and was valued at more than $300 million. O'Brien's twenty per cent stake was worth about $60 million.

It was an incredible achievement. The company he founded in 1991 had almost collapsed in the face of relentless competition from Telecom Éireann and under the pressure to find the enormous amount of money needed to build a substantial telecoms company from scratch. And now it also had a more than forty per cent stake in Ireland's thriving second mobile phone company.

The prospects for O'Brien's telecom empire looked bright and his personal fortune was piling up nicely. He had big plans for how he would spend it.

In between selling the Esat Telecom story to investors he had purchased the Quinta do Lago resort in the Algarve from the British Thompson family for €31 million, almost half the value of his Esat shares at that time, having outbid two other potential investors. The complex, which had changed hands a number of times in previous years, included four eighteen-hole golf courses covering over six hundred acres, stables, a five-star hotel, a large number of luxury villas and several lakes offering sailing and windsurfing. It was an enormous investment that would give him a percentage of the green fees on the golf courses, which included San Lorenzo, and rental income from the properties in the complex. And there was enormous potential to develop many more luxury homes on the plots of land surrounding the four golf courses.

O'Brien enjoyed holidaying in Portugal. He had started to play golf and had rented a villa in the Algarve a few years earlier, inviting his gang to join him in their new outdoor pursuit. Few were still fit enough for the endurance tests in the Wicklow Mountains; now they all played golf. Paul Meagher was shocked when he found out his friend was the owner of Quinta do Lago. 'I couldn't believe it when he told me he had bought the place. I thought, Jesus, we are really going up a league here.'

It seemed that O'Brien was the man with the Midas touch. He had told his gang he would make them all rich and now they believed him. He was the man to spot the lucrative opportunities, the entrepreneur who knew how to make the big money. O'Brien rarely discussed investments beyond the telecommunications businesses outside his close circle of friends, some of whom would be invited to join him in new money-spinning ventures. He was known as the risk taker, hungry to invest his wealth and eager to meet anyone with an interesting proposal.

Together with Buckley and his other close associates, O'Brien now invested in Versatel, a Dutch telecoms company founded by former Esat chief operations officer Greg Mesch and which was soaring in value. Some who knew both men were surprised by the investment as Mesch had left Esat in acrimonious circumstances. They wondered what O'Brien was up to. Certain other investments made by O'Brien during this period might have caused them to raise their eyebrows even higher.

O'Brien's interest in aircraft leasing, whetted by his apprenticeship to Tony Ryan, next led him to establish a new company, Aergo, with a group of friends and business associates that included Paul Connolly and Aidan Phelan. O'Brien had also been acquiring properties in Dublin over the years, investing in houses in attractive locations as well as in commercial property. He now owned Esat Telecom's new headquarters and was looking at further such opportunities at home and abroad. In fact the man with the growing media and telecoms empire was buying up any decent property in Dublin he could. After Conn Clissmann gave Esat his phone business, he says O'Brien, whom he hadn't seen for years, called to thank him for his business. As the old school friends talked, Clissmann mentioned he would soon need to find bigger premises to cope with his company's expansion. The next day O'Brien rang him back with a proposition. 'He said "I went for a walk and looked at your place and I'll take it off you for IR£630,000," ' Clissmann says.

He was surprised O'Brien had moved so quickly to assess this potential opportunity but wasn't interested in selling to him. 'It was a decent offer but he wasn't spilling money over my desk and I thought, if he wants it I should hold on to it. We didn't sell to him but I should have honed my instinct and bought two adjacent properties.'

Northern Ireland businessman Kevin Phelan was a mover and shaker in the property sector, specialising in scouting out properties and sites with development potential in the UK and elsewhere. Through his range of contacts, Phelan brought deals to accountants and other professionals whose clients might be looking to invest. His clients included Michael Lowry, for whom he had identified two development opportunities, in Cheadle in Cheshire and in Mansfield in the English Midlands. Phelan pitched himself as the person who could either manage the site or arrange the resale or 'flipping' of the land to a new owner for a share of the profits or a finder's fee.

In 1998 he spotted another potentially lucrative property deal in south Yorkshire and spoke to accountant Aidan Phelan about it. The two Phelans were not related but knew each other professionally and had both been involved in Lowry's purchase of the two UK properties earlier that year. They decided to bring this investment opportunity to Aidan Phelan's close friend, Denis O'Brien.

Doncaster Rovers was a down-at-heel football club that had long been hoping to build a new stadium. Rovers had played at their home ground, Belle Vue, since 1922. The stadium, known locally as 'The Bell', was located on a valuable piece of land with development potential in the middle of the town. A fire had damaged its main stand two years earlier and the club's chairman, Ken Richardson, whose company owned the site, was keen to sell. It was a far cry from investing in the Quinta do Lago golf resort, yet O'Brien expressed an interest in buying the dilapidated ground. Kevin Phelan proposed to manage the property for O'Brien for a few months and then sell it on to Doncaster Borough Council, making a tidy profit for O'Brien and himself. O'Brien agreed to buy the site, paying for it with money held in a family trust fund in the Isle of Man. He asked his father to oversee the deal. O'Brien was to pay just over €5 million for the site.

Disputes soon emerged between Richardson and Kevin Phelan over fees and payments. When Richardson's and O'Brien's sides disagreed over a final payment, a mediator was called in to broker an agreement, but things turned nasty. In a bid to ratchet up the pressure on O'Brien to complete the sale, Richardson's side declared that it had some potentially explosive correspondence which, if made public, could be very damaging for the Irish businessman.

O'Brien was using an English lawyer, Christopher Vaughan, to deal with the legal aspects of the purchase. Vaughan was also the lawyer Michael Lowry had engaged to process his two UK property deals. Doncaster Rovers' owners now claimed they had a letter from Vaughan that showed he believed the former minister was buying the site with O'Brien. Vaughan referred to Lowry's 'total involvement' in the deal in the correspondence, they claimed, although Vaughan later said he was mistaken. He also said in evidence that the letter was correct in relaying what Lowry had told him. If genuine, the letter could prove a financial link between O'Brien and the former minister, who was currently being investigated for corruption.

O'Brien senior challenged Richardson and his associate, Mark Weaver, accusing them of trying to blackmail his son to settle their dispute. He later lodged a complaint about the pair with the London police. Richardson was jailed in 1999 for an earlier attempt to have the Belle Vue stadium burned down. Kevin Phelan was also in dispute with O'Brien over his fees. It was only after many months that the sale was eventually completed and O'Brien became the new owner of Rovers' hallowed ground.

In Ireland, meanwhile, a new government was settling into office. The Fianna Fáil party had been returned to power with a coalition partner, the Progressive Democrats. The government was now led by Taoiseach Bertie Ahern, who was currently appointing his cabinet. O'Brien rapidly arranged to meet the new administration in order to continue his lobbying for further liberalisation of the telecoms industry in Ireland. He wanted to develop Esat Telecom into a fully fledged telecoms company providing residential, international and mobile phone services as well as data and internet packages. Other new telecoms companies across Europe were being allowed to compete fully with the monopolies; it was only a matter of time before the Irish government would be forced to open up the whole sector to competition.

Mary O'Rourke, an experienced politician, was appointed as the new minister responsible for the sector and soon scheduled a meeting with O'Brien. She remembers it clearly. She knew of Esat's founder through her nephew, Conor Lenihan. 'I had known of him but this was the first time I had a conversation with him. He has an attractive personality and was quite charming. He was brimming with good looks and good health and lots of money and he was naive with it,' she says. 'I don't think he *was* naive but he had a way of saying things naively which if you didn't know him might make him seem a bit dim. But he wasn't dim. I formed a good impression of him.'

O'Rourke was less impressed with O'Brien's cheeky pushing of the boundaries of his licence by continuing to use autodiallers, the technology his company was illegally using to bypass Telecom Éireann's phone network, and told him so. 'You're a pirate,' she exclaimed, to their mutual amusement.

The minister took a dim view of previous deals O'Brien had brokered with a company now under her watch. Esat Telecom's deal with the state's railway company Córas Iompair Éireann (CIÉ) to route its fibre-optic cables along its tracks was, she believed, too generous to his company, and she told him how she felt: it was 'far too cheap' and bad value for the state. 'CIÉ made what I would have called a bum deal with him.' But at this point, according to O'Rourke, the contract couldn't be undone.

Nor did she undertake any investigation of the mobile phone licence when she took charge of the Department, although she felt apprehensive about it. The officials, she says, were 'uneasy' about the matter but didn't confide in her. Instead, being progressive, and keen to embrace further changes to open up Ireland's telecoms industry, she was preparing to dismantle the last vestiges of Telecom Éireann's monopoly. Soon other companies could start offering a residential phone call service to the public in Ireland. It was good news. Finally

Esat Telecom could compete with its mighty rival in every segment of the market.

When the new licences were issued O'Brien and his chief operations officer, Seán Corkery, went along to the Department to collect theirs from the Minister, wearing pirates' hats to mark the occasion. Later that day they launched Esat Clear, a new company headed by Lucy Gaffney, to compete with Telecom Éireann for residential business. The Esat crew were amused to hear O'Brien mistakenly introduce Gaffney by her nickname, 'Lucy Gaddafi'. The new venture was heralded in true Esat style with a big party at a Dublin late night venue where musician Jools Holland and his band entertained the crowd.

And there were other milestones to celebrate. In 1998 O'Brien was crowned Ireland's Entrepreneur of the Year in a competition run by Ernst & Young. It was, he says, one of the proudest moments in his business career. 'If you are an entrepreneur and someone says: "Hey, there's an award for it," you say: "Jaysus, that's fantastic. That's brilliant." It's like winning a Nenagh Bumper,' he told the *Irish Times*, comparing the accolade to winning a National Hunt race in County Tipperary.

O'Brien was riding the crest of a wave, but he would soon have to return to the bunker and wage another war. This time he would be fighting the enemy within his ranks, his Norwegian partners Telenor.

The telecoms industry across Europe was being transformed. Not only had thousands of new telecoms companies been launched, a wave of mergers was also triggered as the big players began to forge alliances.

In Ireland too the environment was changing. Having deregulated the residential phone network, the government was preparing to sell off Telecom Éireann. As a first step Minister O'Rourke sanctioned a partnership between the state telecommunications company, Swedish telecommunications group Telia and Dutch group KPN. The Irish government was loosening its grip on Telecom Éireann and soon it would have to fend for itself as a public company with international investors.

The repercussions of the merger mania across Europe would

quickly impact on Ireland's two rival telecommunications companies in an unexpected way. Telia, Telecom Éireann's new partner, was itself preparing to merge with Esat's partner Telenor, something neither Irish company was pleased about. There was an expectation that one or other of the Nordic partners would have to disengage from its Irish counterpart. And, given the fragile relationship between the Norwegians and O'Brien and his investors, Esat was hoping Telenor would be the one to retreat.

O'Brien and his team therefore upped the ante, hatching a plan to buy out the Norwegians and finally secure control of Digifone. Their first approach, in April 1998, was rebuffed, and repeated efforts over the following months came to nothing. So Leslie Buckley travelled to Oslo in the hope of persuading Telenor to reconsider Esat's offer.

From the minute he arrived, it was clear the prospects of cutting a deal were remote. 'I was kept waiting for quite a while even though they knew I had travelled over from Ireland,' Buckley says. 'I spent quite a number of hours there without making progress. I really knew I wasn't going to make any progress when they said "You are staying at that hotel over there" and I had to walk in the snow for about half a mile.' It was a discourteous way to treat a senior figure from its Irish partner but was indicative of the naked hostility that now existed between the two sides. 'They would behave like that,' says one person who observed Telenor's business dealings with its Irish colleagues. 'They were tough and could be every bit as uncompromising as Denis.'

The merger of Telenor and Telia, partner of eircom – the privatised company formerly known as Telecom Éireann – was now complete, increasing the strains between Digifone's shareholders. O'Brien was concerned that commercially sensitive information might end up being passed on to eircom's mobile phone operator, Eircell, Digifone's competitor in Ireland. He sought assurances from Telenor that no information would be exchanged but was dissatisfied with its response. In the prevailing atmosphere of mistrust, it seemed the company had no option but to take legal action against Telenor, alleging that it was leaking commercial information to its competitor.

By now Esat Telecom was itself being mentioned by various analysts as a takeover target. There was speculation that the expanding telecommunications company would fit well into British Telecom's operations, valuing it at almost €320 million. The success of Digifone had greatly enhanced the value of its parent company; it was estimated that Esat Telecom's stake in the mobile phone business now accounted for half of the company's value, or about €160 million.

O'Brien and his management team were well aware of how valuable the company was, and no one valued it more highly than its founder. Esat Telecom's shares had fared well on the stock markets and by early 1998 were steadily rising. Kevin White, a recruit to the company, remembers giving O'Brien a lift home from the office one evening and listening to the business news on the radio on the way. RTÉ reported that Esat Telecom shares were trading at $22 on Wall Street that day, well up on the flotation price of $13. After the bulletin, O'Brien told White the shares would go all the way to $100. 'I remember I thought he was mad,' he says. At that price he was valuing Esat Telecom at a staggering $2.5 billion.

O'Brien had in fact started to mention to investors a price of $90 a share as the ballpark figure the company would expect in a takeover. His valuation was based on the strength of the company's business, he explained. It was now a thriving telecommunications company operating in a booming economy. Esat Telecom had built its own phone network, rolling out a fibre-optic network and a submarine cable to handle international calls and data, and was continuing to win more and more customers.

O'Brien and his lieutenants knew they should prepare for a takeover bid. With military precision the chairman again led the war games, anticipating all the likely scenarios they might face in a bid situation. 'Denis was the main driver here,' recalls Esat's finance director, Neil Parkinson. 'We knew we needed to be ready for a bid and developed a plan in the summer of 1999. We considered all the options. What if someone makes a hostile bid? What would we do and who would we go to? That work was done by August or September and effectively left on the shelf. At least we knew we were prepared whatever happened next.'

Paul Connolly recalls a meeting with US bank J.P. Morgan around this time, at which it was outlined how a publicly quoted company should behave if it became embroiled in a hostile takeover. He put a copy of the presentation in his briefcase, intending to read it on a flight somewhere. He would need it sooner than he expected.

The relationship between the Irish and the Norwegians continued to fracture, their tolerance of each other growing ever thinner. Some credit Dermot Desmond and Michael Walsh, his representative on the Digifone board, for helping to maintain the company's momentum regardless of the intense power struggle between the two factions. IIU had proved loyal supporters of O'Brien in the boardroom but equally were unafraid to disagree with him and block certain of his proposals at board meetings if they felt they were not in the company's best interest. 'Denis didn't always get his way in the boardroom,' according to one source. Others suggest that the company thrived because of the mix of shareholders, despite their disagreements. 'Maybe it was the perfect blend,' one said.

But Telenor was tiring of IIU's presence in the boardroom and went to court to have Walsh ejected. Desmond's company had continued to reduce its shareholding, selling off its shares in equal measure to O'Brien and his investors and Telenor. By November 1999 IIU held just one per cent of the company. But this was still enough to give it the balance of power in any bid, and it still had two seats on the board. In court Telenor claimed IIU had no right to the level of influence it continued to wield in the boardroom, but it failed to alter the arrangement.

In fact board meetings had generally been businesslike affairs, if punctuated by bitter rows. The Telenor executives spoke fluent English but from time to time incensed O'Brien and others by breaking into conversation among themselves in their native language. Now, four years into their uneasy partnership, there was no prospect of reconciliation. The court battles displayed very publicly the depth of their domestic strife, but this was only a taste of things to come. Soon the hostilities would intensify to outright warfare.

Esat Telecom's plan to defend itself in a takeover bid didn't have time to gather dust. Within a few months O'Brien and his troops were poring over it and assuming battle stations.

The drama unfolded as O'Brien and Connolly were meeting

investors in London before travelling on to the USA. On the evening of 29 November 1999 O'Brien received a message that Telenor's chairman, Terje Thon, wanted to speak to him. It was urgent.

That morning's newspapers had carried reports speculating that both Telia and KPN were preparing to sell their stakes in eircom. O'Brien thought Thon wanted to talk about this and relayed a message that he would speak to him in a few days when he returned to Ireland. But Thon couldn't wait. He would meet O'Brien in New York the following day, he said. Clearly something serious was afoot. On the transatlantic flight O'Brien and Connolly tried to anticipate what Telenor wanted. Had it finally decided to accept Esat's offer to buy them out? All would be revealed at lunchtime the next day.

When O'Brien and Connolly arrived at the Palace Hotel in Manhattan they were surprised to find Thon was accompanied by Telenor's chief executive, Morten Karlsen, and a senior banker. It was a more formal meeting than they had expected and without delay Thon opened the discussion by reading a prepared statement. For the next few minutes he detailed the breakdown of the relationship between Digifone's two shareholders, including the latest spat that would soon see them heading to court.

O'Brien was relieved to hear the sentiments expressed and felt Telenor had finally decided to throw in the towel. Thon and his colleagues were meeting to negotiate the price, he thought, right up to the statement's last sentence. 'And so,' Thon concluded, 'the best way of solving our differences is for Telenor and Telia to purchase Esat's shares.'

O'Brien and Connolly were shocked. They could only listen in shock as Thon went on to say Telenor's offer for the company would be 'generous'.

During the war games, they had never considered a bid for the company would come from Telenor. They couldn't believe the Norwegians' audacity in attempting to take over the tele-communications empire they had built.

O'Brien managed to compose himself and brought the meeting to a formal close by flatly rejecting the offer. As he headed for the door, he turned back and calmly invited Thon and his colleagues to enjoy the sandwiches that lay untouched on the table. They were off to their next meeting with investors.

Despite his composure, colleagues say, he was stunned. 'When Telenor launched the bid they really put it up to Denis. They [Telenor] felt they had been ridden over by an Irish guy,' says Eileen Gleeson. 'He got a shock.' Others involved with the company at the time say they never expected something so overt to happen. 'It was a bit disappointing,' one said. 'You expect people to work together and the business was doing very well. We were all surprised.'

Fuming, O'Brien resolved not to hand control of his company to his old enemy. He was hoping his emphatic dismissal of the offer would persuade them of its futility. Or perhaps, now the relationship had irretrievably broken down, Telenor might even think again about selling its stake to O'Brien and his investors.

But things didn't work out that way. For all of their military manoeuvres, they had been caught unawares. Telenor was determined to move forward with its bid for Esat Telecom.

At 2.30 the following morning, O'Brien was awoken by a call from Thon. His message was brief. Telenor was mounting a hostile bid to take over the company and would issue the terms of its offer to the stock market and the media within the hour. It was offering $72 a share for Esat's stake, valuing the company at almost $800 million (€779 million).

According to Connolly, O'Brien rang his room immediately to convey the shocking news, saying, 'They have fucking made a bid. Jesus they have. We had better get up.' Connolly searched for the J.P. Morgan file he had tossed into his briefcase and they tried to compose themselves.

O'Brien rang RTÉ business journalist Geraldine Harney, who would shortly be broadcasting the morning business news, to announce the bid and said he wouldn't be selling for less than $100 a share. This was against the rules and would subsequently get him into trouble with the Takeover Panel, the body charged with monitoring the takeover of companies traded on the Irish Stock Exchange, but he had got his price out into the market.

'I am now up and in my suit with the J.P. Morgan book out,' says Connolly. 'We were surprised but at least we had it. We knew we had to ring the board and Denis was asking "Who else do we have to fucking ring?" ' They took a Concorde flight in order to arrive quickly back in Dublin to round up the troops.

The bid was soon announced. Telenor publicly declared that it was making a generous offer and urged Esat Telecom shareholders to accept it. The bid valued O'Brien's shares at almost €200 million if he accepted but he had no intention of taking the Vikings' money. He would be rejecting it himself and his advice to shareholders was to do the same. The hostile bid demonstrated 'an extraordinary lack of understanding of the business and value of Esat', he said, and would be 'contested vigorously'. Shareholders should just ignore it. They could rely on him to defend them from these Norwegian corporate raiders.

O'Brien's mantra when planning an assault is 'prepare, prepare, prepare', and he demanded ferocious discipline from himself and his team as they once again went into battle, focused on working together to extract as much money for themselves and the other shareholders as possible. Alongside their advisers, they drew up a list of businesses that might consider mounting a counter bid to buy the company. Thriving as he always did on war games, O'Brien was once more marshalling the troops and barking out the orders. 'There is nobody better to be in the middle of a battle than Denis,' Eileen Gleeson says. They once again adopted the bunker mentality, operating amid tight security and with precision. O'Brien gathered his war cabinet and they executed the defence plan precisely the way he demanded.

He divided them into two cells, one to concentrate on defending the company against the Telenor bid while the other went in search of an alternative bidder, a so-called 'white knight', who might pay a higher price. Again his obsession with security came to the fore and he dictated that neither cell could communicate directly with the other. O'Brien would check on their progress early each morning. He, Lucy Gaffney and Connolly all obtained new phone numbers; they also travelled by private jet to ensure confidentiality.

Venture capitalist Massimo Prelz Oltramonti worked closely with O'Brien, while Tony Belinkoff (nicknamed 'Tony Telecoms' by O'Brien), a telecommunications strategist at US investment bank

Donaldson, Lufkin and Jenrette, worked the phones and set up meetings with likely bidders.

British Telecom was top of the list, with Italy's Vivendi not far behind. Belinkoff ascertained their interest and arranged meetings between their top executives and O'Brien and his team, hoping one of them would get into a bidding war with Telenor and best the Norwegians' offer. 'We were right on our game; we were razor sharp and we'd everything prepared,' O'Brien has said of the operation. 'We hit the purple patch at just the right time. You see it in football where a team does really well coming into the end of the season.' United in their goal, determined to sell the company to the highest bidder, they would all make a fortune as a result. O'Brien's price, as he had so often repeated, was $100 a share.

His army of advisers were ordered to find a bidder that would pay up to $100 a share for Esat Telecom and were offered incentives to achieve that lucrative price. O'Brien told them they would get their normal fees if the company was sold for up to $99 a share. If it went for $100 or more they could claim a fifty per cent bonus. It was an extraordinary sweetener, but to earn it they would have to secure an extraordinary price of $2.5 billion for the company.

As the battle unfolded Telenor showed no sign of retreating, even when its merger with Telia fell apart. It pledged to see the takeover bid through and returned to the skirmish with an improved offer of $85 a share. It didn't believe O'Brien and his lieutenants would find a rival bidder to top that price.

O'Brien once again told shareholders to reject the bid. To emphasise the message his team placed the image of a computer keyboard on the documents circulated to shareholders, urging them to press the 'reject' button on the front cover. The shareholders were generally happy to sit back and wait to see who would be the victor. The hostile bid was steadily driving Esat Telecom's share price higher. They had hit highs of $99, edging closer to O'Brien's valuation.

Esat and its advisers now believed British Telecom was the 'white knight' to rescue it from the Vikings' clutches but they would have to play a clever game to entice the UK's biggest telecommunications provider to pay such a hefty price. BT had tentatively opened for business in Ireland the previous year and was going head-to-head with Esat Telecom and Eircom to gain a substantial foothold in the Irish market. The acquisition would immediately bring it more customers and allow it to expand at a faster pace. It would surely make perfect sense for the British company.

It wasn't the first time the company had eyed up Esat. Shortly after it had won the mobile phone licence BT had approached O'Brien about buying his fledgling company but had been rejected. And sure enough, as Telenor raised its bid for Esat, British Telecom finally came into view. Its financial director, Robert Brace, and chief executive, Sir Peter Bonfield, were ready to talk about a possible deal. 'We liked each other from the first meeting,' O'Brien has said. 'Straight away we struck up a good relationship.'

Massimo Prelz Oltramonti was among those who always felt BT would do the deal. 'Denis, with Tony Belinkoff, did a fantastic job,' he says. 'They maintained the pressure on BT and convinced them there was an alternative bidder.' In the background, O'Brien and his team were indeed talking to Vivendi and Vodafone, trying to entice them to join the bidding, but Esat's hopes were fixed on BT.

Over the Christmas 1999 holidays, they continued to work towards securing a deal with BT. O'Brien and the team returned to work on the deal on 26 December, hitting the phones, leaving messages for investors to maintain the momentum they needed to accelerate the acquisition.

From the outset, British Telecom insisted it would buy out the entire company, including its stake of just over forty-nine per cent in Digifone, where it would replace O'Brien and his investors as a joint shareholder alongside Telenor and IIU. The price was the only sticking point.

Time and again O'Brien and his advisers discreetly entered and exited BT's London headquarters for covert meetings at which they squared up to Brace and his team. With many voices contributing to the discussion, O'Brien adopted a tactic that had worked for his old mentor, Tony Ryan. In an attempt to close the deal, he invited Brace to move to a separate room to talk about the offer man to man.

There they to-ed and fro-ed some more, with O'Brien persistently nudging Brace towards the magic $100 a share he wanted. 'All right,

Robert, $100 on the nail,' he said, reaching out to grasp Brace's hand to shake on it before he could pull it away. They had a deal.

On 6 January 2000 BT agreed to pay almost $2.5 billion for Esat Telecom. It was an incredible price, way beyond what many of the shareholders believed would materialise. 'We had a target of $100 and we got it,' Prelz Oltramonti says. 'Frankly I was surprised.' It was a knockout bid that decisively blew Telenor out of the water.

BT had also been negotiating with Dermot Desmond and had struck a deal to pay him €23.5 million for his remaining one per cent shareholding, which would give it over fifty per cent of Digifone and control of the company. It had beaten Telenor to claim Esat Telecom and had also outmanoeuvred its bid to control the mobile phone business.

The Norwegians were bruised after the encounter, smarting that the lethal blow had come from BT, the company with which it was in partnership in Sweden, Germany and Finland. BT's chairman, Sir Iain Vallance, knew the news would be discomfiting for Telenor. 'I'm quite sure this will be a little surprise for them this morning,' he said. Soothingly he suggested that Esat would be staying 'in the family', as he very much hoped Telenor would remain in Digifone 'in one form or another'.

The Norwegians were having none of it. As the news was reported in Scandinavia, one reporter spluttered: 'You say it is staying within the family but this is like the first cousin running off with the bride!' It was a humiliating defeat.

O'Brien and his loyal crew were ecstatic. They had beaten the enemy and made a fortune. The company's forty-one-year-old founder was about to pocket €317 million (IR£250 million), just nine years on from his initial onslaught on the telecommunications sector.

12 Life in Exile

Denis O'Brien was the new poster boy for Ireland's Celtic Tiger money-worshipping generation. Days after he announced the sale that would give him a €317 million fortune, O'Brien was eager to talk about his achievements on Ireland's legendary Friday night chat show, *The Late Late Show*. 'You're an extraordinary man,' Pat Kenny declared when he introduced his celebrity guest.

Always a man to tell a good story, on television that night O'Brien explained that his achievement was all the more extraordinary since Esat Telecom had almost gone bust as it awaited the outcome of the mobile phone licence competition five years earlier. Things were so bad, he said, he had asked a nun to pray for his consortium to win the bid and sent her IR£3,000 when it won. 'She must have been praying for me this week too,' he laughed.

It was an exuberant performance, where O'Brien confirmed for the first time that his company had almost collapsed in those anxious days before it won the licence. The company had always angrily dismissed rumours to that effect as malicious gossip generated by the other licence applicants. And as those applying for the licence were expected to be financially robust, it was a surprising admission. The losers in that competition watched the victor revel in his great fortune and could only wonder what might have been.

He now had an awful lot of money, O'Brien acknowledged, and he was considering the impact it would have on his family as he and his wife Catherine awaited the birth of their first child. 'Money is the root of a lot of unhappiness,' he noted, and promised he wouldn't be burdening his children with great wealth. They might inherit just a few thousand each, he suggested.

The Revenue would be rubbing its hands in anticipation of a big cheque from O'Brien for the tax due on his payout, Kenny suggested. O'Brien even paid tribute to the fact that the government had recently cut the rate of capital gains tax to twenty per cent as a stimulus to investors. That was a great idea, O'Brien said, now everyone was playing the stock markets.

Of course many others were also counting their wealth in the light of the biggest corporate takeover in Irish history. O'Brien's friends and associates had all made lots of money.

Leslie Buckley, the man who advised Dan Rogers that 'If Denis says he will make you rich, he will', was set to receive €7.6 million for his shares. Paul Connolly had a windfall of more than €6 million to look forward to. Esat Telecom executives Seán Corkery and Neil Parkinson each got almost €7 million. Mark Roden, who started the company with O'Brien in 1991, had options worth €5 million, as did Esat director Padraig OhUiginn, while Lucy Gaffney received almost as much. O'Brien's father was also a beneficiary, netting close to €4 million.

Indeed, everyone at Esat Telecom was looking forward to a cash bonanza. Almost all of its largely twenty-something workforce had share options. Seventy-seven Esat Telecom staff became millionaires as a result of the BT bid. Outside the top earners, many were looking at payments of about €130,000.

The staff at Esat Digifone could only gaze in envy at their colleagues' good fortune. There was no cash bonanza on their horizon. They never had options to buy shares in Digifone and many felt cheated out of a windfall. The same couldn't be said for Digifone's chief executive, Barry Maloney. O'Brien had given him generous share options in the mobile phone company to ensure he would take the job in the first place. He was sitting on a €40 million fortune. While the pair never made up, in just five years Maloney had become exceptionally rich.

And 'the Kaiser', Dermot Desmond, had done even better out of his investment. The man who secretly joined the consortium after it had submitted its application for the licence had steadily sold his share to his fellow shareholders before finally surrendering his remaining one per cent to BT. In total Desmond made a

€127 million profit on his Digifone investment.

Dan Rogers, the American executive O'Brien had so earnestly pursued to join Esat only to quickly change his mind, was also looking for his share of the spoils. His case for wrongful dismissal was quickly settled after the BT deal and he was reported to have received €4 million. It was a court victory but the final payment was shy of the €24 million his one per cent of Esat Telecom would have been worth if things had worked out differently between himself and the telecoms tycoon.

O'Brien, who could be taciturn and aggressive at times with the media, said his next goal was the pursuit of happiness. 'And if you have fun, you are happy – you have to have a bit of craic.' He would be staying on with the company for a short period and had no plans to retire. 'It's a little bit eerie, to be honest,' he said.

The mobile phone licence for which the government had charged just €19 million had proved to be a licence to print money. While the various media organisations lauded O'Brien's success, however, some tempered their comments by referring to the controversy about the awarding in 1996 of the licence that had proved so lucrative.

The *Sunday Tribune*, part of the stable of newspapers owned by Tony O'Reilly's Independent News and Media group, was at the forefront in reviving the controversy. In its editions that weekend, it carried a photograph of former minister Michael Lowry on its front page above a piece headlined 'Lowry defends "early" licence award to O'Brien'.

Editor Matt Cooper asked Lowry about O'Brien's admission that his company had almost gone bust while it waited for the competition's outcome. Lowry, by announcing the licence winner two weeks early, had surely thrown a lifeline to the failing business, he suggested.

But Lowry rejected any suggestion of impropriety. 'Everything was done impeccably,' he said, claiming he had been unaware of any financial problems at Esat Telecom when it won the licence. 'I was satisfied and the Department was satisfied that he had the financial backing and funding and resources to perform as required and to put the infrastructure in place to roll out the service in accordance with the terms of the licence.' The reason O'Brien's group had won the competition was simple. It had 'taken the place by storm with its presentation', Lowry said.

In a lengthy feature inside, the paper referred to three 'lucky breaks' that had helped Esat to walk away with the licence. First it mentioned the knockdown price of €19 million the government had placed on the licence when analysts believed the bidders were prepared to pay up to €100 million for it in an auction. Second was the extension of the deadline for applications to the Department for the licence; coming just as Esat's partnership with Southwestern Bell foundered, this had given the group more time to bring Telenor eventually on board. Third was the early announcement of Esat's success in the competition, which effectively saved O'Brien's empire from disaster.

In an editorial, the paper focused on Dermot Desmond's late arrival as an Esat Digifone shareholder. That, it claimed, had never been adequately explained. 'Why Desmond instead of the other potential shareholders?' it asked. 'O'Brien has taken brave chances and been lucky,' it continued. 'Hopefully O'Brien is not a man who will fall victim to all the hype and believe his own publicity. Hopefully he will realise that those who get rich have a responsibility to the community and he will spend some of his money in a philanthropic fashion without looking to boost his ego or corporate activities.' The newspaper expressed the hope that O'Brien wouldn't develop a 'persecution complex' like those which often afflicted businessmen when asked how they had accumulated their wealth.

After a brief stay at Esat, O'Brien moved on to focus on other businesses. He was held in such high esteem for his business acumen and success that companies were eager to bring the telecoms entrepreneur on to their boards of directors. Arguably one of the most prestigious invitations came from the Bank of Ireland, the bastion of the country's blue bloods of the business world. And O'Brien was delighted to join their ranks, taking up his new role on the bank's court of directors, as it is known, in 2000.

The appointment to this conservative banking group raised a few eyebrows at the time, particularly in the light of the mobile phone licence controversy and the investigations of the Tribunal of Inquiry.

But the bank was delighted to have a dynamic entrepreneur on board at a time when investors were increasingly focused on how financial institutions would adapt to the internet. It was viewed as a positive development. O'Brien could only boost their fortunes.

And he was busily building a new and more diverse empire. He had worked to a clear objective in building Esat Telecom, creating a fully fledged telecoms company. But, open to new ideas as he was, his strategy for the future often seemed unclear. Some describe him as taking a 'scattergun' approach, displaying an almost frantic need to quickly reinvest his great wealth.

Telecommunications would still be a major source of investment, and O'Brien invested in a range of companies in that sector. He put some money into e-via, a company laying fibre-optic cables throughout Europe, and more into a similar business in Argentina, commenting that more than half of his investments were in this sector. He was showing his mates where they could next make money. 'I'd have pals and we'd all invest together, we would go into different things and take a punt on things,' he said in an interview with the *Sunday Business Post*.

He established Island Capital, a venture capital group, to invest mainly in technology companies, including Datalex, Norkom Technologies, Eontec, Twelve Horses and 360 networks, a company laying submarine and land-based cables around the world, where according to himself he made a 'big investment'. There was also an investment in mobile software operation Mobileaware, which O'Brien described as a 'super company, it's a cracker, a cracker'. To add gravitas to Island Capital he invited former Guinness Peat Aviation executive and European Commissioner Peter Sutherland, who went on to become chairman of BP Amoco, to be chairman.

Paul Connolly, Leslie Buckley, accountant Aidan Phelan and Denis O'Brien senior were also involved in Island Capital. O'Brien claimed they weighed up investment opportunities collectively and had ground rules about investing: 'If one person gives the thumbs down, we don't go with the project.'

He also purchased a stake in the PGA European Tour Courses, the London-listed company that operated golf courses in Britain and continental Europe, and invested many millions in the internet through his Communicorp group.

Still obsessed with beating monopolies, he and Leslie Buckley were ready to take on another. Together they were preparing to launch an assault on the Irish electricity market, setting up ePower, a joint venture with a US company, to compete with Ireland's Electricity Supply Board (ESB). O'Brien was relishing the prospect of another battle against a mighty competitor, saying it felt much like Esat four or five years earlier. 'Obviously there's a big regulatory issue,' he explained in a newspaper interview. 'We don't think the market is being opened up quickly enough and we think there's a general softness towards the ESB. It's the state protecting the state again.'

Raising money for ePower was much easier than it had been at Esat, for they had a lot of money themselves and had proved they could build successful ventures in fields of emerging competition. 'We have our own capital, whereas before we didn't,' explained O'Brien. 'Leslie has his own capital, I have my own capital; it's a different ballgame. It's easier to raise money when you have your own capital – and when investors have made money from different projects over the years.' Lots of people were willing to bet their cash on following O'Brien into his next business.

There were investments in a recruitment website, Irishjobs.ie, that O'Brien believed was an 'absolutely brilliant' business. He also took stakes in the Irish Film and Television Network and ICAN, an internet advertising company. It was a diverse portfolio.

With plenty of money in his pocket, O'Brien wanted to expand his radio business. His ambitious plans for Communicorp had never been realised and now he was keen to build a growing radio group in the sector that fascinated him most, the media. Friends say he enjoyed not having the executive responsibilities that came with running a company listed on the stock market, but he was missing the cut and thrust of the Esat days. He would hand the money back, he said, to do it all again, and he believed many of his colleagues felt the same way. 'If you took the top ten managers in Esat and asked "Would you hand back your cheques and continue to do the job you were doing beforehand?" I'd say a lot of them would prefer it the old way,' he has said. 'We never wanted to sell Esat.'

*

Despite his comments on *The Late Late Show*, O'Brien did not want to have to pay tax on his fortune to the Irish Revenue authorities. Before the sale he had told his advisers to find a way for him to take the full €317 million without paying any tax at all. Otherwise he could have been facing a tax bill in Ireland of as much as €50 million. They came up with a scheme whereby if he moved to Portugal he could avoid paying any tax on his spoils and still be free to travel in and out of Ireland to oversee his radio and other businesses. He would become a tax exile.

The Irish tax authorities allowed tax exiles to spend a generous number of days in the country without becoming liable to hand over any money to them. Effectively tax exiles could spend every weekend in Ireland in a full year without any liability to pay tax, once they provided evidence to the Revenue that they were not permanently living on the island.

To move abroad permanently was a life-changing decision, one that O'Brien, Buckley and other members of Esat's millionaires' club were considering. 'I had no problem with me doing it or with Denis doing it,' says Buckley, who did move abroad for a while as part of a tax arrangement. 'To be quite honest, if that's what somebody wants to do, why not?'

O'Brien's decision to emigrate, though, took some of his friends and associates by surprise. One even cautioned against the move, suggesting he might regret it. 'I was surprised from a family point of view,' says his Esat colleague Seán Corkery, although he adds, 'From an entrepreneurial point of view I understand it. If I had made IR£250 million (€317 million) I would look at what I could do with that, what I would invest in. He would get a return on the capital. He would get no return if he paid it in tax.'

In contrast, his close friend Paul Meagher was alarmed by the news and urged O'Brien to reconsider. 'I gave him my views. He didn't agree with me. It was a short conversation,' says Meagher. 'His view is very different. He felt he was entitled to every penny of it. He created a huge amount of jobs, directly and indirectly, and created a lot of wealth for others. I thought at the start, it was fundamentally wrong.

'You pay your taxes if you want to live in Ireland and you want to be a citizen of the state. I think you have got to contribute, but Denis takes a fundamentally different view and he is entitled to it. He has a view that he can live wherever he likes in the world.' O'Brien's decision to move abroad to avoid paying tax on the fortune he made from a licence awarded by the Irish government could prove damaging to his friend's image in Ireland, Meagher believed. 'It has caused him a lot of difficulty on and off and I don't think that is fair. As I feared they would the media have used it to flog him.'

Public relations consultant Eileen Gleeson recalls some discussions about O'Brien becoming Ireland's newest tax exile, saying there were plenty of advisers ready to point out how much money he was paying in other taxes at that time and how much money so many other people had made from the company's sale. 'Nobody looked at the long-term perspective,' she says. 'Tony O'Reilly, Tony Ryan and others had all become tax exiles and there wasn't much of a deal made about that. Nobody saw what was coming down the road. Nobody said if you do this you are going to be seen as a bad boy. The other guys weren't.'

O'Brien had made his decision. He was moving to Portugal and would be settling into a magnificent home at the Quinta do Lago golf resort with his wife and young son. He was going to enjoy himself and regularly invite the 'rat pack' over to play golf.

13 Jousting with the Knight

Before he left Ireland, Denis O'Brien had made a commitment to lead the country's bid to host the Special Olympics World Games in 2003. On the business front, meanwhile, he was preparing for his next battle.

The Special Olympics World Games was a huge event. For the first time the Games were to be hosted outside the United States and the whole of Ireland, from Taoiseach Bertie Ahern to the thousands of volunteers, wanted it to be a success. As chairman of Special Olympics Ireland, O'Brien had taken on responsibility for leading the efforts to raise a staggering €60 million to stage the games, having accepted the role in the midst of Esat Telecom's battle with Telenor after other prominent Irish business figures turned it down.

Mary Davis, chief executive of Special Olympics Ireland, had heard of O'Brien but never previously met him. The reason why his name hadn't been mentioned as a candidate for the role at the outset, she says, was because of the organisation's long association with Ireland's biggest telecommunications company, eircom, the company formerly known as Telecom Éireann. It had sponsored the Special Olympics since 1985.

When Davis first met O'Brien, she was keen to assess how engaged the new chairman was likely to be in such an ambitious project. 'I said to him, "What is the best way for me to communicate with you? What do you like, email or whatever?" He said, "Whatever is best for you, but a phone call is the best for me. Here is my mobile phone number and you can ring me any time." I thought, wow. For somebody who had so much going on he was just so accessible.'

O'Brien wanted to find out as much as possible about the Special

Olympics – the scale of the event and what specifically he could do to help. 'That was very helpful. From the first instant you get a sense whether they mean it or whether they are going to be just a figurehead.' That was never the case with O'Brien, she explains. 'He seemed to throw himself into the project from the very beginning.' Indeed, Bank of Ireland quickly signed up as one of the games' main sponsors shortly after O'Brien took a seat in its boardroom.

And the organisation's relationship with eircom didn't prove difficult to manage, Davis says, despite the fact that its nemesis was now chairman of the board. 'They realised that he could bring an awful lot of skills and huge entrepreneurial flair to the World Games and that is what we needed. He never did represent Esat. He was Denis O'Brien and he never pushed Esat or mentioned it.' It was agreed to hold monthly meetings at O'Brien's office and over the next four years, Davis says, he never missed one.

In fact, O'Brien had been closely monitoring eircom's fortunes from Portugal. His old enemy had fared badly on the stock markets and was plunging in value. With its share price plummeting, there was much speculation that someone would make a bid for it and O'Brien was planning to do just that. He would launch a €2.25 billion bid for the company.

Esat Telecom's sale to British Telecom had rapidly proved to have been completed at the peak of the telecommunications market. Within months, companies such as eircom and BT were hammered on the stock market as the telecommunications bubble finally burst. Having ploughed much of his new-found wealth into the sector, O'Brien had suffered from the meltdown himself as Versatel, the Dutch firm in which he had invested, filed for bankruptcy protection. At one stage, O'Brien and his associates had owned close to six per cent of the company, with their stake valued at more than $385 million. They had managed to sell some of their shares into the heady market, realising many millions, but would suffer losses on the stake they still held when the shares collapsed. Esat, meanwhile, was now arguably worth only about half of what BT had paid for it. As the company struggled in the unforgiving market, many of its top executives – including finance director Robert Brace, the man who shook O'Brien's hand on the deal – resigned. And to add insult to injury, O'Brien was planning to use some of his windfall to compete against the company he had founded and sold to BT.

By September 2000, eircom's shares were down by more than fifty per cent and the company was struggling against a barrage of criticism from shareholders who had bought the shares in its much-hyped flotation a year earlier. The group was in talks to sell off its mobile phone arm, Eircell, to Vodafone and there was speculation that the company's fixed-line business might also be sold.

O'Brien, who has joked that 'something in his water' was telling him to sell his company when he did, watched his mighty rivals battle against the stock market carnage and weighed up whether he might profit from their misfortune.

Now he wanted to buy eircom's fixed-phone-line business, and he and Paul Connolly were discussing a potential bid with advisers. At the end of October 2000 O'Brien called eircom's chairman, Ray MacSharry, to politely inform him of his €2.25 billion bid. It was huge money, he said, and he was deadly serious about buying the company. 'It's a friendly offer,' he helpfully explained.

To emphasise the seriousness of his offer, O'Brien briefly met eircom's chief executive, Alfie Kane, the man he had battled against for years when he was building Esat, to discuss the bid's merits. He needed Kane and his management team to support his bid for the company and would use all his charm and influence to win them over.

A new company, e-Island, which was to be fifty per cent owned by O'Brien and his former Esat colleagues Leslie Buckley, Lucy Gaffney, Connolly, Padraig OhUiginn and his father, was formed to launch the bid. They would be bringing US venture capital companies on board to help them to fund the takeover.

It was a staggering reversal of fortunes. The company that had tried to strangle Esat at birth was now being targeted by the group who had founded its main competitor almost a decade before. And O'Brien intended to be eircom's chairman and chief executive.

Cathal Magee, one of eircom's senior executives, was among the group to engage with O'Brien on the bid and witnessed one side of his business style at first hand. 'The interesting thing about him is that he is a very charming guy. He is obviously a very tough guy but I have never seen the tough side of him,' he says. 'Denis gets a huge distance of the way through charm. He gets people to want to do what he wants. They don't want to let him down. They want to deliver for him. I've seldom seen him having to crack the whip.'

According to Magee, O'Brien hides traits such as his ruthlessness and toughness well in these situations. 'He has huge influencing skills. He goes hands-on, one-to-one. He makes the phone calls, the contacts, he works it for himself and people are there following up and supporting. It's impressive. He takes it on as a personal goal and a personal agenda. It's not a corporate thing. It's Denis.'

But another successful Irish businessman was also taking an interest in eircom, and was prepared to use similar charm and ruthlessness to get his hands on the company. Media baron Tony O'Reilly was preparing his own bid and was joined by international financier George Soros in a consortium named Valentia.

For the second time in five years O'Reilly was about to go head-to-head with O'Brien to win a business venture. In 1996 O'Reilly's consortium had lost out to O'Brien's in the competition for the mobile phone licence and there had been a perceived deep enmity between the two men ever since. As the owner of a group of radio stations, O'Brien was acutely aware of the power of the media, and he believed O'Reilly's newspaper group had been particularly hostile to him since he had won the licence. The ensuing controversy, he felt, had been reported with more vigour and with more personal attacks in the Independent stable of newspapers than elsewhere.

The *Irish Independent*, along with its sister papers the *Sunday Independent* and the *Sunday Tribune*, had, he felt, made much of O'Brien's decision to become a tax exile after the sale of Esat Telecom. Some of its commentators and columnists regularly launched personal attacks on O'Brien and for years his public relations consultant, Eileen Gleeson, at his request, had meticulously monitored everything that was written about O'Brien in the media.

'Some articles or writers, like Sam Smyth, really irked him,' Gleeson says. 'I would have to get on to them a lot. There could be something in the paper that he didn't like. It would mostly be little things, not that they had got a name or a detail wrong, he felt they were either for or against you and essentially when it came to Denis, that was true. I'd have to explain to him that it was essentially accurate and that you couldn't take a libel action based on the tone of the piece.'

O'Brien's friend and solicitor, Paul Meagher, also compiled newspaper cuttings about him. Offending pieces were illuminated with a highlighter pen and filed in a large area of his office dedicated to his friend's business and personal interests. 'Paul Meagher was always a voice of reason for Denis,' Gleeson says. 'Between us we would launch a pincer action to explain to him why there was nothing he could do about a certain piece. Sometimes he would let it rest after a few days but some just didn't go away.'

When O'Brien read something that annoyed him, he might call Gleeson and say, 'Those fuckers in the *Indo* are at it again,' she says. 'I would have to go back over the cuttings and be able to say whether it was a continued attack on him or whether in fact the paper hadn't written about him for five weeks.'

According to Meagher, his friend has always had an obsession with the media. 'He reads everything. He does get upset about negative coverage. Who wouldn't if somebody had been writing about you constantly since 1995 saying that you didn't get the licence fairly and effectively trying to undermine every single thing that you have achieved?'

Meagher is certain that the constant barrage of negative pieces and comment in the Independent News and Media group was conscious. 'I have never discussed its merits with Denis. It is blindingly obvious they did untold damage to his reputation,' he says. 'I would have my own views on the whole thing from start to finish.' And his friend believed Tony O'Reilly was in some way responsible for this coverage. The newspaper group, on the other hand, always rejected such allegations, while other observers wondered whether or not the *Independent* had been any more vigilant in reporting on O'Brien and his various interests and clashes than, for example, the *Irish Times*. O'Reilly's son Gavin, a senior executive at the company, insists that O'Brien's charge is nonsense, as is the perception of rivalry between O'Brien and his father. 'That is the greatest myth,' he says.

According to others at the newspaper group, there was never an orchestrated campaign against O'Brien. As one person says, 'Denis O'Brien was never on Tony O'Reilly's radar.'

Sam Smyth, the seasoned journalist accused of being among O'Brien's most relentless persecutors, says he did nothing more than his job required in writing about the dynamic entrepreneur. 'My understanding of the second mobile phone licence was that Tony O'Reilly and his crowd just walked away. I could never see and never had any pressure put on me to write about Denis. And the suggestion by Denis that I was being fed and motivated by losing consortia is just plain wrong. It is not true.'

O'Brien's father, however, shared his son's view that O'Reilly was behind the personal attacks published in its various newspapers. It was all the more hurtful for him because he and the newspaper baron had once been close friends, as O'Reilly had acknowledged when he referred to watching O'Brien senior's diving competitions in his congratulatory letter to his son some years earlier.

'I know O'Reilly very well. I've known him intimately for a very long time. We all grew up together and knew each other as young men in the rugby scene,' O'Brien's father says. 'He is not that bad a fellow. He is very bright, very talented. He was a very good rugby player, a beautiful player. It is unfortunate he took on Denis, particularly when he knew me so well. I don't know why he did it. Maybe it's just to make news.'

Whatever they felt about each other, two of Ireland's most high-profile entrepreneurs were now locked in a high-stakes battle for eircom. It was clear the company's new owner would have to win the support of its employees, who collectively owned a crucial fifteen per cent of the company through an employee share ownership trust. So both quickly mounted a charm offensive.

eircom's employees, who were members of the Communications Workers Union (CWU), were alarmed at the prospect of working for O'Brien, a man they had fought against throughout the previous decade. He had always harboured antipathy towards trade unions, aggressively resisting any attempts by organised labour to get a foothold in his empire. In order to secure the confidence of the workforce, he would have to convince the CWU they could do business together. The company's employees were represented on the board of directors by Con Scanlon, a career trade union activist who had worked with the company for many years and was now the CWU's head. He recalls his dealings with O'Brien.

'Denis had always been the enemy. When he was in Esat he was lashing eircom all of the time. Just like Michael O'Leary in Ryanair he was always hammering the incumbent. He showed no mercy.' While the CWU and other trade unions had been decisively dismissed by O'Brien in the past, however, Scanlon says the issue of continued union representation at eircom didn't emerge as an issue during the negotiations. 'He was pragmatic around that. Any issues that might emerge would be resolved. We just wanted to get the best possible deal.' Few observers believed Scanlon would encourage his members to get into bed with O'Brien, but the wily negotiator would play the bidders off against each other to improve the proffered price.

Scanlon says he never developed a personal relationship with either O'Brien or O'Reilly, who both attended meetings to discuss the merits of their respective bids. 'At the meetings you couldn't but be impressed by both sides in different ways. Denis's team was local and we knew a lot of them. Both bids had attractions and there wasn't a massive amount between the two.' Scanlon doesn't recall any obvious personal animosity between O'Brien and O'Reilly at this time. 'They were both anxious to do the business. eircom was a huge prize. It was a national institution critical to the whole economy of Ireland.

'Denis was very personable, a larger than life figure. He was a warm character, very focused and very intense. He covered a lot of ground. He was a formidable presence. He had a ready smile and was a very able individual, the guy you would pick to lead. He had plans for the company and once he came to grips with it he would have made a go of it. I felt if we had done a deal with Denis O'Brien, all things were possible.'

Others believed O'Reilly was always going to win the day. According to Smyth, O'Reilly had tended to work with trade unions in his media empire and at Waterford Wedgwood and stood a better chance at sealing the deal. 'Tony O'Reilly's enemies would say that he always bought off the unions. He wasn't confrontational in that way and when it came to eircom clearly the unions were the decisive figures.'

O'Brien was offering the company's employees a shareholding of almost thirty per cent if he gained control, as well as three directors to represent them on the company's board. It was a generous offer, but there was a catch. If they voted to accept e-Island's bid, the employees wouldn't formally sign the deal for six months after the takeover.

When journalists asked Con Scanlon to assess the state of play he was forthright. 'There is not a hope in hell', he said, that his members could back a deal based on a promise rather than the certainty of a contract. 'How do we know they won't sell up before we even have a stake or a seat at the board?' he told the *Irish Independent*. 'You could have new owners who would say in six months' time, we know what Denis O'Brien told you he would give you, but we are not Denis O'Brien.'

O'Reilly's Valentia consortium waded into the public exchanges on the shortcomings of e-Island's bid, with one of its big investors, John Hahn of Providence Equity Partners, describing O'Brien's offer as a 'trust me deal' and saying it 'could not be done by a prudent businessman'. O'Brien responded by pointing out that he and his colleagues were 'people of their word' and took a pot shot at his rival, suggesting that if O'Reilly added eircom to his shareholding in the telecoms and cable group Chorus it would be 'bad for the country'. It was a comment he would later be forced to withdraw after he was censured by the Takeover Panel that monitored deals.

In the end O'Reilly's bid proved altogether more palatable to eircom. Just as O'Brien had found a 'white knight' in BT to outsmart Telenor, it was Finance Minister Charlie McCreevy who emerged as O'Reilly's knight in shining armour to best the mobile phone entrepreneur. Advisers for O'Reilly's Valentia consortium, together with those representing the employees, successfully lobbied the government to change the tax law, allowing Valentia to issue preference shares that would benefit the company's employees without giving them additional representation in the boardroom. The new tax arrangement would ensure a more lucrative deal for everyone involved.

McCreevy has since admitted that O'Reilly could not have won the eircom battle without the tax changes he introduced in the interest of the company's workers, and which he defended in the face of criticism from opposition politicians. Speaking in the Dáil, he explained: 'If this change had not been made, it would have favoured the Denis O'Brien consortium and the deputy can imagine the hullabaloo that would have caused.'

O'Brien and the rest of the e-Island consortium felt they had been unfairly outmanoeuvred. 'I think we were not honestly outplayed,' says Lucy Gaffney, who worked closely with O'Brien on this deal. Connolly, meanwhile, claims the unions 'double-crossed' them. 'It was a lesson in terms of the highest bidder. There were nine bids and the highest bid didn't win.'

Scanlon says O'Brien quickly retreated once it became clear O'Reilly had won the day. 'That was a big disappointment for him. He vanished once things weren't going his way. I haven't heard from him since but you would never rule Denis out.'

Cathal Magee says O'Brien wasn't a good loser but that was to be expected. 'That's a good sign of him too. He's like an elite sportsman in that respect.' Shortly after the defeat of his bid for eircom, Magee met O'Brien at a gathering to raise money for the Special Olympics. 'I arrived at the Berkeley Court Hotel for a fundraiser and I went into the ballroom early to check out the seating arrangements at my table. And there was Denis doing something similar,' he recalls. 'He looked at me and I thought he was probably thinking "God, I could take that guy's head off". But he parked that completely and came over and shook my hand and said "We have to raise €5 million tonight".

'The remarkable thing was that even though eircom was a negative memory for him, throughout that whole Special Olympics process he went out of his way to compliment eircom. He was very supportive of eircom even though it was a Valentia-owned organisation. He was extremely positive and constructive and gave us every opportunity to leverage from the sponsorship. I thought that was extremely generous and very professional of him.'

The event that night did indeed raise €5 million and O'Brien proved to be a most generous and committed supporter of the Special

Olympics. According to Magee, the eircom staff who worked on the project in the years leading up to the World Games were impressed by O'Brien's involvement and surprised at how well he worked with the company that had slipped from his grasp. 'It did him an awful lot of credit because it was the opposite of what we expected. He connected and he got rave reviews from our own staff because of that. And they would have seen him as the arch-enemy.'

14 The Tribunal

The Tribunal of Inquiry investigating political corruption in Ireland had settled into Dublin Castle. Despite his best efforts, in 2001 Denis O'Brien was set to take a central role in this unfolding drama.

Since 1997 the Tribunal, headed by High Court judge Michael Moriarty, had been investigating allegations of corrupt payments to Irish politicians including erstwhile Taoiseach Charles Haughey. The inquiry had powers to compel witnesses to attend and give evidence in the makeshift courtroom in George's Hall. It could also seek and demand documents that might be helpful to its work. It was now focusing on former minister Michael Lowry, its team of lawyers seeking to establish whether Lowry had received any payments from wealthy business figures that might have influenced his decisions when in office.

Despite the controversy about the awarding of the mobile phone licence in 1996, O'Brien had not initially been in the Tribunal's sights. The spotlight had only gradually shifted towards him after *Sunday Tribune* editor Matt Cooper, who together with journalist Sam Smyth had written a number of investigative pieces about Lowry, revealed Esat Digifone's $50,000 political donation to Lowry's political party as it awaited the competition's outcome. The Tribunal noted the story and did its own investigations. Now it wanted answers.

In the early months of 2001 it looked as if its work was almost done. But as the summer approached, its team was to uncover sensational new information, opening a lengthy new chapter that would haunt O'Brien and his family for the next decade.

The media pack was stunned when in May 2001 the Tribunal dropped the bombshell that it had uncovered four possible financial links between Lowry and O'Brien, totalling more than €1 million. In a detailed statement, the Tribunal's lawyers mentioned the $50,000 donation to the Fine Gael party, a payment to Lowry from party activist David Austin that had come out of O'Brien's bank account in Jersey, and a money trail between the two men associated with Lowry's purchase of properties in the UK. The inquiry was seeking answers from Lowry, O'Brien and Fine Gael on these matters.

The exiled telecoms tycoon flew to Dublin to hear the lawyers detailing the financial links they wished to investigate. Colm Keena, the *Irish Times* journalist covering the Tribunal, remembers O'Brien's first appearance at Dublin Castle: 'I was carrying a couple of coffees and he said to me, "Have you got one for me?" That was the first time I met Denis. I was struck by how informal and easy he was with the media.'

O'Brien hired a heavy-hitting legal team to represent him. It was led by one of Ireland's most experienced senior counsel, Eoin McGonigal, upon whom — likening him to the famous green ogre — O'Brien conferred the nickname 'Shrek'. He brought his own entourage along for the event, including his father, Denis senior, who followed close behind him, and public relations consultant Eileen Gleeson, to deal with the media fallout. There would be lots of headlines that day.

O'Brien sat listening to the Tribunal's statement, growing furious that he had no opportunity to rebut its contents. He would have to wait to be called as a witness to explain under oath what the inquiry had found.

'I thought the information the Tribunal disclosed was very damning of him,' Keena says. 'There were too many coincidences.' And it was clear to everyone that O'Brien was annoyed about what had been said. 'I walked beside him when everybody was going down the stairs that day and he was very angry. He said, "There goes my good name out the window." ' Talking to journalists outside the Castle, O'Brien publicly denied any wrongdoing and pledged to deal with the matters raised to the Tribunal's satisfaction.

In the months and years ahead, the inquiry was to examine the awarding of the mobile phone licence to Digifone, focusing on how the competition was run and investigating the Department of

Communications' decision to award the licence to O'Brien's group, which had expanded at the last minute to include Dermot Desmond. It looked behind Michael Lowry's property purchases and showed that many of the same people were involved in the deals the Tribunal was examining, and that they all had links to Lowry and O'Brien. Its probe later extended into O'Brien's purchase of Doncaster Rovers' ground after a report by Keena appeared in the *Irish Times* suggesting that the former minister was involved in the deal.

And, possibly the biggest blow for the man who prized loyalty above all other virtues, his former best friend and Digifone chief executive, Barry Maloney, publicly revealed the conversation between the two men years earlier during which, he alleged, O'Brien had said he had made a payment to Lowry.

In his stunning testimony, Maloney told the inquiry under oath about the possible payment between O'Brien and Lowry mentioned in a disputed conversation between the two in 1996. He repeated the claim that he believed an intermediary had acted for O'Brien in making the alleged payment to the minister and that the Esat boss later denied that any payment was made, explaining that it had got 'stuck'.

O'Brien had always insisted he had never made a payment to Lowry and had been exonerated by the company's board of directors after it investigated Maloney's allegation. But now the matter was in the public domain and under further scrutiny.

O'Brien viewed Maloney's evidence as the ultimate act of betrayal. Friends say he was deeply wounded by the man whose friendship he had so valued in the past and whom he had helped become a multi-millionaire. Both O'Brien and the 'rat pack' of which Maloney had once been a member were stunned by his statement. Meagher describes the episode as a tragedy.

'I feel that if they had sorted out their differences things would have turned out differently,' he explains.

'Nobody knows what was said apart from them. It's between the two of them, and that's a matter for the Moriarty Tribunal. But isn't it tragic that two friends have ended up in that godforsaken place [i.e. the Tribunal]? I have no doubt that it has been exploited by forces that they have no control over every single day since.'

Almost every day for the next nine years O'Brien would be forced to deal with some aspect or other of the inquiry, providing documents, responding to its queries and appearing when summoned to answer its questions. It was frustrating for the man who ruled his own businesses with an iron fist, tightly controlling everything around him, to be dealing with this tortuous legal process beyond his control that was damaging his reputation at home and abroad.

Gleeson is among those who recall stormy meetings with his legal team and advisers before his appearances at Dublin Castle as he tried to contain the damage: 'When the Tribunal started, everything became much more difficult. I sat in there three days a week for a year and a half. It was really difficult for him, not only because his name was bandied around as someone possibly involved in political corruption but all of those things that he held dear, running and driving a business, were thrown out the window.'

O'Brien would stride into the office of William Fry Solicitors at eight on the mornings he was giving evidence to begin a tension-charged session, thumping the table and barking orders at his legal team. 'He was frustrated with the lawyers. He fell in and out of love with Eoin McGonigal and all of us,' Gleeson says. 'He just couldn't understand this was a deal he couldn't close. That really got to him. It was a loss of control for a "one-page" man who wants things short and sweet. He wouldn't accept that we couldn't make a point for him outside of the Tribunal.' Gleeson had been through a similar process with Dermot Desmond years earlier when he was the subject of an inquiry by a High Court Inspector into a property purchase that left 'the Kaiser' similarly frustrated and powerless to defend his reputation. 'Dermot found that difficult and Denis is very similar to him.'

Keena says it was obvious O'Brien was aggrieved with the Tribunal from the start. 'He was combative and argumentative on occasions and he wasn't deferential in the witness box.' But he had done his homework. 'You could tell he had worked hard at it. He had read his brief. He would go up and put his jacket round the back of the chair; he asked the judge if that was OK. It was like he was at work, like he might be in the boardroom. It was a big job he had to work through.'

Whenever O'Brien felt the Tribunal was treating him unfairly, he was quick to say so. 'He would say "Come on, you have to be fair,"' Keena says.

Of all the tussles O'Brien would engage in with the judge and his team, the row to compel him to appear at the Tribunal following the birth of his daughter Alva in London would upset him most. He asked to be excused from attending to spend two weeks outside Ireland with his wife Catherine and their second child, saying he needed the time to discharge his parental responsibility. In letters to the Tribunal he accused the inquiry of carrying out an 'unwarranted intrusion' into his family life and into his wife's privacy by requesting medical reports from gynaecologists related to the birth. He accused it of having a bias against him, something it denied.

On RTÉ's *Liveline* phone-in radio programme his father publicly voiced the family's distress at what was happening. 'We feel it's a very severe invasion of privacy of the family. This tribunal, as far as I'm concerned, is getting out of hand and is developing into an inquisition. We thought it was incredible that they [thought] he was trying to avoid any further interrogation by the Tribunal that he would use this as an excuse to slip away.'

Denis senior said they felt it was like a McCarthyite witch-hunt of the 1950s. 'It's not like a court of law [where] you can object. You must sit and listen hour after hour to a long list of documentation without comment.' And he blamed the Independent News and Media group for taking advantage of the situation in its reporting of the inquiry when his son did not have a chance to contradict what was being said about him. It was engaged in 'unfair reporting', he claimed, suggesting that this was linked to the battle for the control of eircom that was raging at the same time.

'It's a heck of a coincidence that the main papers, the *Independent* during the week and the *Sunday Tribune*, are the most critical of him,' he continued. 'Only a year ago, Denis was Top of the Pops.' He ended his contribution by saying he was very proud of his son and could not wait for him to be given an opportunity to show that he was 'totally innocent' of all allegations.

This outburst drew a response from O'Reilly's biggest-selling newspaper. In an editorial, the *Irish Independent* rejected any bias on its part. 'Throughout the eircom takeover, and in all our subsequent tribunal reporting, the *Irish Independent* has been at pains to be scrupulously fair to Mr O'Brien. His father, in his outburst yesterday, produced no evidence to the contrary for the good reason that none exists.' The editorial challenged specific claims about headlines that had appeared in the newspaper following sittings of the Tribunal and claimed the newspaper had 'unstinting praise for his son's entrepreneurial skills'. The piece ended by offering some advice to O'Brien senior. 'Before giving in to impulses to shoot the messenger, it behoves the executioner to at least ensure there is ammunition in the chamber.'

His son had often commented to reporters about the eircom takeover outside the Tribunal and Keena says his distress was obvious: 'They were very intense times. You could see the pressure he was under and his anger. He seemed to think the *Irish Independent* had an agenda and he was very angry about that. I think he felt the *Irish Times* was giving him a fair hearing.'

As the years passed and the Tribunal attempted to disentangle a complex web of transactions for evidence of corruption, O'Brien would come to feel he was the victim of a great injustice – one that he would fight to the bitter end.

15 The Sunny Caribbean

As the Tribunal began its investigations into the mobile phone licence that had made him so rich, Denis O'Brien was getting ready to win another phone licence. Just three months after selling out to BT he gathered friends and advisers to Dublin's Morrison Hotel for the start of their next big adventure.

They had celebrated their victory over Telenor and enjoyed many good nights out, posing amid the celebrations for a group photograph to capture their sweet success. Someone draped a Norwegian flag on the ground below O'Brien's feet to display their trophy scalp. They had won the war and were feeling pretty good about the outcome.

But O'Brien was missing the daily cut and thrust of running a fledgling mobile phone company. With plenty of money to leverage in new ventures, he was about to grasp the opportunity to do it all over again, but this time in a sunnier climate.

The countries of the Caribbean had come together in 1989 to plan the region's future telecommunications needs. The Caribbean was one of the last economic areas in the world to liberalise its telecommunications sector, but now each government was preparing to dismantle the monopolistic stranglehold enjoyed for almost a hundred years by the British-based telecommunications giant, Cable & Wireless (C&W).

Governments across the region studied how the new competitive environment was evolving across Europe and in the USA and assessed the economic benefits it might confer. There was much research to show that the deregulation of telecommunications was an important first step in stimulating economic activity, a vital element in a developing region such as the Caribbean. Countries that enjoyed the benefits of two or more telecommunications providers quickly became more prosperous, it seemed. Competition was rapidly slashing the price of phone calls and quickly making a range of services affordable to the entire population.

There were potentially forty million phone users across the Caribbean. It was a huge market that was hungry for competition.

The Cable & Wireless telecoms giant currently generated about twenty per cent of its annual profits in the Caribbean. Those profits were mostly repatriated to the UK, with the company investing very little money in the region. Cable & Wireless was viewed by some analysts as an underperforming operation that had become bloated and complacent in a market where it had no competition.

Telecoms experts were eyeing up the opportunities for new mobile phone businesses in the region. In the months before Esat was sold to British Telecom, one adviser had suggested to O'Brien that he should think about buying C&W's Caribbean operations and running the company himself. Then accountant Ossie Kilkenny, O'Brien's partner in Spin, a new Dublin radio station, met a businessman keen to gather a consortium to bid for a mobile phone licence in Trinidad and Tobago in late 1998. Kilkenny immediately thought of O'Brien. He proposed that O'Brien and the Caribbean company Clico should bid for the licence. This time he would join them as an investor.

O'Brien had learned that there was plenty of money to be made by going up against a monopoly. Just as he had created a lean and fast-paced mobile phone company in Ireland, he relished the prospect of taking on Cable & Wireless. So he agreed to put together a bid.

C&W was in partnership with the government of Trinidad and Tobago in providing the islands' phone service and had fiercely resisted its efforts to be the first Caribbean country to open its tele-communications market to competition. The government persevered, inviting bidders for a new mobile phone licence. But the competition was abandoned with the fall of the political adminis-tration. It would take years for the licence to be eventually awarded.

Down in Jamaica things were more promising. The island's government, led by Prime Minister P.J. Patterson, was ready to embrace the new regime and advertised a competition for the island's new mobile phone licences in the *Financial Times*. O'Brien and Kilkenny decided to bid and set up a new company, Mosel, controlled by O'Brien, with Kilkenny owning a twenty per cent shareholding. They estimated it would cost about €30 million to get the new network up and running. Kilkenny agreed to invest €6 million.

Jamaica was a poor economy with a population of just over two and a half million. A dangerous, hostile and corrupt environment in which to be contemplating building a business, it would be a difficult proposition for O'Brien to sell to banks and potential investors. But he was undeterred.

In Dublin one afternoon in April 2000 O'Brien was monitoring the auction of two new mobile phone licences in Jamaica. Frank O'Carroll, one of the former Esat crew, was in Kingston to handle the bid as O'Brien issued his instructions over the phone.

Patterson says he wanted the competition to be transparent at all stages. As the Irish government had done, the Jamaican government hired international experts to work with its officials to select the winner. In contrast, however, it was holding a straightforward auction, granting a fifteen-year licence to the highest bidder, rather than adopting the beauty pageant favoured by Ireland's tele-communications minister Michael Lowry.

As the bidding got under way it looked as if Mosel had won the licence with a bid of $25 million. Then, after some confusion, the process was restarted. 'Someone put his hand up at the wrong time and it went around again,' explains an eyewitness. 'It finished with Mosel's bid of $47.5 million.' When O'Brien broke the news to Leslie Buckley he just said 'Jesus.' O'Brien's consortium had ended up paying nearly twice as much for the licence this time around, but they were delighted to be back in the mobile phone business.

About one in five people in Jamaica had a telephone and some two hundred thousand were waiting for C&W to install one for them. C&W also had a mobile phone arm with a service mainly in Kingston and the Montego Bay areas, but it was very costly. According to public relations consultant Jean Lowrie Chin, mobile phones were used in Jamaica only by the wealthy: 'A Cable & Wireless mobile phone was very expensive. Only the elite could afford them because you had to make a huge deposit and you had to pay to make and receive calls.

You would keep your phone number to your heart and only give it out to the people that you really needed to.'

The new mobile phone network was to be called Digicel, using Digi from Digifone and adopting the American name for a mobile phone, cellphone. They planned to launch it within a year.

Winning the auction was only the first hurdle in a long and tortuous licensing process overseen by the telecommunications minister, Philip Paulson. It would take many months for the government to award the licence to Digicel because regulatory issues and legal problems persistently impeded progress. Jean Lowrie Chin was among the advisers hired by the new telecommunications company to speed up the licensing process. She worked on the company's communications efforts and also lobbied officials and ministers on the company's behalf. 'They did have some difficulties,' she explains. 'There was a lot of bureaucracy.'

O'Brien was also calling on Ireland's Department of Foreign Affairs for assistance to speed up the licensing process but was annoyed with its response. Impatient as ever with those who didn't work at his lightning pace, the telecoms millionaire launched a blistering attack on Ireland's former ambassador to Jamaica, Paul Dempsey, describing his conduct in relation to Digicel's licence as 'appalling' and accusing him of providing inaccurate information to the authorities.

O'Brien vented his anger in a letter to the ambassador, which was also sent to Ireland's Taoiseach, Bertie Ahern, and foreign affairs minister, Brian Cowen. 'Despite many requests for assistance from the general manager of Digicel, Seamus Lynch, during the negotiations with the Government for our licence, you failed to provide any assistance after we sent you a full briefing document. In fact, your lack of assistance and knowledge of our company's investment in Jamaica is appalling. Quite frankly, I would have expected more from a member of the Irish Foreign Service.' The letter was later published in the *Sunday Independent*. The Department of Foreign Affairs suggested that O'Brien's frustration was due to a misunderstanding between Digicel and the Irish mission in Jamaica. 'We'd been asked to do something, we were doing it but it wasn't apparent how far we'd got,' a source within the Department explained.

Others too attest to Digicel's frustrating wait for its licence. 'There was some targeted action against them,' one Jamaican businessman says. 'They were going against the establishment in Jamaica. I don't think they realised how difficult a time they had.'

As Digicel struggled to overcome the slow-moving bureaucracy, it was also difficult to find local partners and to raise finance from banks in the region. 'They were seen as a bunch of crazy Irishmen,' says one local banker. 'Taking on Cable & Wireless was like taking on the British Empire. People thought they were mad.'

Lisa Bell, executive director at Jamaica Trade and Invest, the country's development agency, remembers the company's difficulties when it started shopping around for finance. 'There was a lot of scepticism,' she says. 'Cable & Wireless had been the giant for so long and Denis O'Brien didn't have an established profile here.'

Eventually O'Brien would persuade the International Finance Corporation, an arm of the World Bank, to help fund the development. 'There were only two sources of money,' says Paul Connolly, 'Ericsson and the World Bank. The World Bank was very cautious and very slow but it took an equity stake and that was critical.'

Rather than sitting back and enjoying their new-found wealth, Buckley, Lucy Gaffney and many of the former Esat crew had by now been conscripted to replicate their Irish success in Jamaica. They were eager to get back to business. 'We would have been bored otherwise,' Connolly says of the group. 'It would be good fun.'

Just as he had so assiduously built up political contacts in Ireland to influence reforms in the telecommunications sector, O'Brien now began to build a rapport with the Caribbean's political elite. He paid regular visits to ministers in the islands where new licences were likely to be issued. O'Brien has been known to bestow such dignitaries with everything from Irish hurleys to fancy ties. Connolly says his friend was happy to be back 'hustling' for licences.

Patterson explains that few people in Jamaica, including himself, had heard of O'Brien or his company when it emerged as the licence winner. 'I didn't meet Denis until after the contract and the licence had been granted. He called on me and introduced himself.' In Kingston, O'Brien informed the island's Prime Minister about the other Digicel shareholders and outlined his vision for the company. 'He talked about his plans for the development of the industry in Jamaica and made it clear he intended to be a good corporate citizen in terms of contributing to the development of the economy in spheres other than the telecommunications industry,' says Patterson. 'He also outlined his plans to expand throughout the Caribbean with Jamaica as the starting point.' Seamus Lynch, who had played a key role in the Digifone licence bid, was moving to Kingston to head up the company, O'Brien told the Prime Minister.

Now that he was regularly travelling to the Caribbean from Portugal it was time for O'Brien to take on the ultimate luxury. He would buy his own jet. As a man who largely eschewed the trappings of wealth and preferred to be seen to be living a fairly down-to-earth life, he struggled with the decision: 'He thought long and hard about it,' says Paul Connolly. But a private jet was becoming an essential item for this newly minted millionaire. In 1998 he and Connolly had clubbed together to buy an eight-seater Hawker 125, using it on fundraising trips for Esat Telecom while also hiring it out to other merchant princes. Now he needed some serious wings. He ordered a Gulfstream G4 jet, for which he paid more than $30 million. 'It was not that easy to get to Jamaica and you could lose a day travelling,' Connolly says. 'The G4 quickly became a critical component of Digicel's ultimate success as it allowed him to branch out more aggressively in the Caribbean.'

Doing business in the Caribbean was a new experience. Everything moved at a slower pace and even today many of the region's islands are listed among the world's most corrupt economies. In 2001, Transparency International began to publish a *Global Corruption Report* and devoted a section to Central America, the Caribbean and Mexico. While noting that the region seemed to be finally coming to grips with the fact that its 'history of corruption' had hindered development and that political efforts against such criminal behaviour were strengthening, it claimed there was still much evidence of corruption: 'Despite the changes, bribery remains widespread across the region. Public administration is bureaucratic and inefficient, stimulating "back-door" tactics . . . Access to political power continues to ensure access to economic privilege.' The heads of state had pledged to 'reinvigorate' their fight against corruption, the report stated: 'anti-corruption offices have sprung forth across the region and are being pursued by activists'. But there was still an acceptance of these practices among the general public: 'Societies in the region tend to view corruption almost fatalistically as an intrinsic part of their lives.'

According to Jean Lowrie Chin, though, there was never any controversy about Digicel winning the Jamaican licence. While the company endured lengthy delays and frustrating obstacles, it behaved 'ethically' throughout the licensing process.

Drafting in more ex-Esat colleagues, O'Brien and Lynch began to build a team for the new mobile phone company. Those who had worked closely with O'Brien on start-up businesses in the past were now regularly boarding his jet for the Caribbean. 'People like the idea of working on a start-up,' O'Brien has said. 'There are people who've worked for me for ten years and all they want to do is start-ups.' He would give them a vested interest in his new business, once again offering share options and the prospect of cashing them in for a bonanza some time in the future.

Local executives working in Kingston were identified and persuaded to join the Digicel team. Lisa Lewis had worked at Cable & Wireless for nine years handling the company's customer care division and was aware that a new mobile phone company was recruiting. She was asked to meet Lynch, Kilkenny and Buckley to discuss their plans. 'Over two hours we chatted about all the experience I had at Cable & Wireless, all of the things I had done and if I had my time over again what would I do differently? It was informal. I thought they were picking my brain. Then the following day they offered me a job as project manager for its billing systems,' she says. 'It was unheard of to leave Cable & Wireless. The following Monday when I said I was leaving I was thrown out of the company within an hour. It was very emotional.'

Lewis was Digicel's seventh employee. Within days she was travelling throughout the USA looking at similar operations, learning how to create a new system. 'It was a whirlwind. I was supposed to be gone for a week and I was gone for three,' she says. 'By the time I came back there were twenty people in the office. That first year was madness. I never saw my family. I didn't see daylight as we tried to launch a company from scratch and none of us knew what that meant.'

Jamaica was a difficult place to build a mobile phone network, with one of the highest murder rates in the world. Most of the population lived around the capital city, Kingston, where gang warfare was rife in many communities. Some of the more dangerous areas were controlled by 'Dons', each of whom headed a heavily armed gang that ran drug, extortion, prostitution and other rackets. Local businesses were often targeted for extortion and forced to hand over money to survive. Political efforts to tackle these elements were gradually being stepped up, however, and politicians like Patterson told Digicel not to give in to extortion or bribes.

The island presented physical difficulties too. It was hard to find suitable sites to erect mobile phone masts in the mountainous landscape and some parts of the island had poor roads and little or no infrastructure. The Jamaican government insisted under the terms of the licence that Digicel must provide a service to the entire country. This meant erecting some of the twenty-five masts it needed for its network in physically challenging sites. Former Esat manager Niall O'Brien was part of the team that travelled around the island nego- tiating with landowners to lease small plots of land to build the masts. Lisa Bell, who was assisting Digicel, says the government wanted to give the company full support. She remembers discussions with Jamaica's indigenous community, the Maroons, who were concerned about the presence of a mobile phone mast on their land. 'They had never seen a cell phone before,' she explains. 'Once they knew they wouldn't get cancer from the masts it was OK. Once they understood the concept of mobile phones it was quickly embraced.'

As the business developed, O'Brien brought more of his former Esat colleagues on his jet to get it up and running. Many were ready to leave the company, finding it difficult to cope with the changed corporate environment under British Telecom. As Kevin White explains, 'A lot of the fun went out of the business when it was sold. I stayed on for about six months. It was a nightmare. It changed dramatically and lost a lot of the excitement of the early days. Denis runs businesses like family businesses and that would have been lost.'

David Hall, who worked with Lucy Gaffney at Esat Clear, was also looking for a change of scene. He remembers how he was lured to the Caribbean. 'Denis said to me, "Get on the plane, I need you to come and have a look at something in St Lucia." So we had a look around and he said, "Have a look here and do a few business models." Then he said, "I'm heading back at 4 p.m., sure I'll leave you here for a few days." '

Having assessed the potential of launching a mobile phone network on the island, Hall rang O'Brien a few days later to say he was returning to Dublin. He was told to stay put. 'He said, "What are you coming home for? Sure you've only just got there."' Hall returned home four weeks later, but he had been back in Dublin only for a short while when O'Brien told him to bring his girlfriend, Liz, down to St Lucia, where he hoped a new mobile phone licence would soon be issued. They were to take a luxury holiday, look around and see if they might move there to work for Digicel.

'We said, this is a great life,' says Hall. A week later his girlfriend handed in her notice and they prepared for a new life on the idyllic island. While they discussed the move, Hall remembers, he kept saying to her, 'At least it's not Kingston.'

Within two weeks O'Brien had altered their plans. 'Denis said forget St Lucia, Jamaica is where it is happening, get your arse over there.' Hall had to break the news to his girlfriend that they would be living in Kingston after all. The poverty-stricken island has come a long way since then, he says. 'The weather was fantastic and the Jamaicans are the nicest people but there were lots of open sewers and a terrible smell. There were only two restaurants in New Kingston [the commercial area].'

The Digicel office itself was equally basic. People shared one large table and everything was done on a tiny budget. 'People were coming from serious jobs to be told they would be sitting up around that table sharing with six others. And we shared cars. So you only left the office when the last person was ready to go, and they were usually the most senior person.'

Harry Smith, a marketing executive who had worked in the USA before returning to his home in Jamaica to handle the marketing of the country's most popular beer, Red Stripe, was one of the new team members. He recalls those early days. 'Denis himself didn't interview me, which could have been a good thing, because maybe I wouldn't have joined,' he laughs. Smith was used to working in a highly structured environment and had to adjust to Digicel's more intimate style. 'I had worked for companies like Diageo and Shell where you usually wouldn't see the board. Here the chairman was actively involved in the company and I was working directly for him. That was a bit of a change.'

For the most part the Irish and Jamaican staff worked well together, but there were cultural clashes that led to tension around the cramped office. 'We struggled immediately,' says Smith. 'It was a function of any group dynamic.' Seamus Lynch proposed a management retreat in the nearby resort of Port Antonio to alleviate the situation. A bruising encounter, it showed how different the two island nations were in the way they related to one another. Smith says Lynch proposed the men would share bedrooms to save on costs, something that didn't go down well. 'I don't want to say Jamaicans are homophobic but the idea of sharing rooms for whatever reason was not going to happen.'

Lisa Lewis remembers those early management retreats and describes them as 'bloody'. 'They thought mixing Irish people and Jamaicans was a marriage made in heaven, but there were some issues.'

O'Brien dropped in and out of the highly charged meetings, at which it was obvious that the use of language was one of the biggest cultural problems to be overcome. 'The Jamaicans said they found it offensive that the Irish cursed so much and the Irish said they found it offensive the Jamaicans used so many sexual innuendos,' says Smith. Lewis explains that while Jamaicans use colourful language themselves, corporate Jamaica was more reserved. It was normal to address senior colleagues as 'Mr' or 'Miss', while everyone at Digicel was on first-name terms; they were shocked to hear people swearing around the office and found that hard to bear. 'The Irish also had major issues with our physical interaction as Jamaicans, which is a lot more touchy-feely,' she says.

The sessions helped them to coexist, according to Smith. 'What we have now is cursing sexual innuendos as everyday parlance,' he laughs.

While they worked incredibly long hours, they went to the Courtleigh Hotel, where Lynch laid on a free bar, to party and blow off steam. 'We used to go there at least three times a week because after work you had to find a way to de-stress really quickly before going home,' says Lewis. And it was around the pool bar that the first ever call on the Digicel network was made. 'That was a historic moment. It was about nine o'clock at night and about twenty-five of us had stopped working and trooped down there. We were just over the moon. It was a milestone.'

O'Brien flew in and out of Kingston regularly, summoning Digicel's staff to meet him, sometimes in the middle of the night. They soon learned how hands-on he was about monitoring and managing their progress, insisting that every member of the management team should become integrated within Jamaica's business community and get themselves appointed to the board of the local chamber of commerce and other networks.

'Denis and Seamus broke your heart about that. At meetings Denis would ask everyone how many boards you were on and take a note of it,' says Hall. 'You were doing this in your own time. It gave you access to people and allowed you to build up a relationship and get a good feel if things were working. He has employed this in all of the businesses. It gets the company integrated into the community.'

Smith and his team had steadily built up Digicel's brand in the months before the launch, telling people they could expect a nationwide phone service and cheaper calls. O'Brien and Gaffney oversaw the Digicel branding and Smith and his team endlessly responded to their relentless demands as to how the brand should be developed.

O'Brien and the other board members travelled to Jamaica at least once a month. The Digicel staff came to dread these encounters. 'We all got to know each other, for want of a better word,' says Lewis. 'You got to know pretty early on you don't go in there unless you know what you are talking about. Don't go in there half-prepared. To be fair we all worked like sons of bitches, so unless you couldn't communicate you were fine. Once you could communicate what you were talking about there was no problem.'

O'Brien mercilessly examined every detail of the business. He would be impatient with those who couldn't immediately answer his questions and quickly lost his temper in frustration if his team was failing to develop the business at the breakneck speed he required. 'Denis gets more involved with some parts of the business than others,' one source explains. 'He would never get too distracted by the technology but he would be all over something like the marketing or the message.'

Smith affirms the chairman's intensity in discussions relating to marketing. 'Denis is very hands on. He only wanted to do things differently. I think a lot of people in Jamaica who didn't know him would have given me the praise for the marketing because they wouldn't have known the process,' he says. Of Denis's interference, he adds, 'I have the marks on my back to show for it.'

Once again O'Brien wanted to build a dominant brand. Digicel's logo bore a lot of similarities to Digifone's. It was a bold red colour with a hint of green to denote Irish involvement and he wanted it prominently displayed all over Jamaica.

O'Brien wanted everything to be done on a grand scale. 'He wanted us to do it on a large scale for less and quicker,' says Smith. 'His vice-chairman, Leslie, was just as bad. He was a quieter version of Denis.'

By 18 April 2001 the new Digicel mobile phone network was ready to open for business. At O'Brien's insistence, a spectacular ceremony had been prepared that would surpass anything previously staged in that part of the Caribbean. Such an event, he said, would create curiosity and hype, alerting the entire population to the new, more exciting and cheaper mobile phone operator. Details of the launch were a closely guarded secret, with O'Brien once again imposing military-style discipline and secrecy.

'It was a very high-pressured launch,' says Jean Lowrie Chin. 'We were bunkered down because we didn't want anyone to know what we were doing. It was very covert.' The company blitzed the media with advertisements featuring a daily countdown to the simul-taneous launch in Kingston and Montego Bay. 'Those who were invited got a mobile phone in a gift bag and the message on the phone was the invitation. All of the phones would be connected to Digicel at midnight. It was very dramatic.'

In Kingston, the Pegasus Hotel was transformed to host the ceremony, which would be attended by hundreds. 'You entered through a tunnel and stepped into history,' Lowrie Chin says. Guests filed past a display of the first moon landing and could listen to the famous 'One small step for man, one giant leap for mankind' recording. It had been a logistical nightmare to organise. 'The launch was live on television, radio and the Internet,' Smith explains. 'It was the biggest launch Jamaica had ever seen.'

When the network went live, it was planned to have a video link to Jamaican reggae artist Shaggy, who was playing in Philadelphia and would welcome everyone to Digicel. The afternoon before the launch there was a problem with the satellite and Smith says they had to come up with an alternative plan. Smith asked Jamaica's superstar reggae entertainer, Beenie Man, to step into the breach. 'The day of the launch he lost a friend of his and I don't know if he was drinking or something, but he was in no shape to do the launch.'

When he explained the situation to Gaffney, she told him he just had to get Beenie Man to perform. 'First he refused to go on stage, then he got into an altercation with a security guard and I didn't know if he was going to perform. But he did. He came on stage in slippers and we kept the camera shots from the knee up.' After all the drama, Smith discovered the next day why the video link to Shaggy had broken down. The technician had been simply pointing it in the wrong direction.

O'Brien attended the show, which was enjoyed by politicians, business people and diplomats. And at midnight two young Jamaican Digicel staff, Jodi-Ann Maxwell and Makonnen Blake-Hannah, switched on the network. 'It was part of the image we wanted to project,' Smith says. 'Normally in Jamaica people would have had the dignitaries but Digicel was brave enough to use two young people.'

They wanted to make the Digicel brand accessible to everybody from the start. 'We put emphasis on putting service into areas that never had service. Prior to that Cable & Wireless only had coverage in the main towns and along main routes. We had island-wide coverage from the get-go.'

*

From the start they knew the Jamaican population was hungry for the new network. A poll on the main television bulletin on the eve of the launch suggested that ninety-eight per cent of the population wanted to sign up. When the Digicel stores opened the next day there were lines of people waiting to buy phones. 'I have never seen anything like that. We hoped to have sold one hundred thousand handsets in a year and we sold one hundred thousand in one hundred days,' says Smith.

As ever, O'Brien's philosophy was that in taking on an incumbent you have to be seen to be totally different. Digicel heavily subsidised the price of mobile phone handsets, making them very cheap or even free compared to those supplied by C&W. Jamaicans were delighted with Digicel's deals. 'It was the first time people were offered a choice,' Lewis says. 'Some bought five and ten phones.'

The Digicel shops were designed to be open and friendly, something that proved problematic in the early days as people scrambled to join the new network. 'We had these lovely phones on display that were dummies and people still stole them,' Smith says. 'Then we chained them on the wall and they cut the chains.' His early market research suggested that having a Digicel phone was a 'badge of achievement', especially among young people, and they struggled to satisfy the demand for new phones.

Digicel charged the same price per minute as its competitor but because customers were billed per second, rather than per minute, it worked out a lot cheaper. This quickly endeared the company to the public. 'People just loved us,' Lewis says. 'An ordinary person could now afford a mobile phone.'

But the reality of being a prominent brand operating in Jamaica soon surfaced. Digicel started to receive threats from the local gangs. Hall says it was decided to heed the warnings about not giving into the gangs' extortionate demands: 'Both political parties warned us of the dangers. They said "If you give in, you're dead".' Now a gang was demanding $10,000 or one of Digicel's phone masts would be burned down.

Hall met with some of the powerful 'Dons' and handed them free Digicel phones to try to keep them onside. The mast that was being threatened had cost about $175,000 to build and was crucial to providing coverage in some of Montego Bay's biggest communities. 'We told them no. We had a security man there and they burned the mast down in front of him and the next week they came back looking for $30,000,' says Hall. 'We told the community leaders that we were very upset, that we would rebuild the mast, but if it was burned down again it would not be rebuilt and that would mean they would have no coverage.' The situation was resolved when the community leaders met with the Don to say they wanted to ensure they would have mobile phone coverage in the future. After that the mast was left alone.

Digicel put a lot of effort into being accepted within local communities, holding street parties in areas where they had erected new masts. 'We would bring two vans, a stereo system, some food and start selling our phones. These parties would often go on until four or five in the morning,' Hall says. 'Every community was hungry for telecommunications.'

Concerns about the health and safety risks associated with the masts would surface every now and again over the following years. As Hall explains, one school closed after claims by its principal that the nearby Digicel mast had made three of its pupils ill. After she appeared on television and radio to talk about the problem, Hall drove to South Manchester to meet her to try to calm the situation. 'Mrs Buckle had gathered all the parents and media to meet me and asked what I was going to do about this mast that was making the children sick.'

There were studies that showed how safe the masts were, he explained, but she pointed to two crows sitting on top of the mast that had convinced her of its potential to be harmful. 'Crows love cancer,' she declared. 'That is what we were dealing with,' says Hall. 'We had to battle through it. It was just after Hurricane Ivan and the water had become infected, which was why the kids got sick. That was the kind of lunacy you were dealing with in certain areas.'

C&W looked on helplessly as Digicel won more and more customers. One media report focusing on the battle between Jamaica's two biggest mobile phone operators described the upstart's aggressive approach as being like a tsunami crashing into the island.

C&W attempted to retaliate by aggressively cutting its prices and improving its customer service but could only watch in horror as Digicel's customers grew in numbers. Within 100 days Jamaica's new mobile phone company claimed to have more than 100,000 customers.

C&W's chief commercial officer, Paul Hamburger, put a brave face on the humiliating assault on its business. 'Clearly, Jamaica is a challenge for us, but we are aggressively winning back market share and have been for the past six to twelve months,' he claimed to journalists. 'They've [Digicel] helped to evolve the market and, frankly, they've helped to evolve us, as well.' Former C&W executives point out that the company's failure to invest in Jamaica for many years made it easy for Digicel to take its customers. 'No money was being spent on the network,' one explains.

O'Brien was again insistent that the company focus on disruptive advertising, antagonising its competitor and emphasising to the public just how much better Digicel was. Its coverage was more comprehensive, it was cheaper, and it was an exciting brand that people wanted to feel part of. Jean Lowrie Chin recalls one famous Digicel television advertisement. 'Jamaican men have a reputation about having their little ladies on the side, so the advertisement shows the wife calling her man to say "Where are you?" He says, "I am driving through so and so and I can't hear you." Of course he is not doing what he should be doing and she says, "I know you have a Digicel phone now and you can well hear me. Just listen to me now." And she gets very firm with him. The advertisement warns you can no longer use bad connection as an excuse.'

According to Harry Smith, Digicel's competitor was arrogant; while C&W had probably spent three times more money on marketing than its rival, the new entrant had created such hype that its employees and the public alike were eager to be part of the new brand. 'At the start I don't think that half of the staff considered working for Digicel a job. In fact it was as close to cultism as I have seen in corporate Jamaica. People enjoyed their jobs and wore Digicel-branded shirts with a pride that I had never seen.'

'The branding is all Denis's influence,' Lisa Lewis says. 'In my mind he has a strong influence in terms of how much marketing you do. I believe he is a one hundred per cent proponent of outdoor advertising. I think he wants you to feel it before you experience it.'

The company's marketing research showed that Digicel was seen by Jamaicans as a 'sexy twenty-year-old woman' whereas Cable & Wireless was viewed as a middle-aged corporate man, making it difficult for its competitor to retaliate effectively. 'So you could see the attractiveness of the brand,' says Smith. 'What was interesting was that if a forty-five-year-old man tries to behave like a sexy twenty-year-old woman it doesn't work.'

O'Brien adopted the same business model for Digicel that had worked in his telecommunications and radio businesses in Ireland. The company hired lots of young staff, giving them enormous responsibilities and demanding roles. 'Denis gave young people a chance and had the confidence to put them in decision-making positions,' Smith says. Again O'Brien offered share options as part of their remuneration. But their basic salary wasn't high compared to C&W and they were expected to work punishingly long hours. In the days before the launch, one staff member employed on the technical side of the business got married on a Saturday and returned to work the following day, such were the demands of his job.

Digicel had made a huge investment in Jamaica. It cost more than $200 million to build and launch the new mobile phone company, way beyond the amount originally budgeted for by O'Brien and Kilkenny. Largely due to the persistent demands to invest more capital, their relationship was now strained. If Kilkenny didn't continue to fund his side of the company, O'Brien would insist that his shareholding be reduced. Their differences would be settled years later in a court action. In the meantime, there were other Caribbean islands to be conquered.

16 A Sticky Wicket

Over the next year, Denis O'Brien spent much time jetting from Jamaica to the paradise islands of St Lucia and St Vincent, getting to know the Prime Ministers of the two islands. He was orchestrating a charm offensive to ensure that Digicel would be the next mobile phone operator in the two small islands where its old enemy, Cable & Wireless, had enjoyed a monopoly for over a century.

St Lucia's head of government, Kenny Anthony, and St Vincent's Prime Minister, Ralph Gonzales, were eager to reform the island's telecommunications systems and accepted O'Brien's invitations to see for themselves how Digicel was transforming Jamaica. P.J. Patterson, for his part, was happy to share the island's experience. 'It's true to say the advent of competition that Digicel brought as a new entrant into the field totally revolutionised our system of communications,' he explains. 'It made a tremendous difference. It was an enabling tool, a source of economic development and social empowerment. It surprised everybody's expectations. The hand cart man, the taxi driver, the nurse, the parson, everybody had access [to a mobile phone].'

Patterson says nobody could have anticipated how successful the company would be. 'Part of it was due to very skilful marketing but most of it was really responding to a felt need of people for communication, including of course Jamaican people abroad.' One man explained to the Prime Minister how his mobile phone had changed his life. 'When he was growing up his father lived abroad and to speak to him he had to go the central phone station and get into a queue for hours. He said "Now I can sit in my house any time of the day or night."'

The economic benefits of having a phone quickly manifested themselves. As Digicel's Lisa Lewis explains, its mobile phone service gave people opportunities to find new ways to earn a living. 'The tow-truck driver could now put his mobile number on the side of his truck and was getting a lot more calls. It was the same for taxi drivers. They could tell their customers, call me anytime, day or night. And the fisherman whose catch would get spoiled could now call to say, "I am on my way in, meet me at my spot at five." That is how you change the lives of ordinary people.'

The potential commercial benefits of rolling out similar mobile phone services in other parts of the Caribbean were obvious to O'Brien and the Digicel team. In the Irish entrepreneur's own words, they were 'coining it'. By 2002 Digicel had signed up 650,000 customers in Jamaica and was on course to make revenues of over $250 million. Patterson says the failure of Cable & Wireless to adapt to the new competitive environment contributed to Digicel's success: 'I suspect Cable & Wireless took them for granted and they were totally overwhelmed by the response. It took some time before they realised there was serious competition.'

With Digicel now determined to expand aggressively across the Caribbean, C&W knew the scale of the threat it was facing. It would do everything possible to keep its enemy at bay and prepared to doggedly resist political moves to introduce competition in its other markets. O'Brien warned of a 'vicious' battle.

The Irishman needed Anthony and Gonzales to push through regulatory and legal reforms to allow Digicel go head-to-head with C&W in their islands, and he seemed to have their full support. 'When we were trying to get the licences in St Lucia and St Vincent at the time, he struck up a great relationship with the Prime Ministers there,' says Kevin White, head of Digicel's business in the two islands. 'Denis would be up and down to these guys and does put a lot of effort into meeting the people who run these countries.' And it was paying off.

Thanks to C&W's failure to invest in upgrading its network in the Caribbean ahead of liberalisation, not only was using a mobile phone expensive, but the signal was weak; phone conversations in certain areas were prone to come to an abrupt end. This caused huge frustration for mobile phone users and led to bitter criticism of the company. Anthony was among those who attacked Cable & Wireless in public, at one point branding it St Lucia's 'most hated' company.

The island was truly ready for competition and O'Brien believed Digicel would quickly win new customers. And, given the public hostility towards the company and Digicel's success in Jamaica, C&W knew it was facing a drubbing. An internal report leaked to the media revealed that C&W expected Digicel to take more than fifty per cent of Jamaica's mobile phone market by 2005. It wasn't going to make it easy for Digicel to come into its other territories and poach its customers and refused to cooperate with government efforts to pave the way for competition.

Any new mobile phone company needed to gain access to C&W's network to enable customers to make and receive calls between networks, but the incumbent was in no mood to broker any such agreement. With delays in reaching an interconnection agreement proving frustrating and expensive for Digicel, O'Brien ordered an all-out offensive against its competitor.

Disruptive advertising has always featured among O'Brien's favourite weapons and soon local newspapers in St Lucia and St Vincent were carrying full-page advertisements from Digicel, complaining that Cable & Wireless was stalling competition and depriving people of a cheaper and better mobile phone service. Suddenly radio and television talk shows were debating why C&W was afraid of competition. And Digicel's attacks continued.

It was a gamble to expand in the islands. The advisers who had cautioned against opening in Jamaica were predicting an expensive disaster. 'At the time everybody was saying "Don't do it." They told Denis, "You are never going to make a viable business in St Lucia, St Vincent and Grenada,"' White says. 'I remember advisers, consultants, financial advisers writing ten-page documents telling Denis not to do it. But he would tread fearless. His own gut was telling him different.'

Having won a licence on the same day as Digicel, the US giant AT&T was also preparing to launch in St Lucia, and the two companies were racing to be the first to get their new network up and running.

Buckley recalls the urgency to open the business; he and O'Brien piled pressure on White and his team, calling them at least once a day to hurry things along.

Mark Linehan, who had moved to the Caribbean from Ireland to oversee the development of the new networks, says they faced many of the same issues in each of the islands when trying to acquire sites to erect masts. Communities were concerned about the safety of living near such huge fixtures and there were often other unforeseen logistical issues. 'There was one guy who had some land in a rural part of one of the islands where I had selected a site for the mast,' Linehan says. 'When our guys went to build the site, brought in the digger, he came running out saying "You can't build there." They pointed out that he had agreed to release the land, then he said his wife was buried there. Thank God they didn't start digging. We had to move the site on to another part of his land.'

St Vincent was Linehan's first posting. He fondly remembers when the Digicel network was switched on. 'The mobile phone coverage came from St Lucia. I remember a guy with a satellite trying to get the signal and suddenly, bang, Digicel comes up on the screen and you could make a call. Then you knew you had built a network. It was one of the most pleasing moments for me.'

While Digicel's network was ready, however, Cable & Wireless was continuing to resist all efforts to allow Digicel to interconnect with its own network. O'Brien turned to the island's top politicians for help. 'Basically you are left to sit down with the monopolistic operator and you try to hammer out a deal,' White explains. 'Sometimes the politicians get involved as well because it is prescribed under the Telecommunications Act. It's a battle of wits.'

O'Brien appealed directly to Anthony and Gonzales to intervene and they agreed. 'He'd get people to do things,' White says, referring to his boss's persuasive nature. 'Denis managed to get the Prime Ministers of those two countries to attend those meetings. Those guys stayed up all night in a hotel with us and they were trying to mediate between us and Cable & Wireless. The fact that he managed to get heads of state involved in his business to help you to get over the line and get your business launched is due to his incredible powers of persuasion.'

And when Digicel's exhausted troops looked as if they were wilting, O'Brien, blessed with boundless energy, rallied them back into action with a familiar refrain. Over the years he had instilled an underdog mentality into those who worked for him, energising his troops and strengthening their loyalty to him and the company. It was time for another battle cry.

He gathered his weary bunch and made a speech. White recalls what he said. 'It was along the lines that it was history repeating itself again.' The multimillionaire businessman successfully presented himself as the representative of the downtrodden. 'It's the English,' he said passionately. 'We are the oppressed here. We have to rally around the flag and show that the underdogs always come through.' Finally that night agreement was reached. Digicel was ready to conquer new territories.

The mobile phone operator replicated in St Lucia and St Vincent virtually everything it had done in Jamaica. It sponsored sporting events, its top managers infiltrated local business networks and the bold red Digicel logo was visible on every street corner. Its 'Bigger Better GSM Network' was advertised everywhere.

And people responded enthusiastically to the hype, scrambling to sign up. 'Within two to three months St Vincent had a huge base. It had a population of over one hundred thousand and in no time we had thirty thousand customers,' says Linehan. They knew from the start that the new mobile phone company would quickly win lots of new customers from C&W, but such was the rush that they struggled to cope with the demand. 'We had a fantastic start,' he says. 'We ran out of phones, out of SIM cards, we had to get them flown in from Jamaica.' Eventually eighty per cent of the island's mobile phone users became Digicel customers. O'Brien's gamble had again paid off.

Linehan says Digicel's forceful marketing and brand-building were driven by the company's founder: 'Denis is very much a sales and marketing guru. His vision is very simple. If a market is going to liberalise every person should have a chance to have a handset in their hand. Make it affordable and accessible and people will use your product, and of course behind that you have to build a state of the art network.'

Kevin White, who had been part of the Esat Telecom crew, was now running a mobile phone company for the first time. Having quickly risen through the ranks, he had been rewarded with a challenging role. 'That is the great thing about Denis: he will give you a chance to do anything,' he says. 'We used to say in board meetings that someone had done very well, had become a general manager of a business within I don't know how many years, and Denis said, "Sure you can do that in six months in our business." And you can. If you show the enthusiasm and work hard enough, you can do whatever you want to do.'

Yet O'Brien tightly managed everyone who worked for him, constantly testing their loyalty. 'It is micro-management,' David Hall says, 'and that is the hard part. That is the choice you make. You have a lot of flexibility but run all of the major decisions past the board.'

O'Brien managed the rollout of the new business particularly closely so as to ensure it would not prove to be the disaster some had predicted. 'Denis had gone against all of the advice he was getting and so was paying a lot of attention to the business,' White says. 'He was visiting every two to three weeks, often travelling on his own on the jet, and he would go through the nitty-gritty detail of the business. His attention to detail was unbelievable.'

White explains that he closely followed Seamus Lynch's business plan, which had worked so successfully in Jamaica. 'We made it up as we went along. We copied whatever went on in Jamaica that we thought was useful.'

White intended to stay in the Caribbean for two years but would end up as one of O'Brien's longest-serving lieutenants at Digicel. It took a while to adjust to living in the Caribbean, he says, but O'Brien smoothed the transition by always ensuring they had comfortable living conditions and arrangements. 'It [living in the Caribbean] does take a while to get used to, but to be fair the company ensured that you were well sorted out in terms of accommodation, transport, flights home and all that. It was an attractive package put together to entice you out. A lot of the guys were single and O'Brien made an extra effort to make sure we were OK.' When they arrived they would work long, punishing hours and many say they had little opportunity to spend the money they were earning.

*

With Digicel now up and running in St Vincent and St Lucia, O'Brien's appetite for expansion was insatiable. His list of engagements with Prime Ministers across the Caribbean was growing as he lobbied them to issue new mobile phone licences. More and more politicians were travelling to Jamaica as O'Brien's guests to view his success there. And new licences were up for grabs in Grenada, Aruba and Barbados.

According to Buckley, O'Brien could be holding discussions with up to six Prime Ministers at any one time as the company chased new licences across the region. 'Prime Ministers and ministers were open to Denis because they were aware of what he had done in Jamaica and had probably met him there,' Linehan says. 'If Denis was to drop in they would make time to meet him. They understood he was investing a lot of money in their country and would assist where they could.'

Lewis, who worked closely with O'Brien on winning new licences across the Caribbean, says they spent a lot of time courting politicians. 'We bring a lot of politicians to Jamaica. They are people who can help learn about Digicel so they can go back and explain about it in their own country. We buy them the most expensive phones and take them to the shop. It costs a lot of money but those things are important because you are making a good impression.'

Some, however, were less accommodating than others and proved resistant to O'Brien's charm. From time to time Leslie Buckley weighed in with the politicians himself, and he was responsible for sorting out Digicel's licence in Grenada. 'We knew we were being given the licence,' he explains, but it was taking a long time to materialise. 'The paperwork was sitting on the minister's desk but we were not sure why he was not issuing it, so I decided to go down there and stay until we got it.' For the next couple of days Buckley 'camped' outside the minister's office, but was told he was too busy to speak with the Irishman. 'I stayed the weekend and was back again at his office on Monday,' he says.

The minister had scheduled a press conference at his office for later that day, and as a means to engage him Buckley decided to hijack it. 'I put a big table in front of the lift and sat there for five hours,' he says. His intention was to block the journalists, threatening to hold his own press conference to tell them the minister was stalling Digicel's arrival in Grenada. 'I said the minister should come and discuss it with me or I'd be calling a press conference.' Eventually the minister relented; Buckley recalls the two men staring at one another for a long time as they attempted to resolve the remaining problems. 'Four hours later the licence was signed,' he says.

Some of the region's politicians were shocked by Digicel and O'Brien's aggressive business style. While he forged firm friendships and relationships with many of the political elite, there were politicians who preferred to avoid him. One Prime Minister confided to a prominent businessman in the region that O'Brien was one of a handful of international tycoons with business interests in the Caribbean whom he refused to let into his office.

Things ran more smoothly in Barbados, where in February 2004 Digicel won a mobile phone licence and was preparing to launch its service in this more affluent part of the Caribbean. White moved there to run the new business, which was to be launched in Digicel's traditionally spectacular style.

By now the group had a template for a successful start-up in each new country, borrowing from the experience in Jamaica. It would also adopt successful marketing ideas from other parts of O'Brien's business empire.

In Ireland, the 98FM radio station was gaining notoriety via the 98FM Fugitive competition. Listeners were teased over the air every hour with clues as to the whereabouts of a 'fugitive', with a substantial cash prize for the person who identified him. In Barbados, customers were invited to find the Digicel Spy, with phone credits and other prizes for the winner.

O'Brien spends a lot of time in Barbados, holidaying and playing golf at the Sandy Lane hotel owned by his friend Dermot Desmond and associates J.P. McManus and John Magnier. Over the years these visits would challenge Kevin White and the Digicel crew in ways they hadn't foreseen.

'We had frequent visits,' White recalls. 'Denis used to visit to see how the business was going, but he also went there on holidays, so he would often call from Sandy Lane, saying "I'm at breakfast, the signal is not great down here." Or he would be out playing golf and he would ring me up and say, "I've just converted a customer from a prepaid to a bill-paid phone." He would give me the details and say "Can you get him sorted out?" And by the time he was finished playing golf there would be about ten people that he would have promised phones to, upgrades, free credit. They would all think he was a great fella. He was giving out phones all over the course.'

White introduced O'Brien to some local Barbadian businessmen with whom he was friendly and would gain an insight into how his boss operated in these social settings. 'Denis would say to them, "We'll watch a rugby match or play golf" and they would tell me he was a great guy. He was a great laugh; he'd be telling jokes, cursing and drinking. He is a great lad's lad but I have no idea what that's like.' Unlike staff who had enjoyed his hospitality at 98FM, those who worked for O'Brien these days didn't see the gregarious side of his personality too often.

Barbados was already a challenging business environment, according to White. 'You have a lot of well-off people coming into the country, including Irish people, who if they have any problems are very quick to call and say "Hey, your network isn't working in Barbados."' But no one would test the Digicel network more thoroughly than its owner.

O'Brien's signal tests became legendary. He regularly drove around the Caribbean islands to make calls from the most remote spots and there would be trouble if his experience was bad. His insistence on using an old Nokia phone was particularly annoying. White was not the only one to explain that with a newer phone he would have no problems connecting with Digicel. But he was relentless. 'When you hear he is coming to your country on holiday you think, OK, you are definitely not on holiday,' says Lisa Lewis. 'Those coverage tests are brutal. He still does that.'

O'Brien liked to keep a close eye not only on how the business was being managed but how it was presented to customers in each of the islands. As well as testing the mobile phone signal, he would randomly inspect Digicel shops. By now he was visiting Jamaica and the other markets at least once a month, and sometimes every couple of weeks. Harry Smith recalls one trip that proved a particularly painful experience for the management team.

When he stepped off the jet, O'Brien said he wanted to see one of Digicel's phone shops. While everyone had prepared for his visit, they had not anticipated this request and had to quickly arrange the trip. Digicel's regional manager, Joy Clarke, travelled to the selected store with O'Brien but it was closed for the evening when they got there. 'Joy, in her normal Digicel style, finds the owner and opens the store,' Smith says. But her enthusiasm to please her boss created a nightmare as the store failed to live up to his expectations.

'Denis just beat us up,' Smith says, describing the verbal assaults that followed. 'The red in the Digicel brand was wrong, everything was wrong. I was called the following day. David Hall got beat up, the head of retail got beat up. You learn that it's not personal; it's about the brand. We learned that whenever he wants to see stores you know there is going to be blood on the walls.'

On another trip O'Brien asked Smith to show him one of Digicel's satellite stations. This time, the marketing director wanted to ensure it would be a successful visit: 'Knowing how Denis is, in terms of his sense of quality, I made sure all of the billboards on the way were pristine.' Or so he thought. 'Denis looked at one board and said, "Harry, that is not perpendicular; it is slightly off." This is a steel structure. I had to call and get them to go and straighten it. You shrug your shoulders and say I thought I did it right. What do you do now? You look to see if it is straight.'

O'Brien's unpredictability and attention to detail would create great anxiety among the staff ahead of his regular visits. Like Esat, Digicel was a tough environment where you had to learn to survive. It was clear to everyone that if they failed to be responsive to O'Brien's demands they would be shown the door – or, as Lucy Gaffney puts it, be 'pushed off' the fast-moving train. As Paul Connolly says, in such a rapidly developing business people can get 'kicked' along the way: 'If they don't like it, it's a nightmare.'

Some who made a hasty exit say O'Brien was an impossible taskmaster. Others resented the micro-management, often of very senior roles, that left them wondering if he trusted anyone to run parts of his business.

By now Digicel was expanding into the Cayman Islands where a new licence was being offered by the government. Lisa Lewis prepared the licence application under O'Brien's close scrutiny. 'He wanted an update every week,' she says. And when the document was finished, Lewis was under orders to send it to Digicel's boss immediately.

'He wanted me to fax it to a restaurant that he and his wife and kids were eating at,' Lewis recalls. 'I remember the fax machine wasn't working properly and it was over one hundred pages. He wanted to see the document to make sure it was saying what he wanted it to say. I think we went to bed at six that morning and he called me at eight.' And they were surprised when the chairman asked how they intended to deliver the bid to the minister. 'He wanted to know were we getting a horse-drawn carriage to deliver it like the Esat bid in Dublin. He wanted to know what had we thought of, did we have any actors or actresses? This kind of thinking outside of the box was definitely a new thing for us.'

The competition for the new licence in the Cayman Islands was similar to that held in Ireland, where applicants were invited to appear before officials to explain their plans and answer questions. O'Brien, a veteran of such events, prepared his troops for the occasion. 'He coached us and we rehearsed,' Lewis says.

And he personally selected the sites for Digicel's new shops on the islands. 'I remember the whirlwind visits,' continues Lewis. 'The plane would touch down and you would meet Denis and drive around for three hours and he would rush back to the plane. Denis would be in the front of the car and we were in the back, driving around Cayman looking for sites for our stores. You couldn't sign a lease on a store until Denis said to you, "Yes, this is where I want the store to be."'

Cable & Wireless was also getting used to Digicel's aggressive business style, which was decimating its business in this part of the world. It needed to retaliate forcefully and sought to hire someone who had waged war with O'Brien in the past. Stephen Brewer, the executive who in the 1990s had headed Eircell, Digifone's competitor in Ireland, seemed an obvious choice.

'Cable & Wireless had a real problem with Digicel,' Brewer says. 'Denis was eating their lunch and breakfast, so they headhunted me to go down there to take him on. I was flattered.' Brewer was to manage fourteen of the Caribbean countries in which the group was operating, and was to focus on those suffering most at Digicel's hands. 'I had to pick out the difficult ones, places where Digicel had gone very well, and see how we could fight back. I enjoyed doing it. Denis and I had our run-ins but they were competitive.'

Brewer was not alone at Cable & Wireless in believing that bad investment decisions over the years had helped Digicel to attack its customer base. 'C&W just didn't believe in competition. It appeared to me before I got there that they had let Digicel in. Denis saw that gap in the market and went for it,' he says.

Brewer crafted a plan of attack against C&W's rival, but it was a difficult task. 'Digicel is a relentless competitor,' he says. And O'Brien's close involvement in the company, he believes, was a huge factor in the company's success. 'Cable & Wireless was never led by a hands-on executive with a solid management team behind him. If you want to wish a competitor badly, you have got to plan badly for that competitor. You have got to be relentless and to keep your staff with you.' Brewer was ready to lead a counterattack.

O'Brien too had plans to escalate the war. The telecoms entrepreneur admits he loves plotting his competitors' downfall. Now he was working on a plan to inflict further humiliation on Cable & Wireless. For almost nine months he and Seamus Lynch, the man colleagues say O'Brien always drafts in for 'covert' operations, prepared the ground to wrest away C&W's most prestigious sponsorship.

Cricket, the game invented by the British in the sixteenth century, had long been considered the force that bound the English-speaking Caribbean together. The West Indies cricket team — familiarly known as the Windies — that dominated the sport from the mid-1970s to the early 1990s is a multinational team comprised of players from a dozen English-speaking Caribbean countries including Jamaica, Trinidad and Tobago, Barbados, Grenada, St Vincent, St Lucia, Guyana and Antigua. The region has produced some of the world's top cricketers, such as Andy Roberts, Everton Weekes, Gary Sobers, Brian Lara and Sir Vivian Richards.

Sponsoring major sporting events was a fundamental part of Digicel's business model and had proved a winning formula in enabling the company to connect with its customers. In Jamaica Digicel's first sponsorship was the country's Special Olympics team, reflecting O'Brien's association with the World Games. Its red logo was now dominant at many sporting events – with the exception of the region's best-loved sport.

Cable & Wireless had cornered that sponsorship and for eighteen years had been the 'proud sponsor' of the team that spanned its markets in the English-speaking Caribbean. Its deal was up for renewal in 2004 and O'Brien wanted Digicel to replace its arch-rival as the team's new sponsor. He wanted to use this sponsorship to beam the company's bright red logo across the Caribbean.

The West Indies Cricket Board (WICB), the sport's governing body, was preparing to enter into fresh negotiations with Cable & Wireless, and according to its president, Teddy Griffith, the talks began in July 2003. All seemed to run smoothly and within a couple of months the WICB and Cable & Wireless agreed a new three-year sponsorship deal, subject to formally agreeing the contract.

But the deal would soon unravel and ultimately slip from C&W's grasp. Griffith claims that problems arose because conditions not discussed or agreed during the negotiations were included in the new contract. Further negotiations between the two sides proved equally difficult and within a couple of months C&W's sponsorship deal was in jeopardy. The WICB was obliged to tell Cable & Wireless if it intended to start negotiations with another potential sponsor and the telecoms company was to be given the opportunity to match a rival offer. And Cable & Wireless quickly realised that the WICB was indeed talking to another potential sponsor.

Paul Aspin arrived from Britain in 2003 to run C&W's operations in the Eastern Caribbean. One of his first tasks was to deal with the renegotiation of the Windies' sponsorship deal. C&W reminded the WICB of its obligations under the existing contract, he says, but received no information. 'I would imagine that O'Brien said to them that Digicel was keen to do it,' says Aspin. 'The WICB have always been and remain a disorganised bunch. We were suspicious for many months. I kept calling Teddy Griffith, saying "Look, we think you are talking to someone. If you are, you do realise that you are in breach of contract unless you tell us." He was obviously between a rock and a hard place and didn't want to tell us anything.'

Aspin eventually persuaded Griffith to meet him, but the WICB president insisted it had to be discreet. 'He flew from Barbados for an "unofficial" meeting,' Aspin explains. 'It wasn't to be in my diary and he didn't want anyone to know. Before anything was announced or before any deal was done he actually asked me if Cable & Wireless would be prepared to come back in and talk to them.' Aspin says he played 'hardball' with Griffith, who said of Digicel, 'The other lot are horrible to deal with.'

Digicel had informally mentioned its interest in the cricket sponsorship to a WICB representative at a golf tournament in late 2002. Since then O'Brien and Lynch had been honing their plan to become the new sponsor. Digicel, which had worked with London-based brokers International Sports Marketing (ISM) on similar deals in the past, hired the firm again to secure its most ambitious sponsorship. But the brokers would not deal directly with the WICB on Digicel's behalf for fear of alerting Cable & Wireless to its enemy's intentions. Instead, they negotiated with the WICB through a company known as SBI, which was to get ten per cent commission on the deal.

David Brookes, director of International Sports Marketing, explained when asked about the deal that SBI was used to 'mask the identity' of Digicel to Cable & Wireless. Knowing the competition between the two companies, Brookes said he assumed C&W would not want to lose the sponsorship deal to Digicel and would automatically match his client's offer if they were aware of it. 'I felt this put Digicel at an unfair disadvantage and because ISM had worked with Digicel in the past, ISM could be easily linked to them. To avoid this, I hired the services of SBI simply for client confidentiality reasons with the aim of ensuring that the Digicel offer was viewed fairly, reasonably and on a level playing field. Cable &Wireless was therefore given the right to match this offer.'

In a further effort to maintain confidentiality, Digicel's offer was made to Griffith and WICB chief executive Roger Braithwaite, whom Brookes described as the 'driving force' behind the negotiations to

secure Digicel as the main sponsor. They both gave a legal undertaking not to disclose details of the deal being discussed, including the
potential new sponsor's identity.

As these discussions moved towards agreement the WICB
informed Cable & Wireless of SBI's alleged sponsorship bid. The
company has claimed it was asked to match a $30 million deal. It
declined to do so, instead offering $4 million to sponsor the Windies
home series, a figure that was turned down. Griffith told C&W
executive David Austin that he was unable to consider the offer
because of a twenty-one-day exclusive discussion agreement with
another potential sponsor.

In March 2004, Digicel's business development director, Liam
McDermott, said the company was told Cable & Wireless 'had
declined to match its offer' and that the WICB was ready to negotiate
terms for Digicel to become the new principal sponsor of West Indies
cricket. Two months later the WICB's chief marketing officer, Darren
Millien, was told to 'hammer out the contract' with the new sponsors
and travelled to Jamaica to meet Digicel's lawyers and its broker.

With Cable & Wireless about to lose its coveted sponsorship deal to
an unknown company, it began to salvage what it could from the
situation. It clinched a deal to become one of the main sponsors of the
2007 Cricket World Cup, which was to be held in the West Indies, and
found other ways to maintain a presence in the game.

Cable & Wireless had a long-standing endorsement deal with West
Indies captain Brian Lara, who had a contract that ran for another
year to promote the company regardless of the new sponsorship deal.
And he was about to be joined by seven other team members –
Ramnaresh Sarwan, Chris Gayle, Dwayne Bravo, Omari Banks, Fidel
Edwards, Ravi Rampaul and Dwayne Smith – who also signed
personal endorsement contracts with C&W.

The WICB, concerned about potential conflicts of interest, urged
the players not to sign the contracts ahead of the new sponsor's
arrival, but failed to persuade them. And it was relieved when the
board finally announced Digicel as the new 'proud sponsor' of the
West Indies cricket team in July 2004. 'Our partnership with Digicel
represents a new era for the sponsorship of West Indies cricket,' said
Griffith. 'We look forward to a long and rewarding partnership.'

Cable & Wireless was horrified by the news and demanded an investigation. The deal went against its contractual agreements with the WICB, it argued. It felt the company had been unfairly treated when it was asked to match a new sponsorship offer worth $30 million rather than the $20 million now being pledged by Digicel. And so the war of words continued. The vicious battle between the Caribbean's two largest telecoms companies would continue to affect the region's beloved sport for years to come.

But Digicel was delighted with its victory. O'Brien was in London to announce to journalists his company's new $20 million five-year deal, which would begin from the Windies' tour of Australia in 2005. 'Digicel takes enormous pride in becoming the official main sponsor of the West Indies cricket team,' he said. 'We believe in the future of the Caribbean and its cricket. We will add new energy into West Indies cricket through our incentives and youth programmes. This will encourage more great performances and foster future cricket legends. We are excited about the future of cricket in the Caribbean. Our sponsorship will help enable West Indian cricket regain their dominance of the sport.'

In Jamaica, Seamus Lynch invited the local media to Kingston's Sabina Park cricket ground to announce the deal. The bargaining process had been a 'sticky wicket', he said, as his team batted for nine months of negotiations. He played down Cable & Wireless' controversial sponsorship arrangements with eight of the players, insisting that this wouldn't cause a problem for Digicel: 'Captain Brian Lara has signed up with our competitor for a year. While he is engaged and while any of the players are engaged in West Indies Cricket Board activities, they are available for use to Digicel at all times.' And, he explained, Digicel would be offering Lara 'an enhanced individual sponsorship contract' when his existing one expired.

According to Harry Smith, snatching the cricket deal was the last straw for Cable & Wireless. 'It was akin to pulling down Saddam's statue. It was the last bastion of their regional visibility.' Digicel had seized the region's most visible sponsorship. It had toppled its great rival and was winning the war.

17 'Santa Claus'

Seventy-five thousand athletes and spectators gathered in Dublin's Croke Park Stadium on 21 June 2003 for the star-studded opening ceremony of the 2003 Special Olympics World Games. Nelson Mandela, Muhammad Ali and rockers Jon Bon Jovi and U2 joined Eunice Kennedy Shriver and her family, including son-in-law Arnold Schwarzenegger, to formally open the games. Manchester United star Roy Keane accompanied Special Olympian Catriona Ryan as she took the Games oath on stage.

Denis O'Brien was proud to stand among the celebrities and took the opportunity to urge the Irish government to continue to embrace initiatives to support those with disabilities. As a first step, he wanted it to sign up to the UN Convention on the Rights of Disabled Persons, proclaiming the treaty as 'perhaps the single most important event ever in the history of the United Nations with respect to disabilities'.

It was a magnificent ceremony and the start of what was hailed far and wide as a highly successful event. According to their chief executive, Mary Davis, O'Brien had played an important role in Ireland's staging of the Games, incidentally acknowledging the contrasting aspects of his character: 'He had both sides really, a very soft side and a business-nosed side. He viewed the games as a business that had to raise €60 million in cash or kind. We were all daunted by the amount of money that had to be raised, Denis as well, but he was very clever in understanding that unless you brought a business sense to it, it was going to fail abysmally. And none of us wanted that to happen.

'He got a really good board together and effectively made things happen. He wasn't slow about delegating positions to people when something needed to be done. He gathered good people around us that were then able either to influence or assist us in terms of what we needed, whether it was logistical or fundraising.'

O'Brien's long-term business colleagues, including Lucy Gaffney, Leslie Buckley, Padraig OhUiginn and P.J. Mara, were drafted in to help Davis and the team. Maria Mulcahy, O'Brien's friend since their university days, also played a central role. Many years after O'Brien's eviction from Tim Shriver's twenty-first birthday party at the Kennedy family compound at Hyannis Port, the pair made Shriver's reacquaintance that summer when they welcomed him to Ireland as the Special Olympics international chairman.

Davis paid tribute to O'Brien's support for her own efforts, pointing out that, as a sports enthusiast, his was a natural association with the Games. 'He was a generous donor. He never left us stuck [for money] and definitely assisted us in raising money. But the most significant thing for me was the amount of support that I felt behind me, which for an event that size gives you incredible confidence. You need huge self-belief that you can do it. You never felt you were doing anything alone. You were doing it in the knowledge that you had a team led by him behind you. He had that incredible self-belief and in turn he was telling me that I had it.'

O'Brien was popular with the volunteers, and despite living outside Ireland and being involved with his company's war against Cable & Wireless in the Caribbean, he attended many fundraising and other events to show his support. 'He forged a pretty good relationship with all of the volunteers,' says Davis. 'I remember I always admired him for doing this.'

His involvement in the Special Olympics showed O'Brien at his very best. He readily weighed in to bring Iraq's twelve-strong team of Special Olympians to Ireland when, at the last minute, they were allowed to leave their war-torn country. After difficult negotiations to gain permission to land in Baghdad, he sent his jet to collect the team and personally paid for their stay in Ireland.

And he showed particular support for the journey of the Games' 'Flame of Hope' from Athens to the official opening in Dublin, in which the torch was carried in a series of relays run by two thousand law enforcement officers from the Irish and Northern Ireland police forces. Davis says O'Brien liked to be there to greet the runners as they arrived in towns and cities around Ireland on their journey to Croke Park. Witnessing the Torch Run, he has said, was 'the most moving experience' of his life. 'He went to every location he could to support the people. He was an incredible believer in what people did,' says Davis. 'He really did want to show that he cared about the effort that went into the Torch Run.'

Davis is not alone, however, in recalling one episode where O'Brien's plans to attend the Torch Run in Athlone were almost derailed. He stepped from a helicopter into a field close to the town but found no one there to meet him. Thanks to a mix-up, O'Brien had been left alone in the countryside some miles from the event. 'Instead of having a head-throw he got out onto the road, hitched a lift in a van then hopped on a bus that dropped him at the edge of the town.' The roads were blocked to traffic for the Torch Run so the marathon runner ran the rest of the way to get there in time. 'He took that in his stride. He wouldn't stand there with a phone wondering who was going to collect him,' says Davis. 'That's the thing about him, he is always resourceful.'

As the pressure built, O'Brien did whatever Davis asked of him, she says. 'He would hop in the car and come and see a sponsor. I remember we were trying to get more money from Tesco and he said, "Come on, we'll squeeze more money out of them." He loves that. He gets a buzz from that.'

In the midst of his involvement in the Special Olympics, however, O'Brien was to become embroiled in a controversy that would once again highlight the paradox of his determination to go into battle on behalf of the underdog. O'Brien's movements in and out of the country were closely monitored by the Irish tax authorities. His tax exile status meant he could spend only a specific number of days in Ireland during the year and his commitment to the Games would quickly add up. O'Brien had gone to some lengths to prove he was not liable to pay tax to the Irish Revenue. A large house he owned in Dublin's Raglan Road couldn't be classed as his main residence, it was revealed, because it didn't have a kitchen. And records showing the thousands of air miles clocked up on his Gulfstream aircraft formed part of his proof to the Revenue of the vast amount of time he spent outside the country. News of his dealings with the Revenue was revealed in the weeks before the Games commenced, when the *Sunday Business Post* carried a front page story headlined 'Revenue Probe into O'Brien's Tax Residency'.

The article revealed significant details about O'Brien's tax affairs, specifically a dispute with the Revenue about whether or not his residency in Portugal exempted him from paying tax on the vast profits made when he sold his Esat mobile phone company to British Telecom.

The Revenue's challenge to his tax residence was ultimately unsuccessful after O'Brien appealed it. But the story left him fuming and, revealing once again his prickly side, he was quick to convey his displeasure to the newspaper through his lawyers. He believed he had a right to confidentiality in his dealings with the State's tax collector and launched a blistering attack on what he described as a prevalent 'negative culture' towards politicians and entrepreneurs in Ireland.

Speaking to an *Irish Times* journalist after a telecommunications conference in Dublin, O'Brien said he was so frustrated with the prevailing negativity that he would not move back to Ireland in the foreseeable future, adding that he wouldn't apologise for where he lived. 'I can live anywhere in the world and nobody is going to stop me . . . This is not China in the 1970s or 1980s. People can move and live wherever. People can invest and move their capital.'

He was much happier living outside Ireland, he continued, as 'there is too much shite going on inside Ireland at the moment. I think people are too negative towards politicians, Government, and entrepreneurs. We are fast turning into a communist state. We are fast moving towards communist doctrine. People in this country should be thankful for what they have achieved in the last ten years. Instead, I come back to Ireland and people are screaming like spoiled children.'

And when it came to his tax affairs, he believed in the basic right that people's tax position should be between themselves and the Revenue. 'People leaking details is just totally unacceptable.'

A year later, after much legal wrangling, the *Sunday Business Post* apologised to O'Brien for the story. 'We accept that Mr O'Brien has a right to confidentiality in his dealings with the Revenue and that we are not entitled to make use of any confidential information relating to those dealings,' the paper stated. 'We have undertaken to Mr O'Brien that we will not do so again.' As a 'mark of regret' it made a donation to the Aisling Foundation charity at his request.

In the view of *Irish Times* columnist Fintan O'Toole, the controversy was potentially 'the most serious threat' to freedom of the press to emerge in decades. 'A serious and well-respected newspaper has been forced to accept that the media has no right to deal with the relationship between any individual and the Revenue,' he wrote. 'The implications for the public purse, for ending tax evasion and for investigative journalism are enormous.'

There is 'a genuine public interest in Denis O'Brien and Esat', O'Toole explained. 'The profits were made on the back of the granting by the State of a mobile phone licence to Denis O'Brien's consortium in circumstances which are being investigated by the Moriarty Tribunal. The broader issue of State policy on tax exiles is a live political question. The problem is, however, that Denis O'Brien has now effectively established that the public interest in such matters is completely outweighed by the right to confidentiality.'

When faced with an extremely expensive court case, the paper accepted it had no right to report on these issues, O'Toole claimed. 'This sets a precedent for a blanket ban on reporting . . . If this precedent stands, it will make it extremely difficult to report on a whole raft of issues concerning business, politics, and the relationship between them.'

Journalists at the *Sunday Business Post* were aware of the ongoing row with O'Brien. Some say he and his associates openly referred to it by the unflattering nickname of the 'anti-Business Post'. They were shocked some months later when the paper's editor, Ted Harding, resigned. This raised some concern with the paper's owners that Harding's departure was in some way linked to O'Brien's ferocious onslaught.

Seamus Dooley, head of the National Union of Journalists, also voiced concern, describing Harding's departure as a 'very disturbing development'. Dooley went on to state that 'Ted Harding was a very courageous journalist. He exhibited a lot of bravery in stories concerning the relationship between big business and politics, notably in relation to Denis O'Brien and Esat. He was centrally involved in investigating the financial affairs of businessmen like Mr O'Brien. He was also consistent in highlighting the various business links of Independent News and Media through Tony O'Reilly, and used his position as editor of a non-IN&M-linked Sunday newspaper effectively. This departure could be seen as sending a signal to brave editors who take such stances that they could be vulnerable.'

As a result of the dispute, some people bristled at the congratulations being heaped on the controversial businessman for his extensive and genuine commitment to the Special Olympics. Many of his friends feel his efforts in that direction were never fully appreciated. O'Brien took on the chairman's role that other prominent business figures had turned down, they say, in the months before he made his great fortune from the sale of Esat and long before the start of the Tribunal's investigations into the award of the mobile phone licence to his company. Maria Mulcahy insists that O'Brien's contribution to the Special Olympics was genuine and feels it was never publicly acknowledged. 'He got no credit for the Special Olympics. I have no idea how much money he gave but he does these things for the right reasons.'

Some people nevertheless believed that O'Brien's involvement in the Special Olympics was a deliberate effort on his part to rehabilitate a reputation that he felt had been badly damaged by the Tribunal's investigation. Former Telecommunications Minister Mary O'Rourke shared this view. 'It was a good move,' she says. 'It got [sic] that edge to him that he didn't always have. I thought it might have been Bertie [Ahern] that might have advised him to give that dent to his character. He did marvellous work. He really threw himself into it but it helped him as well.'

In answer to those who may have been cynical about O'Brien's involvement, Davis says she can only speak from her experience. 'I only know what I saw and dealt with, day in day out, for those four years and since then. I can only judge Denis on that. He went from one state to another in a financial sense but otherwise the person never changed from that time right up until now, and that's admirable.'

It was O'Brien, she says, who encouraged the organisation to develop a plan for the future. 'When we were finishing in the last six months the main emphasis was on ensuring the Games were successful, but Denis was saying we needed to start working on a legacy plan, because that was why we were holding these Games. We weren't doing it just for this massive event.

'I think that is a really good example of his commitment. If someone thought he was cynical he'd just have been interested in getting the event over, but he was very keen to leave something behind after the Games in Ireland.' It was O'Brien, she said, who had urged the organisation to form a separate group, even before the Games finished, that would be able to continue its work once they were over. 'We had developed a strategy that was ready to go the next day. That was his incredible vision and the reason why we did the Games in the first place. And he remains a strong supporter.'

He also wrote a letter to each of the thirty thousand volunteers and insisted on signing each one personally, adding a handwritten note to those he knew. It took four months to sign them. 'People can think what they like but there aren't that many people that would actually do that,' says Davis. 'You could digitally sign them but I think that would be cynical. It was a nice touch, a very personal touch.'

One of O'Brien's close friends was moved to publicly acclaim his contribution to the Games. In a letter published in the national newspapers, Patricia Tsouros suggested the media should examine its 'moral ethics' in the light of its coverage of her good friend after his tremendous work.

'Denis agreed to take on the daunting prospect to chair the 2003 Special Olympics World Games when no one else in Ireland was prepared to do it,' she wrote. 'He put the money where his mouth was and wrote the cheques when funding fell short. Denis along with other leading Irish businessmen ensured that the funding was in place to provide for a very high-standard World Games production. But most importantly Denis never attempted to hijack the games to achieve his own means.'

O'Brien knew funding was simply the catalyst for the Games, she

continued, and that the real success would come from the determination and commitment of the many athletes and volunteers. 'He
revelled in their achievement, not his own. He embraced their success
with selfless joy. That is Denis at his best. It is unfair to judge Denis on
the fact that he did not have to pay twenty per cent capital gains to
the Revenue.'

Her letter pointed out that it was 'legitimate and logical' that after
selling Esat, O'Brien would move to Portugal, where he had invested
in Quinta do Lago. 'In making the choice to live in Portugal, he did
not make the choice to turn his back on Irish people. Denis has a
group of close-knit friends and he continues to remain loyal and
supportive. He is a committed family man. He is privately compassionate and supportive to many organisations and individuals and
remains a major investor in many companies in this country. He has
never abused his financial situation and has a very strong work ethic.'

He was, she suggested, entitled to expect that his tax issues, home
address and family matters should be kept private. 'He is
understandably exasperated by the biased, ill-informed, manipulated
information that is being put into the public domain by the press. I
think it is about time that all media people look at the standard of
journalism that is being written and said about Denis O'Brien and
question their moral ethics to their profession.'

O'Brien would receive praise from many quarters for his hard work
in contributing to the Games' success. Even Gavin O'Reilly, chief
executive of the Independent News & Media group and son of Tony,
sent his congratulations and best wishes. 'Dear Denis,' he wrote, 'I
fully suspect that I might be the last person you'd expect to get a
letter from, but I just felt I had to write to congratulate you on, and
thank you for, the Special Olympics. Saturday evening was a really
unbelievable showcase – like never before; that owes to your
incredible perseverance, drive, creativity and generosity.'

The letter continued: 'It may sound corny to utter it – but I felt
truly proud to be Irish – and from the reaction of everyone I met, it
will certainly go down in the annals as the night Ireland Inc played
the leading role in such a wonderful and inspirational undertaking as
the Special Olympics. Our involvement – as media sponsor – was
fairly modest in comparison to others, but we were, and are,

delighted to have played our part.' And O'Reilly seemed to extend an olive branch to the man who complained so bitterly about what he believed was an orchestrated campaign by the newspaper group to damage his reputation.

'At some stage (at your choosing), we should get together . . . as I detect that absence has not been our greatest ally!' O'Reilly wrote. 'In the meantime, renewed congratulations and my personal best wishes to you and Catherine.' The letter was signed, 'yours sincerely, Gavin O'Reilly'.

Some of O'Brien's other 'enemies' were also impressed by his recent endeavours and publicly paid tribute to him. When he appeared before the Tribunal of Inquiry at Dublin Castle once again, Justice Michael Moriarty took the opportunity to congratulate him for his efforts with the Special Olympics.

By the autumn of 2003 the Tribunal had, much to O'Brien's annoyance, begun delving into his purchase of Doncaster Rovers' ground. Having lost a challenge in the courts to its right to examine his personal affairs, he was already being bombarded with requests from the inquiry team for documentation. Now he had to attend to give further evidence.

Welcoming O'Brien back to the inquiry on 10 November, Judge Moriarty assured the businessman, who had complained so bitterly about this intrusion into his life, that his findings would be fair. It was no secret, the judge said, that in the past relations between O'Brien and his advisers on one hand, and the tribunal on the other, had had their 'low moments' and that O'Brien believed it had been unfair to him. That day Moriarty said he wanted to welcome O'Brien to the Tribunal 'to hear your side of these important events' and promised to pay 'close attention' to his evidence.

His report, the judge said, would be based on the evidence heard in public from witnesses. If he found that O'Brien had won the State's second mobile phone licence 'fair and square', the judge assured him, he would subscribe to that form of report 'as gladly as any other'. And he went further: 'Last thing, and I say it not as a vacuous or cosmetic formula,' he added, 'I do note that since we last met in this place you have been very significantly involved in the very commendable and great success of the Special Olympics and I think it would be churlish of me not to acknowledge and commend you for that success and your own not inconsiderable role in it.'

O'Brien is undoubtedly a curious mix that intrigues colleagues and acquaintances alike: ruthless in business, obsessive about loyalty, the worst imaginable foe in a battle and dogged in his determination to get value for money, yet legendary for his generosity to people in need of help.

Friends say he never talks about such matters, but many have been astonished by his gestures to people he has never met but who were in distress. His generosity has ranged from financial contributions to making his jet available to them.

Some of these acts are facilitated through a charitable foundation, the Iris O'Brien Foundation, named after his mother, established in Ireland in 2000 and run by Maria Mulcahy. Over the years, the foundation has made large amounts of money available to many people and causes. 'He is a Santa Claus figure,' Mulcahy says. 'He just can't say no. Some of the things he has done are staggering.'

The foundation has helped with providing medical treatment for those battling with various illnesses, but O'Brien's main interest is helping to provide educational assistance, whether for people with special needs or those living in difficult economic circumstances. 'He likes to say yes. He might hear of a sick child and the next thing they are at the Mayo Clinic. He makes decisions on the spot. He doesn't spend time over it,' says Mulcahy. 'He is not looking for a legacy.'

Mary Davis also learned of the financial support he gave in a private capacity to some of the Special Olympic athletes during the Games. 'I never knew he was involved in that way,' she says. 'Some people are always boasting about what they do but you would never hear about it from Denis. He has supported an incredible amount of stuff. People may criticise him for being a tax exile but he gives in another way.'

Some of his new-found wealth was also channelled into projects in Africa, where he had been providing help and support since the 1980s when he joined with Fred O'Donovan to coordinate aid for the famine in Ethiopia ahead of Live Aid.

O'Brien's father says he is often surprised to learn about the extent of the financial support and assistance his son gives to various causes. 'I don't want to boast about him in this regard, but he is incredibly generous in giving money away. He is unbelievable, what he does in Africa and so forth. I am talking about millions. I have priests and nuns coming up to me and saying "How wonderful your son is." He doesn't tell me. Actually he never talks about it. Maybe he thinks I would say to him that he should slow down.'

The successful businessman's long-standing support of organisations such as Amnesty International is also perplexing to some. His father says this is influenced by his mother, a serial protestor against injustice. According to Conor Lenihan, O'Brien's support for Amnesty was evident from his college days. 'In the early days when 98FM was starting, colleagues were bemused by this. When we were struggling and had no money he was heavily involved in Amnesty. Cynics in the company were saying "What is this about? Mr Capitalist Left-winger." People were genuinely perplexed.'

Amnesty International's former Dublin head, Mary Lawlor, remembers O'Brien from that time. 'He asked me to meet him in the early nineties when he was at 98FM to discuss some ideas. He was very approachable, friendly and wanted to help. He was asking what he could do and when I gave him ideas he said yes to them all and we went from there.'

O'Brien undertook to promote Amnesty's work through his radio station, also stepping in to fund a sculpture in the Dublin International Financial Services Centre after the collapse of his former mentor's company, Guinness Peat Aviation. GPA had sponsored a public art competition for a piece of sculpture to highlight Amnesty's work but could not honour its commitment when it needed to provide the €18,000 to cover its cost. 'I asked Denis if he could help us and he agreed. He gave us the money,' Lawlor says.

The giant ball of chains encloses a constantly burning flame and is surrounded by the inscription: 'The candle burns not for us but for all those whom we failed to rescue from prison who were tortured, who were kidnapped, who disappeared. That is what this candle is for.' According to Lenihan, O'Brien saw the project as a bit of a challenge. 'It was a way to put up a piece of sculpture that would be of public value and to give Amnesty's message. He doesn't go around making a big public relations exercise out of it. He doesn't promote that side of it because he believes that is essentially private.'

O'Brien is a very generous donor to the organisation. He donated the record damages of almost €330,000 he won in a libel action against the *Mirror* newspaper to Amnesty International. For many years he organised the annual Amnesty International lunch in Dublin, selling the tables and handing over the money, and immediately pledged some of his new-found wealth following the sale of Esat to BT.

Lawlor later persuaded him to back a programme she was keen to establish to protect and assist those defending human rights. He gave the new organisation, Front Line, headed by Lawlor, €3 million to get started and continues to support it in a financial and personal capacity.

And as his Caribbean empire thrived and prospered in islands where poverty was rife, O'Brien set up the Digicel Foundation to support educational and other good causes. It began its work in Jamaica, the first Caribbean country conquered by Digicel. O'Brien set aside some of his millions and encouraged Digicel staff to participate in its projects.

'Denis has a very generous spirit,' says public relations consultant Jean Lowrie Chin, who joined the foundation's steering committee. 'Ordinary members of the staff were on the board from day one. It was a team effort, not just the big boys who would be deciding how the money would be spent.' The foundation is focused on the areas of greatest need, such as education and activities to promote harmony in communities.

Digicel's head of marketing, Harry Smith, took on the chairman's role and Major General Robert Neish, the former head of Jamaica's army, stepped in as its chief executive. 'Everyone had a clear idea about what we wanted to do,' Neish says. 'I didn't meet Denis until we finished the first project but we were all clear about what the foundation would do. He had set clear guidelines. We were to find an education project as soon as possible and to encourage Digicel's staff to think of projects and to bring applications from their own communities.'

Neish explains that O'Brien is supportive of providing facilities for children with special needs. 'Denis has a very genuine feeling for kids and getting them to develop their full potential. We really want to make an impact in areas to broaden education and are hoping within a short period of time to eliminate illiteracy at primary school level.'

Smith recalls the foundation's first project, the construction of a new elementary school in the Lake Pens area of Jamaica. The school, with spacious classrooms, was built and ready to open within six weeks. 'It was a very poor area,' Smith explains, one where the children attended school in a single room at the back of a church. 'We had a lot of enthusiastic people and Digicel staff painted murals on the walls.'

O'Brien attended the school's opening. 'We made a videotape of the opening. The little children sang Bob Marley's "One Love",' says Neish. 'Denis was besotted with them. He was giving out books and reading to the kids. I don't think I have ever seen him so happy.'

Smith saw a different side to O'Brien through his work with the Foundation. 'He has a hard exterior but he has a soft underbelly. He is a pussycat,' he says. Within four years Digicel contributed $7 million to the Foundation, funding over forty projects in parishes all over Jamaica. It constructed a physiotherapy unit and computer training centre in St Ann, set up an information technology lab at the José Marti High School and repaired schools damaged by hurricanes.

Former Jamaican Prime Minister P.J. Patterson says O'Brien was among the first to call him when the island was battered by hurricanes, asking what he could do to help. In 2004, after Hurricane Ivan, Digicel contributed almost $3 million, the single biggest ever corporate donation, to the island's hurricane relief fund.

'Denis has invested in almost every facet of national development, whether it be education, culture, sports, charitable causes, times of natural disaster, encouragement of talent, innovation. It's hard to think of any aspect of national development in which Digicel has not participated in a positive way,' Patterson says. 'A lot of it is to do with the kind of person Denis is.'

18 A Mobile Fortune

It didn't take long for Digicel's sponsorship of the West Indies cricket team to turn into a public relations disaster for Denis O'Brien's mobile phone company. The $20 million, five-year deal that was supposed to endear the company to the entire English-speaking Caribbean quickly threatened to destroy their beloved sport, fuelling bitter conflicts between Digicel and the region's legendary cricket stars that would fester for years to come.

As part of the controversial deal agreed between the West Indies Cricket Board and O'Brien's company in 2004, captain Brian Lara and his team would, when they toured Australia in January 2005, be expected to warmly embrace the new sponsor and work with Digicel to promote its brand through their cricket exploits. But, thanks to the personal endorsement deals some of the top stars had recently signed with Cable & Wireless, the entire team was embroiled in the turf war between the Caribbean's rival telecom companies from the start.

The West Indies Players' Association (WIPA), the body representing West Indian cricketers in negotiations with the WICB, expressed concerns that players were being 'exploited' for commercial purposes and urged them not to join the forthcoming tour unless the difficulties created by the rival sponsorships were resolved. At the last minute the players accepted the decision of an independent adjudicator, Justice Adrian Saunders, to break the impasse, but the fundamental problem remained unresolved.

In the light of the threat to the tour, Digicel attacked C&W for deliberately attempting to undermine its sponsorship deal by signing the personal contracts with players, claiming this had been done 'in the full knowledge their actions would create great difficulty for the WICB, the seven players and the title sponsor, Digicel'. It accused C&W of 'bad sportsmanship'. Cable & Wireless in turn accused Digicel of 'ambush marketing' and the verbal assaults continued.

If the players refused to support Digicel in garnering maximum publicity from them, the company's $20 million coup could ultimately prove disastrous. So O'Brien gathered some intelligence to find out just how difficult the sponsorship might prove to be.

Englishman Richard Nowell, a former professional cricketer who was working with Digicel on its crucial new sponsorship, would be going on tour with the Windies to Australia. He was under orders to compile a confidential report for O'Brien analysing the sponsorship benefits. And he found plenty of material.

Tensions between the new sponsor and the team emerged as soon as they landed in Australia. According to Nowell, Lara and the six other team members signed to Cable & Wireless were uncooperative with Digicel's demands to appear in photographs and at other events to promote the team's new sponsor. Excerpts of Nowell's report appeared in the *Trinidad Guardian* chronicling the difficulties experienced during the tour and he concluded by questioning the value of the sponsorship for Digicel. The West Indies players were, in Nowell's view, 'lacking sponsor/media savvy' and were poor ambassadors for the company.

He was equally troubled by other aspects of the team's performance. Their conduct on and off the pitch, he said, was providing little value for Digicel. Had certain members of the team 'scored as many runs as they had women's phone numbers during the tour', he told O'Brien, they would have won the series comfortably. In his view, the WICB needed to seriously examine the 'nuts and bolts' of the sponsorship contract or it would be pointless for Digicel to continue to invest so heavily in the team. The WIPA president rejected the comments, which he said contained 'unjustified imputations on the character and behaviour of West Indian players.'

The report's contents were explosive, however, and showed once again just how ruthless O'Brien could be when seeking value for money. Digicel would use its findings to demand a greater show of support from the WICB for its sponsorship or risk losing the lucrative deal. Publicly, though, Digicel insisted the deal would stand.

Everyone from the team's loyal supporters to politicians across the Caribbean was horrified by the ongoing public squabbles. The political establishment was particularly concerned that these problems might damage the West Indies' successful hosting of the 2007 Cricket World Cup. Each of the islands was building a new stadium for the event which, it was hoped, would bring thousands of tourists to the region and restore the West Indies to the sport's top echelons.

But instead of getting better, the situation steadily worsened. The team's next outing, a tri-series against South Africa and Pakistan, showed the world just how divisive the sponsorship deals continued to be. Perhaps emboldened by Digicel's demands, the West Indies selectors announced a twenty-two man squad that excluded the seven players signed by Cable & Wireless, including captain Brian Lara. Having refused to sign fresh contracts with the WICB, they lost their place in the team as a consequence.

The following month the WICB again picked a second-string squad for the tour of Sri Lanka after some players continued to refuse to sign new sponsorship contracts. Angry and frustrated with the way they were being treated, the players publicly aired their views. 'I just want to play cricket really,' Lara told journalists. 'It's very important for me and for West Indian cricket that I'm out on the field playing. The war is a telecommunication war.'

Cable & Wireless was outraged by the dropping of the squad's top players. 'Frankly it is outrageous that Digicel can, with a straight face, claim to support West Indies cricket out of one side of its mouth, while wanting to destroy it out of the other,' a company spokesperson told the media. The WICB should fulfil its mandate to field the best team, it said, calling on Digicel to stop its 'capricious behaviour' and its attempts to 'bully and buy' to get what it wanted. Digicel responded that C&W's comments on the row were full of 'half truths, mis-statements and blatant lies'.

The WICB was under siege from two directions. Digicel was pressurising it to bring the players into line, while C&W was fighting with it to maintain its contracts with the players, and was still demanding an investigation into the circumstances surrounding Digicel's sponsorship deal.

Politicians, many of whom O'Brien had courted during his rapid expansion of Digicel, also weighed into the debate. A Prime Ministerial Cricket Committee was formed to offer assistance in the dispute, with Grenada's Prime Minister, Keith Mitchell, assuming the chairman's role. But the Caribbean's political elite were divided, taking turns to snap at each other, according to media reports, as they meddled in the cricket row. Jamaica's former Prime Minister, P.J. Patterson, whose government had initially forged such close ties with O'Brien and his company, was perceived as lending strong support to Digicel, something that angered the Prime Minister of Barbados, Owen Arthur. 'Back off,' he said, a remark perceived to be aimed at Patterson. He and other Prime Ministers were concerned that the dispute could ultimately splinter a team created from the best players of up to a dozen islands. 'A few thousands of dollars should not be enough to stop us from seeing a common purpose of the only thing, really, that has not only effectively held the Caribbean people together but has given us a global sense of accomplishment for more than fifty years. Obviously, the game has been, in many respects, destabilised to some degree.'

As the controversy raged, Mitchell summoned all sides to a meeting in Grenada to broker peace between the warring factions. Representatives from Digicel, Cable & Wireless, the WICB and the WIPA were invited. O'Brien flew to Grenada for the session.

Paul Aspin, the C&W executive in charge of the sponsorship deal, would come face-to-face with the man who had stolen it from under him. He vividly recalls the meeting and O'Brien's demeanour throughout. 'We all sat around a big table and it was very states-manlike. The Prime Minister of Grenada said his job was to sort out where they would go from here. We must all be prepared to compromise to break the impasse, he said.' Mitchell opted to meet each delegation individually for a discussion before calling them all back to, he hoped, reach an agreement. Cable & Wireless was the last group to meet him that day.

'We told him what had happened in a very calm way,' Aspin says. 'We told him that we had the right to be told about another sponsor and that we had been given no right of reply. We also explained that we would have put more money into the cricket board than the deal on the table. We thought that we had done a very good job.'

When they reconvened, Mitchell said all sides, with the exception of one, had shown willingness during the discussions to make concessions. 'You can imagine who the exception was,' observes Aspin, implying that Digicel was the party at fault.

'The Prime Minister then said some interesting things that we didn't know before and before he got any further Denis threw the toys out of the pram. He was accusing Cable & Wireless of being a colonial power, of misusing the people of the Caribbean for a hundred years,' he continues. 'I assume nobody was quite surprised at his conduct, but it was very unseemly.'

Having signed the $20 million sponsorship, O'Brien was obviously unhappy that C&W was now trying to undo it and that the row had escalated to this level. Why would Digicel cede any ground in these negotiations?

When the Prime Minister invited C&W to respond to O'Brien's outburst, Aspin got to his feet. 'Prime Minister, if I may say so,' he said, 'you started things with a voice of calm in trying to sort everything out to the benefit of West Indies cricket and I hoped that we had all come here with that intent. The diatribe that I have just listened to bore no part in the proceedings. I wouldn't even lower myself or my employer to refer to any of the nonsense that has been spoken, so I appreciate the opportunity, but frankly I would be wasting my breath.'

Aspin says he glanced across at O'Brien, who he said was 'purple' with rage. At the end of the meeting O'Brien approached him and extended his hand but Aspin ignored the gesture. 'I just turned the other way.'

With no truce in sight, the WICB appointed an independent official to probe its deal with Digicel in the hope that this would finally end the controversy. WICB president Teddy Griffith, one of the driving forces behind the negotiations, established a Sponsorship Negotiations Review Committee, headed by Justice Anthony Lucky and joined by accounting professionals Gregory Georges and Avondale Thomas.

For the next couple of months Lucky's committee examined and reviewed all correspondence, transactions, communications, minutes, contracts, records, arrangements and any other relevant information concerning the WICB's switch of sponsor. In August 2005 Lucky presented his findings to Ken Gordon, who by now had replaced Griffith as WICB president. The report concluded that Digicel's sponsorship deal could be declared 'null and void' because of the way the WICB had approached the negotiations and its dealings with the previous sponsor, Cable & Wireless. The sponsorship agreement, and the ten per cent commission payable to the SBI brokerage used to mask Digicel's identity in the negotiations, 'cannot be in the best interest of West Indian cricket', it stated.

The negotiations that resulted in the finalisation of the agreement were conducted 'in secret under a guise of confidentiality', Lucky continued. The board had done all it could to disguise the identity of Digicel, thereby breaching its own contract with Cable & Wireless, which required openness in all negotiations. The result of this secrecy, Lucky concluded, was that the players and the West Indies Players' Association were unable to negotiate with the board because they were unable to find out the exact terms of the contract.

The board noted the findings but shelved the report. It decided there was nothing contained in its conclusions that would undo Digicel's sponsorship deal. Lucky resigned in protest, saying the WICB had failed to meet him and the committee it had established in the wake of 'widespread public concern across the Caribbean' about the implications of the 'still secret' sponsorship contract signed with Digicel. The board, he claimed, had chosen simply to criticise his report in a 'self-serving' manner.

Cricinfo, the website devoted to the Caribbean's best-loved sport, summed up the state of play. It was a case of 'corporate telecoms giants hurling boulders at each other whilst the naive ship, the WICB and its hapless passengers, the players' association, try to float through the barrage'. And so the battle between the WICB, the players and the two telecoms rivals continued. Everyone hoped a final resolution would materialise before the 2007 World Cup.

All the while O'Brien's Caribbean empire was growing. Trinidad and Tobago, the islands that were to have been the launch pad for his Caribbean adventure, had proved the most difficult for Digicel to enter so far. Now, six years after it first set its sights on a licence in 1999, the company was finally preparing to open for business.

Again, its old enemy Cable & Wireless was the dominant telecoms company on the islands where, through a joint venture partnership with the government, it owned Telecommunication Services of Trinidad and Tobago (TSTT). It had done everything in its power to block new entrants and, via lengthy delays in sharing infrastructure and striking agreements over interconnection costs, had until now kept its rivals at bay.

Stephen Brewer, whom O'Brien had recruited after a stint fighting Digicel at C&W, was in charge of setting up the new mobile phone operator. The task was to prove more troublesome than anyone in the company believed possible.

O'Brien travelled to Port of Spain almost every week for six months to help break the costly deadlock. Brewer explains that when O'Brien wasn't in Trinidad he was on the phone: 'When I was talking to him on the mobile he was in Portugal with his family and could have one of his kids on his knee during the conversation.'

TSTT had plenty of time to prepare for Digicel's arrival and by now was familiar with the tactics it used when entering a new market. Its mobile subsidiary, bmobile, was ready to go head-to-head with its new competitor. The ongoing cricket row, it hoped, might also help to ensure an unfriendly welcome for O'Brien and his crew. Cricket enthusiasts had been vocal critics of Digicel in the preceding months. The dropping of the islands' hero, Brian Lara, from the team during the sponsorship conflicts angered many of Digicel's potential new customers and signalled that the new mobile operator might enjoy a more lukewarm reception than it had received elsewhere in the Caribbean.

And while Digicel prided itself on its spectacular launches, its arrival in Trinidad was decidedly low-key. O'Brien described it as a 'soft launch' as Digicel 'tested' the market. 'This is a long game and it's going to be very competitive,' he told journalists. He played down the likely impact of the highly charged cricket spats on his company's prospects in the islands: 'We sent a package to the WICB and they accepted. So they [Cable & Wireless] got upset. I can't help that. And so you move on and we're very happy with the sponsorship. We're very pleased with Ken Gordon, who is really moving the WICB into another level.'

He wasn't expecting any fallout from its potential new customers, although he admitted: 'This is not the toughest market we've been into but it has been the longest one that we have fought for. I've been here over one hundred times. This is a marathon and Digicel is a marathon runner.' The company had a five-year and a ten-year plan to recoup its $1.9 million investment in the local market, he added.

Digicel's publicity machine cranked up, announcing that its more than 200 shops would open at 6 a.m. the following morning with promises of cheaper phones and call packages for new customers. Before dawn hundreds of people gathered in the expectation of free phones and other promotional goodies. But the openings didn't go according to plan. Some shops were still closed after 9 a.m., while those people who had waited patiently for freebies left only with Digicel brochures illustrating its phones and the cost of making calls on its network.

One hour into the long wait for the opening of Digicel's shop at Independence Square in Port of Spain, local media reported that potential customers were leaving and walking to the nearest TSTT outlet, which had just launched a new range of packages. 'The frustration of people squashed in the mêlée crowding the sidewalk, was evident,' the *Trinidad Guardian* reported, and those waiting outside had plenty to say about it. 'But them is ah bunch of fakers. What happened to the six o'clock opening? They done start bad already,' shouted one man as Digicel employees pushed their way through the crowd at 7.30 a.m. 'Aside from cries of outrage, loud enquiries to all and sundry, from time to time the air was punctuated with an assortment of phone rings and people could be heard informing the callers of their disappointment. When a woman, wearing the trademark Digicel red T-shirt, but covered with a jacket, squeezed through, she was tugged at and boldly asked by a young man: "When all yuh really opening?"'

There was plenty of entertainment on display as Digicel and TSTT's bmobile both created a true Trinidad carnival atmosphere to mark the formal opening of their hostilities. Over on Brian Lara Promenade, bmobile's neon green-attired dancers were joined by local footballers who handed out promotional gifts to bemused onlookers. Close by, Digicel's red tents, flyers and music boxes belted out popular hits. Cable & Wireless had learned a few of Digicel's tricks and was ready to play O'Brien's crew at their own game. And it would win significant victories. Within a few months, Digicel closed some of its dealerships as it wrestled to win customers amid fierce competition.

Over in Haiti, however, it was all systems go. By May 2006, Digicel had spent more than $100 million on creating a new mobile phone network, the biggest corporate investment ever by an international group on the troubled Caribbean island. Within weeks of launching in Trinidad and Tobago, Digicel was ready to open for business. It expected a rousing reception in one of the world's poorest and most dangerous countries.

O'Brien's arrival in Port-au-Prince triggered a full-scale military-style security operation. Digicel's owner was met at the airport by an armed private security force, including former Irish Army Rangers, who ferried O'Brien and his entourage into the capital in armour-plated vehicles and guarded them throughout their stay. Murder and kidnappings for ransom were commonplace in Haiti, with company executives offering rich pickings for its vicious criminal gangs, known as bandits. And Digicel's owner was about to become one of Haiti's most influential business figures, joining with a former US President, among others, in a development plan for the country's future long before it was devastated by an earthquake.

O'Brien has described Haiti as one of the most entrepreneurial regions in the world. This struck him as he watched the buying and selling carried out on the streets on visits to the island. 'It was like a bazaar,' he said. Lucy Gaffney, who accompanied him on these first trips before the company put in its bid for the mobile phone licence, says there was plenty of commercial activity. 'We were flanked by bodyguards,' she recalls, as she and O'Brien walked through the streets of Port-au-Prince. 'The place was buzzing. We looked at all the trade that was going on. 'Denis likes to wander around countries where he is thinking of doing business,' Gaffney continues. 'He always walks around a city and goes into the retail units. He doesn't sit in five-star hotels and weigh things up. He can very quickly sense what we need to do from a marketing perspective. What is the biggest sport, what are the biggest social issues? He likes to get involved in people's lives in a multi-tentacled way. He will go to sports events and concerts.'

In the months before the launch, Digicel's red-and-white painted masts were rising throughout the island, bringing coverage to even the most remote spots. Making such a huge investment in a country where its more than eight million people survived on less than $2 a day and most had no formal job or electricity or running water was a huge risk. But from the first day Digicel's prospects looked bright.

They were lining up before dawn on the morning Digicel opened for business in Port-au-Prince. Everyone, it seemed, wanted a Digicel phone. For weeks now Digicel had promised cheaper call rates, a reliable phone network and free phones for anyone who cancelled their contracts with Haiti's biggest mobile phone provider, Comcel.

Jamaica-based public relations consultant Jean Lowrie Chin travelled with O'Brien to the capital for the launch and witnessed the Haitians' eagerness to sign up with Digicel. 'You would say, why is he going to this poor country to launch his business? They are poor. How can they afford to have a phone?' But the demand for tele-communications was evident. 'The Haitians were saying they could not afford not to have a phone,' she explains. 'This is how they would make contact with family members in North America.'

And they were treated to a spectacular launch. 'It was the biggest launch Haiti had ever seen,' according to Lowrie Chin. 'Denis flew in an act from the Cirque du Soleil from Las Vegas for the event.'

O'Brien was delighted to launch his new business in the country that was potentially Digicel's biggest. 'For too long the people of Haiti have had to put up with a terrible service, bad networks, high prices and total unreliability,' he declared. 'From today, we see a new beginning in Haiti.'

Within days, Digicel's bold red brand was visible throughout the island's main cities. Keith Collister, a journalist who travelled there from Jamaica just three days after the launch, described the scene in the *Gleaner* newspaper. 'Stepping into the entrance of Port-au-Prince's sleek international airport on Wednesday morning, the welcoming band clad in Digicel's red colours led to an immigration entrance almost entirely covered by Digicel advertising, followed by porters with Digicel emblazoned across their caps' brows.' The company had even branded some of the street signs in parts of the city, he noted.

Digicel quickly sold hundreds of thousands of its mobile phones, with reports of pushing and jostling in many of the shops as they struggled to cope with the swelling crowds. O'Brien was concerned about those waiting in line to get into the shops in the blistering heat and reprimanded his staff for failing to consider their discomfort. As Mark Linehan, a member of Digicel's start-up team in Haiti, explains, 'He was surprised that we didn't spot this. "Look at the queues outside the door," he was saying. "You should have seen this. Get them water. You can't have people hanging out in the hot sun. Give them umbrellas, make sure they are comfortable." It's that human touch. He has it. He is constantly thinking that way.' Good business it might have been, but it was also a glimpse of O'Brien's humanitarian instincts.

Digicel would sell its phones through a network of more than two hundred dealers, including the 'Allo' chain established by one of the former Digical employee, Bernard Henry. One of the dealers told Keith Collister business was booming. 'If I had more phones, I could sell one thousand a day,' Jean-Max Garoute explained from his shop just two minutes from Haiti's notorious Cité Soleil slum. As Collister reported, fifteen armed guards surrounded the complex where Garoute's shop was doing a roaring trade, with another six guarding his business.

Its cheapest phone, the Motorola C115, was the biggest seller, said Garoute, and was now popularly known as the 'huit million' (eight million) to reflect the fact that the entire Haitian population wanted to own one.

Mark Linehan, who would spend almost a year in Haiti, saw how quickly the business developed. 'Denis realised the importance of having expats in first to build the network and then for the locals to take it over eventually,' he says. 'Six months later local staff took over the responsibility for the running of the company. That is great to see.'

The lack of infrastructure and the dangers of everyday living presented particular problems for the Digicel staff. Linehan and his team were ferried to and from work by security guards in armoured vehicles. 'They were serious security guys,' he says. 'You couldn't go anywhere without them. It was a difficult environment to live in but it was well worth it to see the progress that we made. Denis would always tell Seamus [Lynch] that when people were moving here from Ireland and the UK, they would work hard but their living conditions should be comfortable. We were living in a beautiful house. It was one of the nicest houses in the Caribbean I have lived in.'

Like Cable & Wireless, Digicel's competitors in Haiti, Haitel and Comtel, failed to see the potential of the mass market, providing a service mainly for wealthy Haitians, explains Lenihan. 'They only realised that potential when we launched and then they went head-to-head with us. We came into the market at the right time.' By the end of 2006 Digicel claimed to have won one million customers in this new market and was determined to become the biggest mobile phone company in Haiti.

Digicel was by now operating in twenty-two countries in the Caribbean, including Antigua, Trinidad and Tobago, the Turks and Caicos Islands, Bonaire, Guyana, Martinique and Guadeloupe, with more than four million customers and 1,500 employees. Having expanded both by acquiring new licences and by spending hundreds of millions purchasing existing businesses, it had now extended its reach beyond the English-speaking territories.

Given his micro-management style, the size and spread of the company presented a challenge for O'Brien, so he and his team developed structures and training programmes which he hoped would allow him to retain close control of his empire. Colm Delves, who joined the company in 2004, was now running the group. He and his management team would meet O'Brien at least once a month and he would call them without fail every day.

'He has business interests in other areas but Digicel is by far his biggest investment and his biggest focus,' Delves says. Everyone at Digicel is to some degree 'micro-managed', according to Delves, a style that creates a challenging working environment in which new recruits often struggle to cope. 'I find that people when they come in can be set in their ways. In Digicel it's all-encompassing in terms of the focus that is required and the amount of dedication that goes right throughout the organisation.' Often new recruits 'don't like the intensity of the management style we have at Digicel', says Delves. Over the years Digicel has hired people with impressive experience who, Delves says, have resented that type of management approach and that level of accountability and have quickly exited.

Digicel's finance director, Lawrence Hickey, was well acquainted with O'Brien's management style, having been part of the Esat Telecom crew, and quickly adjusted to his new role. Nowhere would O'Brien's management style be more evident than at the monthly board meetings where the management teams were grilled on their performance. They were bruising encounters that everyone at Digicel grew to dread.

Every month O'Brien gathers his board of directors on his jet to travel to the Caribbean. 'It's miserable being a director of Digicel,' he has said. 'We have a practice of meeting our management teams and probably having a monthly board meeting in every market. That is excessively demanding but worth doing.'

David Hall is among those who agree that these meetings can be ferocious. 'You learn to leave your dignity at the door and collect the shreds of it on the way out,' he says. 'This is the way it happens; it's effective.' According to Harry Smith, it was impossible to predict how these meetings would develop. At one presentation, Smith recounts, he told the board about a current marketing campaign in Jamaica, bringing branded T-shirts and other Digicel merchandise to show them the concept. 'While I was waxing away thinking I was doing pretty well, Denis gently placed the shirt in front of me and said the registration of the colours was slightly off. How could I be doing that to his brand, he asked. To say that puts you off is an understatement. I was thinking I didn't have to take the shirt. I was asking myself, Why did I bother? I had to come back and give all of those shirts to charity and get them all redone.'

They learned everything had to be done to O'Brien's high standards. 'As a professional you are going to feel bruised, because the higher you go in an organisation, the more the criticism of your job is about you, because you are so aligned with it. But it makes you better.'

The phrase 'It makes you better' or 'I was better for it' is one readily uttered by O'Brien's lieutenants. Maybe it is a mantra they have adopted that allows them to withstand these relentless attacks.

Initially the meetings were held in Jamaica, but as the group expanded, teams from the various islands would gather either in the Caribbean or in Miami or Los Angeles. O'Brien believes it is essential to grasp even the smallest details in each business. Most months the board will 'hit eight markets in three days. Each management team will come to a central place and they will all get a slot for two hours to tell us how they are doing, and to show us how they plan to create more upset for our competitors.'

As Delves explains, these are more operational meetings than board meetings. 'Denis very much leads the meeting as chairman. Leslie Buckley will focus on the costs, Lucy focuses on marketing and Seamus Lynch on the commercial side. Greg Sparks looks at audit controls procedures, Julian Horn Smith, the former chief executive of Vodafone, looks at operational aspects and David Sykes focuses on finance, structuring and cash needs. P.J. Mara will offer words of wisdom and has a great nose for the marketing side and particularly on messaging. They all play those roles. The one who is most unpredictable in the meetings is Denis.'

O'Brien and Buckley push people very hard, Hickey says. 'Leslie and Denis both know when they have pushed people to the limit. Both recognise there is only so far you can push a guy. They are not unreasonable in that and I think they are quite good at sniffing a guy, asking if he is delivering as much as he should be or how much pressure you can put on someone.'

Delves believes O'Brien often underestimates his power to set a tone or an atmosphere at those meetings, a subject he has discussed with him. And the chairman has been known to change his personality to suit the situation. 'At times he can be very strong. He can be hot-headed on specific issues, particularly if he feels somebody is trying to pull the wool over his eyes. At the other extreme he can be jokey and get his point across to get people to do things on a much more relaxed basis. He can switch from one to the other depending on who the person is. He might lure someone into a trap. He might for instance ask, "What about that person who is working for you in marketing, are they any good?" "Oh yes, very good," you reply. He'll ask "How long have they been with us? Do they have languages?" And then he might say, "OK, will you get them down to Haiti. They have been transferred."'

One employee had a unique strategy for dealing with O'Brien at these sessions. She later shared the secret of her success. 'She had a voodoo doll of Denis,' says Delves, with pins targeted at strategic points if things turned ugly.

Delves, who sits next to O'Brien at the meetings, says, Digicel's chairman pores over all of the management reports for hours during the flight. 'He then summarises everything on one page in tiny writing, by market, with little boxes for each market and the points he wants to focus on.'

O'Brien expects his management team to be well read, and is exasperated with their shortcomings in this area. Delves remembers a meeting where he enquired how many of his lieutenants had read a book by Jack Welch, former boss of General Electric. When it became clear that it hadn't formed part of their reading material, he wearily ordered copies for them all.

It was Welch – known as 'Neutron Jack' for eliminating employees while leaving buildings intact, rather like a neutron bomb – who took over GPA, the company founded by O'Brien's mentor, Tony Ryan, following a disastrous stock market flotation in the mid-1990s. Welch drove a hard bargain and Ryan famously accused him of having 'raped' GPA. Welch was swift to reply: 'What do you expect when you're walking around with no clothes on?' While Ryan had taught O'Brien almost everything he knew about business, O'Brien was highly impressed by the man who bested his mentor.

Lawrence Hickey says that the pace within Digicel can be gruelling. 'We launched Haiti and Trinidad within a month and launched Panama and Honduras within a month of each other. They are difficult, stressful things to do and take their toll on everyone.' It's not an easy lifestyle, he says. 'People get burned out. There is a lot of travel, long hours and constant pressure and it's not for everyone. There are lots of businesses like that now. Denis does expect and demand loyalty from his senior guys and they are and like being part of his empire. He doesn't take prisoners. If you are not producing the goods, you will know about it. If you keep not producing the goods, you will be shown the door. That brings its own pressures. There is no place to hide.'

Harry Smith had a ready answer for those who complained about the gruelling pace they were expected to maintain. 'I said if you can't take the pace, my recommendation to you – and people thought I was harsh – was that they should go and work somewhere else. Because it wasn't that the pace was going to change. That was the environment for success. We just kept driving and driving. There was no let-up. Some people can do it and some can't. I dare say that some of those people might find working in a steady-pace job boring.'

And according to David Hall, O'Brien always operates at this same high pace. 'It's not like Denis is someone sitting there taking the dividends. He is a serious worker. If you got a good swift boot in the backside you would turn around and say, "What in the name of Jaysus am I still doing here?" But everyone was very loyal to the man and there were lots of fun days as well.'

And of course the staff were well rewarded for their hard work and loyalty. O'Brien used the same reward system he had adopted in Esat Telecom, offering share options to the management team and beyond. Lynch, Harry Smith, Lisa Lewis, Hall and White, who had all been there virtually from the start, had seen the value of their shareholdings increase as the company thrived. Being granted share options was a rare phenomenon in the Caribbean and Digicel was the first company to launch a company-wide scheme in 2006. It would divvy up almost one million shares to employees across the group. Jamaica's Finance Minister, Dr Omar Davies, congratulated the company on the initiative and urged other companies to follow its example.

Lawrence Hickey agrees that O'Brien was very generous when it came to recompensing his troops. 'He rewards people and looks after them. He will be fair. It's a two-way thing. That's what you get for loyalty.'

Hall says that as you continued to work hard to build the business you would be keeping an eye on how much your shares might eventually be worth. 'You could see the company progressing and you were thinking, Maybe there will be a pay day at the end of it. So you kept going.'

The share options were definitely an attraction, says Smith. 'Those of us who came in early all came in at similar salaries. The kicker was the share options. It was a gamble, but from day one I just considered this was a good thing to be involved with. It wasn't the money at all. You didn't have time to spend it.'

Someone else who started out on the Caribbean adventure with O'Brien was also carefully monitoring Digicel's success, but would have to fight to get his share of what he felt he was due. Ossie Kilkenny, the musician-turned-accountant who first encouraged O'Brien to apply for a mobile phone licence in Trinidad, and who invested in the business and did a lot of the groundwork, had now fallen out with the mercurial entrepreneur. They were heading to court for a very public showdown over Kilkenny's claim to his shareholding in Digicel.

In 2005 the case opened in Dublin's High Court and the high-profile clash excited much media interest. Kilkenny claimed he owned just over thirteen per cent of Digicel and was seeking an injunction against his former business partner to prevent him from taking any steps to dilute his stake. He also demanded damages for breach of contract. O'Brien issued a counterclaim, denying parts of Kilkenny's assertions and in turn seeking damages from him arising from their contract. The case was abruptly halted and quietly settled between the two men without disclosing the terms of that settlement.

While the company was privately owned and its shares weren't traded on a stock market where employees could see how they were faring, the ease with which Digicel continued to raise money from investors by issuing bonds was evidence of the company's success. It raised hundreds of millions of dollars in this way, many of the bond issues attracting more investors than was required. The company attracted a lot of attention in the media, and there had been speculation at one point that it was being eyed up by an Egyptian group that was interested in acquiring it once it had rolled out in Trinidad and Haiti. Digicel denied the rumours, insisting that the multinational company was not for sale.

Nevertheless, given this level of enthusiasm, O'Brien started to consider bringing Digicel to trade on the main US stock markets. There was speculation that the company he had founded five years earlier could be worth up to $2.5 billion, valuing O'Brien's eighty per cent stake at around $2 billion.

O'Brien had successfully led Esat's journey to the New York Stock Exchange some years earlier and has said that running a public company was one of the most onerous tasks he had ever taken on. Now, once again, he was planning a potentially lucrative stock market outing and was working with a team of advisers to develop a successful strategy.

In 2006 Colm Delves and a group of experts were told to weigh up the pros and cons of a stock market listing for the company's chairman. Within Digicel this exercise was known as 'Project Courtleigh' after the New Kingston hotel where they had enjoyed so many celebrations.

'The investment banks were saying this was a great time to take the company public,' Delves says. 'A number of private equity firms had also approached us.' As they mulled over the options, O'Brien considered how the aggressive private equity firms would structure their investment in Digicel. 'They would put a small amount of their money in and then they would leverage that up,' adding a large multiple of their investment in the form of debt, Delves explains. 'That got Denis thinking.' Instead of floating the company on the stock market, O'Brien opted to act like a private equity firm, devising a deal that would allow him to increase his shareholding in Digicel while at the same time taking an astonishing amount of money out for himself.

In a complex structure, a new company, Digicel Group Limited, was established in Bermuda to purchase Digicel Limited, the company owned by O'Brien and his fellow investors. The deal, announced in 2007, valued the new company at $2.4 billion.

O'Brien was planning to reinvest $1.1 billion of his $2 billion Digicel shareholding in the new company, which would also borrow another $1.4 billion from investors. And he would pocket $800 million in cash for himself. He had made another massive fortune.

His loyal lieutenants and Digicel's staff were also in line for handsome payouts ranging from between $5 million and $70 million. The company's vice-chairman, Leslie Buckley and O'Brien's father, Denis would each receive the biggest payments. Lucy Gaffney's stake was worth $35 million and Seamus Lynch would get $20 million. P.J. Mara and Greg Sparks both received less than $5 million. Those of Digicel's staff who had share options shared $90 million as part of the transaction. The early crew, such as Hall, Smith and Lisa Lewis, all made a lot of money. It was another incredible deal, creating many more multi-millionaires.

19 Settling Scores

Flush with $800 million in cash from the refinancing of Digicel, Denis O'Brien had plenty of ammunition with which to wage a battle against his enemies. He was ready to settle a few scores.

One person who knows O'Brien's business style suggests that, given his great propensity to leverage up or borrow additional funds to make his fortune go further, his plans for spending his war chest would have been wildly ambitious. '$800 million would be like $800 billion in Denis's hands.' O'Brien has said that entrepreneurs never know when to leave the casino, and he was intent on casting his money far and wide.

O'Brien had moved to Portugal to avoid paying tax on his Esat windfall. He did not want to pay tax on his second fortune either, but this time his tax advisers suggested he should move to Malta.

The tiny Mediterranean island operated some of Europe's most generous tax arrangements for its residents, charging no tax on assets or income earned outside the country. By simply renting or purchasing a property with a certain minimum value, which he would visit at least once a year, Digicel's founder could legitimately avoid capital gains tax.

News of O'Brien's new address appeared in the *Irish Times* some months later and was widely commented upon. One person in particular noted the information and saw an opportunity for a cheeky publicity stunt.

Ryanair's Michael O'Leary had only a passing acquaintance with O'Brien, even though they had a shared history. The low-cost carrier's truculent chief executive had, like O'Brien, served his apprenticeship with Tony Ryan, the airline's founder, stepping into the role a few years after O'Brien's departure.

With Ryanair preparing to launch flights between Dublin and Malta, he decided to use O'Brien's move to his adopted home to generate some publicity. Newspaper advertisements announcing cheap fares on the new route featured a photograph of O'Brien. Above his picture a bubble caption read: 'Just heard 'bout Ryanair's free seat sale! I'm moving to Malta!' The advert encouraged readers to book now for free flights. 'All you pay is taxes.'

According to O'Brien's friends, he went 'ballistic' when he saw the advertisement poking fun at him and once again highlighting his tax exile status. But he would soon have one up on O'Leary in spectacular fashion.

He was still battling with the Tribunal of Inquiry and had become so frustrated by the process that he told a group of business people in Dublin early one morning in 2006 that he wished he had never won Ireland's second mobile phone licence. Ten years after he had celebrated that great victory, the forty-eight-year-old telecoms billionaire was still haunted by allegations that the licence had been awarded corruptly.

It was taking a great toll on both him and his family and to date had cost him almost €8 million in legal fees and expenses. He had unsuccessfully challenged the Tribunal's right to examine some of his personal dealings, including the purchase of Doncaster Rovers, but had lost each time. These challenges had served only to lengthen the inquiry and add to his expense, as he also had to pick up the Tribunal's legal costs.

Commentators watching the years of often mind-numbing proceedings were now suggesting that the Tribunal's findings might prove disastrous for O'Brien. *Irish Independent* columnist Sam Smyth suggested that if Justice Michael Moriarty chose not to accept O'Brien's and Lowry's sworn evidence that there was no impropriety surrounding the awarding of the mobile phone licence, it could precipitate the biggest corporate and political scandal in Ireland's history.

Smyth, one of those accused by O'Brien of deliberately working to damage him as part of a wider campaign within the Independent News and Media stable of newspapers, insists that his views about the

Tribunal's likely outcome are solely based on the evidence it has gathered, and that there was no agenda on Tony O'Reilly's part to discredit O'Brien through his media group. If there was, he was unaware of it. 'I reported on the Tribunal as fairly and objectively as I could,' he says, explaining his consistently harsh assessment of O'Brien's dealings with Lowry. 'And as someone with some knowledge and experience of it, I have followed a line that was going in one direction. And eventually others agreed with me.

'If a team of very highly paid and skilful lawyers and one of the most respected judges on the bench are coming to the same conclusion I am, then I think that is where it will probably end up,' he continues. 'I never had any reason to change my mind on that and I don't see how anyone can come to any other conclusion based on the evidence.'

Thanks both to what people had informally told him and to his own dealings with the tycoon's media handlers over the years, Smyth was well aware of O'Brien's attitude towards him. The pair have never met socially, even though they share many mutual acquaintances, but Smyth recalls a brief encounter with O'Brien in a Dublin coffee shop. As Smyth waited for a table, O'Brien, who was just leaving, rushed past him 'very brusquely', toppling the startled journalist who fell back on some chairs. 'I can't say he did it deliberately but normally people would say sorry if something like that happened,' he says.

Occasionally his columns hit a nerve with O'Brien that was immediately communicated to the columnist by his media advisers. Eileen Gleeson, who played that role for many years before relinquishing it some time after Esat's sale to British Telecom, says the Tribunal and the reporting of its evidence has always been upsetting for O'Brien. 'It really bothers him that he is seen to have done something wrong, which he genuinely truly believes that he didn't.'

O'Brien is annoyed that people have questioned his motives, according to Gleeson. 'Not in a "how dare you" way, but he just can't understand how people can't get it – that the licence award was done fairly and squarely by the civil servants.

'People are never going to understand the personality of the guy. He is a unique character. If he was going to meet Michael Lowry or was going to do whatever he wanted to do – as in non-corrupt things – he wouldn't be thinking: This might get me into trouble. He is not built like that. He doesn't really care. He just does the right thing or the fair thing for people, and that is the hard thing for him to understand.'

As details of the convoluted money trail came to public attention, they often created 'a sideshow', Gleeson says, one that just added to O'Brien's hurt. 'People jumped to conclusions because they didn't have the time or interest to go into the detail. People were only interested in the top line. If you ask people what the Tribunal is about they would say that Denis paid off Michael Lowry for the licence. That is one sentence out of ten years of investigations and hearings. That's the most frustrating part for him.'

According to his close friend and lawyer, Paul Meagher, O'Brien simply doesn't trust the Tribunal's workings. 'He doesn't trust the process. He doesn't trust anybody in it and in particular he has absolutely no time for lawyers, including myself. He holds them in contempt at this stage and thinks we are a self-serving profession. He just thinks the whole thing is a sham.'

He is fearful of the Tribunal's findings, Meagher says. 'Has he told me that he is fearful? No he hasn't, but wouldn't anybody be? He thinks the Tribunal is determined to down him no matter what he does. That would be devastating for him in terms of what he has achieved, his good name and reputation and for his family.'

Former journalist James Morrissey stepped in to handle O'Brien's dealings with the media after Gleeson's departure and took Smyth to task about his reporting of some of Denis O'Brien senior's testimony to the inquiry. Noting their striking resemblance, Smyth had said Denis senior could have been a 'digitally aged' photograph of his son when he took the witness stand at Dublin Castle. And their personalities, he suggested, were also similar: 'At 76 years old, the old block is as chippy as Denis jnr.'

'Morrissey told me Denis didn't like it and thought it was very ageist,' Smyth says. The 'ageist' criticism was particularly amusing to him, because by now O'Brien was himself embroiled in a battle with another feisty septuagenarian whom he believed had held on to the reins of power for too long.

*

Tony O'Reilly, having received a knighthood from the Queen in 2001, was now known as Sir Anthony. The knight of the realm had only recently disengaged from a bidding war with O'Brien for Irish mobile phone company Meteor, a struggle won by eircom, the company O'Reilly chaired.

O'Brien had already dusted himself down and was preparing for his next joust with Sir Anthony.

His first reaction to the congratulatory note sent by O'Reilly's son Gavin after the successful staging of the Special Olympic World Games in 2003, he said, had been to 'throw it in the bin'. Subsequently he sent a strongly-worded letter to Gavin in reply: 'As far as I'm concerned, Independent News and Media have spent the last seven years trying to destroy my reputation. Some of the coverage of my affairs, both business and personal, in the *Sunday Tribune*, *Sunday Independent*, *Irish Independent* and *Evening Herald* have caused hurt and enormous damage to my reputation, not to mention the emotional distress suffered by my wife, Catherine, and my family. I very much doubt whether you or any member of your family could have survived a similar onslaught. Control of the media brings privileges and responsibilities.

'While I am waiting for the appropriate time to rectify the damage, I note and appreciate your gesture and in a spirit of goodwill I am willing to meet you to see whether we share any common ground.'

Three years on, that time had come. O'Brien stunned everyone when, just two weeks into 2006, he spent a staggering €57 million buying a three per cent stake in the company run and partly owned by his long-standing business rival. Despite his love of military-style covert operations, the telecoms entrepreneur was happy to let everyone know he was the proud owner of a small slice of Sir Anthony's empire.

There had been earlier signs of O'Brien's ambition to become a media mogul. Just like other wealthy figures before him, he had been aware for some time that owning a slice of the fourth estate would yield great power and afford plenty of opportunities to enhance his image and reputation. In 1995 he had attempted to buy the Irish Press group, a long-established company that published the *Irish Press*,

Evening Press and *Sunday Press* newspapers. Despite its long tradition – the group was owned by the family of one of the Irish Republic's founders, Eamon de Valera – by June 1995 the group was ailing and close to collapse.

In a last-ditch effort to save it, a group of journalists convinced the High Court to appoint an interim examiner to keep its creditors at bay for a few days in the hope of finding a buyer. Various business figures were identified as potential investors and one young entrepreneur was keen to meet the staff who were desperately trying to fend off liquidation.

O'Brien met Colm Rapple and Chris Dooley, who were leading the rescue efforts, to explore his chances of becoming a press baron. The discussions were fruitless and the newspaper group folded within days. It is questionable, given Esat Telecom's own financial troubles, whether he could have raised the money to save the paper, but it signalled his interest in maybe one day owning a newspaper and wielding the power associated with this ultimate trophy asset.

There were also rumours in 2001 that O'Brien had expressed an interest in purchasing the *Irish Times* newspaper, which was at the time in the midst of a serious financial crisis, although his proposal never progressed to any extent.

Now he had a shareholding in Independent News and Media. Purchased in his own name rather than by an investment company set up to mask his involvement – a practice often favoured by investors – his stake was below the level at which a formal announcement to the Irish Stock Exchange was required. He could have kept the purchase under wraps, but he had chosen to make it public. Indeed his spokesman, James Morrissey, suggested that O'Brien would be an enthusiastic supporter of the group and was in the market for even more of its shares.

Friends and close colleagues who knew of O'Brien's distress at some of the stories and comments that appeared in the group's stable of newspapers were stunned, if intrigued, by the move. It was something he had never discussed or mooted with most of them beforehand. Paul Meagher says he was shocked by O'Brien's tentative move and was fearful it might be the start of another all-out war between the two business rivals.

Gavin O'Reilly had received quite a few letters from O'Brien over the years, but nothing like this. 'I was genuinely surprised. I didn't have to write a letter to Denis and I don't do these things lightly, but I genuinely thought that the Special Olympics had been a great tribute to him and to Ireland and I was of course happy to be there. So I sat down and penned the letter,' he says. 'You get a response like that and you know it is unfortunate but I didn't do anything with it. I just put it in the drawer and said, "That's it, there isn't much I can do." It says more about him than me to be honest.'

O'Brien had written to O'Reilly before to complain about stories that had appeared in the group's various newspapers, mainly concerning the Tribunal. 'On occasion he would write to me about what some of our journalists were writing about. I know nobody wants to believe it but journalists write what journalists want to write. They don't pick up the phone and say, "Gavin, is it all right for me to write about something?" People fail to realise that Tribunal reporting is pretty consistent in the *Irish Times*, the *Independent* and the *Examiner*. Now some of the commentators may take a different angle but the Tribunal is a public forum, a truth forum, and journalists report what they hear. Stories come up and they get reported. The accusation that has been inferred that INM has prosecuted a campaign against Denis or any of his interests is a complete fallacy.'

According to O'Reilly, O'Brien is no different to other successful figures who get upset when they read unflattering stories about themselves in the paper. 'My family has been in the public eye all of my life. You have got to take the good with the bad.' The booming Celtic Tiger economy that fostered swathes of swaggering business figures had also produced a powerful group who preciously guarded their profile. A new generation who had generated wealth never before seen in Ireland, they were growing ever more powerful. 'It's been an interesting time,' says O'Reilly. 'Celebrity chief executives and chairmen courted the press enormously on the way up and took great offence when the press took a less than positive view of them. I am not talking about Denis, but this sensitivity tends to be more prominent in Ireland. Here it's almost like Dr Jekyll and Mr Hyde. If it's in a foreign paper it is dismissed as being "anti-Irish", but maybe Ireland is so small it is a particular issue for people here and it really hurts when they have to read it.'

O'Reilly claims not to have paid a great deal of attention to O'Brien's initial share purchase. He noted that the telecoms billionaire wanted the whole world to know he was an investor but insists that the O'Reillys had no sense this might be the start of a takeover bid for the group. 'We didn't really hear anything from him until 2007.'

The news caused much consternation elsewhere, however. Stockbrokers scratched their heads and asked what O'Brien was up to now, while the media speculated about his motives. Was it the start of a battle for control of the group Sir Anthony had led for decades or was it just mischief-making on a grand scale?

Irish Times business editor John McManus suggested in his newspaper column that O'Brien had been reading von Clausewitz's treatise *On War*, which advocates the use of surprise to sow confusion among your enemies as to your real intentions. And while there was no shortage of reasons why O'Brien might spend almost €57 million just to annoy O'Reilly, such an analysis painted him as 'some sort of impetuous madman' hell-bent on revenge. 'This does not really square with what we know of him, although he is without a doubt hot-blooded.'

The alternative – that O'Brien was having a tilt at gaining control of the company – was also hard to digest, continued McManus. 'O'Reilly's position at IN&M is thought to be impregnable. He controls twenty-eight per cent of the group and has had thirty-three years in which to organise a board, the loyalty of which is unquestioned.' There was no doubt that O'Brien could raise the money needed to buy the company, but he would have to destabilise it first, to force its shareholders to consider another offer.

'If O'Brien's intention is to build a stake in IN&M of sufficient size that he can force it to put itself on the block, then he can look forward to the fight of his life,' wrote McManus. A more likely scenario, he suggested, was that O'Brien was positioning himself to benefit from future events, including a bid for the company by another media group. 'Perhaps O'Brien is happy to wait,' he concluded, 'and if he causes his old enemy a few sleepless nights into the bargain, all the better.'

Paul Meagher says he can't honestly say whether he believes O'Brien's assault on Independent News and Media is simply a cold-hearted business decision or not. 'I have never discussed its merits with Denis. It is blindingly obvious they did untold damage to his reputation. I would have my own views on the whole thing from start to finish.'

By this time, O'Brien had fallen out with another of his close friends, Paul Connolly. The man who had worked with O'Brien for many years raising money for his various business ventures says they had a row in Jamaica in September 2005 that 'built up' over a couple of things. 'I am quiet and headstrong in a different way. He would be more outspoken,' he explains. 'We just bounced off each other.' The pair didn't speak to each other for two years, causing tension and strain within O'Brien's gang.

Commenting on O'Brien's assault on the Independent group, Connolly says the telecoms tycoon had previously talked to him many times about investing in the company, but that he would have urged caution. 'I wasn't around to stop him but he would have gone ahead anyway. David Sykes would have done a lot of the share trading. Denis would have been making that decision himself. He likes the media sector.'

O'Brien was buying into a successful international media group that was making about €250 million a year. Its shares were rapidly rising in value in the wake of his buying spree, rising to highs of more than €3.60, valuing the group at €2.8 billion. It was also a company that traditionally rewarded its shareholders very handsomely with large dividends. O'Brien was looking forward to reaping the rewards of his investment.

While engaged in taking a stake in Ireland's biggest media group, O'Brien was also active in other areas. First he was gearing up to rapidly expand his radio empire. As he complained about the damage to his reputation inflicted by certain sections of the Irish media, he seemed determined to control more and more of it.

Having acquired new stations in Bulgaria, the Czech Republic,

Estonia, Finland and Hungary, the Communicorp group now consisted of almost forty radio stations in Eastern Europe and Ireland. Unlike O'Brien's telecoms businesses, his radio empire was making a loss; at the end of 2005 the group had racked up losses of €22 million and its day-to-day operations lost €6.6 million that year. Yet O'Brien was primed to invest more and more of his wealth in building the company. His next goal in Ireland was to control a national radio station as well as his growing number of local stations.

He had controversially gained control of Dublin news and current affairs station Newstalk, having won a power struggle with the other shareholders. The deal was criticised by the Competition Authority, which concluded that Communicorp had broken the law in the way it had wrested control, but the company would face no penalty. The Authority had 'insufficient evidence' to seek a criminal penalty, it said; it was not apparent that anyone involved had 'knowingly and wilfully' broken the law. Once again O'Brien had pushed the boundaries and achieved his objective. He had persuaded the broadcasting authority to allow it to extend its reach and let Newstalk become a national broadcaster in an ambitious plan to go head-to-head with RTÉ's main radio channel.

So far O'Brien and other shareholders had invested €14 million in the Dublin radio station and he said it would need another €6.2 million to broadcast its programmes nationwide. The station would struggle for years to attract a significant audience and burn up more and more of O'Brien's cash.

And when British group emap put three of its Irish radio stations on the market, Communicorp was immediately keen to buy them. It was an attractive lot that included nationwide station Today FM, Donegal-based local station Highland Radio and 98FM's old rival in Dublin, FM104. If Communicorp bought these stations O'Brien would control two national radio stations in Ireland as well as the two biggest local stations in Dublin.

Others in the radio sector were also chasing these attractive stations and a fierce bidding war erupted. However, in July 2007 Communicorp's €200 million bid trumped them all, rapidly increasing O'Brien's control over Ireland's radio market.

The purchase would attract the scrutiny of Ireland's Broadcasting

Commission, which forced O'Brien to sell the Dublin station FM104 to dilute his influence in the capital. Within a year the station was sold to UTV for €52 million, while he also disposed of Highland Radio for another €10 million. But he held on to the nationwide radio station he had wanted all along, Today FM, although in total the acquisition of his second nationwide station cost him €138 million.

And despite his first unsuccessful attempt to create a television channel in the 1980s, his company was preparing to apply for a licence to operate a new digital channel being offered by the Irish government.

Outside his media interests O'Brien was investing in a Chinese jobs website and also emerged as a shareholder in the Irish airline, Aer Lingus. With this investment he intended to use his financial muscle to thwart Michael O'Leary's ambitions for Ryanair to take over the nation's flag carrier.

The budget airline made an audacious swoop to buy a stake in Aer Lingus immediately after it began trading on the Irish Stock Exchange in 2006. Ahead of the flotation there had been much speculation about another airline becoming a major shareholder in the former State-owned airline, but no one considered it would be Ryanair.

O'Leary's blatant antipathy towards trade unions and his constant criticism of the airline which, like Telecom Éireann with Esat, had tried everything to prevent Ryanair's take-off in previous decades, made them unlikely bedfellows. If O'Leary got his way, Ryanair would control many of the major routes out of Ireland, a prospect that was frightening for many Irish people, given the airline's aggressive business style and its unique customer service concepts.

A group of Aer Lingus pilots were so concerned by the prospect of having one day to work for Ryanair's boss that they raided their own pension funds to build up a blocking stake in the airline. Their small shareholding, they hoped, could keep Ryanair at bay for the time being.

They were heartened to find a new ally keen to wade into the battle, but were surprised to find themselves aligned with Denis O'Brien, a man who shared much of Michael O'Leary's business style and antipathy towards trade unions. Now the man who had made a fortune by attacking monopolies was spending €30 million buying more than two per cent of Aer Lingus, weighing in to add his shares to the Irish government's more than twenty per cent stake and that of the pilots to derail – at least for now – O'Leary's plan to control Aer Lingus.

Speaking about his investment at a conference in December 2006, O'Brien pledged to resist O'Leary's efforts to control Aer Lingus. Describing Ryanair as the 'evil blue', he said it was important for Ireland to maintain the two airlines. Although he had long since stopped using commercial flights, he felt himself able to comment: 'I think Ryanair is a terrific product, but I also think Aer Lingus has a terrific product.'

It was an unusual investment for O'Brien. Given his success at Esat and Digifone, backing O'Leary's efforts at Ryanair should have come more naturally to him. It was the attacker brand that took on the establishment and was winning. Instead O'Brien was protecting the former monopoly from Ryanair's assault.

This time, he explained, he was weighing into the battle to prevent Ryanair becoming a monopoly in Ireland. As the owner of a large leisure complex in Portugal, he had a vested interest in ensuring that Irish people could easily fly to the Algarve at competitive prices. In his view this was best maintained by the operation of two Irish airlines.

Was it a coincidence that O'Brien had come to the aid of Aer Lingus so soon after Ryanair's cheeky advertisement mocking his tax exile status in Malta? Whatever his reasons, in the months and years ahead, as Ryanair launched a series of takeover bids, O'Brien aligned himself closely with Aer Lingus, supporting its fight against a common enemy at every turn. And his loyal lieutenant Leslie Buckley would soon take a seat in the airline's boardroom, bringing his influence to bear on its future direction.

All the while O'Brien was spending more and more money increasing his shareholding in Independent News and Media and the speculation about his intentions heightened. If he mounted a successful bid, he could soon own four of Ireland's national newspapers, two national and a number of local radio stations as well as a plethora of local newspapers. Some commentators and many journalists working in the Irish media began to ponder about O'Brien as Ireland's new media tsar. If he was using his wealth to settle scores with the likes of Sir Anthony O'Reilly and Michael O'Leary, how might he use his potentially huge media empire in the future?

In O'Brien's kingdom, journalists are viewed as the lowliest in the pecking order; the interests of advertisers and the stations' marketing team, according to those who have worked there, are always the top priority. And just as he micro-managed Digicel, O'Brien's attention to the day-to-day operation of his radio empire stunned some of his employees.

Broadcaster Eamon Dunphy, former host of Newstalk's flagship breakfast show, worked at various times for both Sir Anthony and O'Brien, and wrote a lengthy piece in the *Irish Times* comparing his experience of the two. He describes his time working for O'Brien as 'traumatic'. 'As editor and presenter of *The Breakfast Show*, I operated in the constant shadow of a man with strong opinions about the content of the programme. His name was Denis. O'Brien's misgivings were not conveyed in person.' O'Brien's people, Dunphy claimed, let him know when he wasn't happy with some of the contributors invited on to the show to talk about current stories in fields as diverse as the war in Iraq and business events in Ireland. 'Although, with a small team of gifted and committed young journalists, we increased audience share exponentially, our view of what *The Breakfast Show* should be was at odds with the proprietor's. The hassle, though low-level, was constant and utterly demoralising.'

Newstalk executives finally 'lost patience' with Dunphy over his stand on a decision to increase the price charged to listeners to text the show, after Dunphy made comments about the decision on air. 'I told our listeners what was going on and expressed disapproval. All hell broke loose. "What do you think you're doing?" the managers wailed when I came out of the studio. "Journalism," I replied.' The new charge was being introduced to generate much-needed money for the perennially loss-making station. Dunphy says he prepared to pack his bags and was soon followed by all bar one of the show's team. 'O'Brien didn't care,' he said.

O'Reilly, on the other hand, was an 'old-style' media baron, who understood the importance of a free press. Dunphy, whose tenure at the O'Reilly-owned *Sunday Independent* also ended acrimoniously, paid tribute to Sir Anthony's continuing support for the campaigning journalism at the loss-making London *Independent* despite his opposing views to some of the major stories it campaigned on, most notably the invasion of Iraq: 'Tony O'Reilly was in favour of the invasion of Iraq. The London *Independent* has vigorously opposed the invasion.'

Those who cared about freedom of the press, said Dunphy, should root for O'Reilly over O'Brien in the power struggle at INM. 'Denis O'Brien's capacity to absorb the pain, much less the responsibility that comes with media ownership, is a matter of grave concern as his bid to take control of INM reaches its decisive phase. As a journalist and a citizen, I'm with the old-style mogul.'

Newstalk's chief executive, Elaine Geraghty, who had started out as a presenter on 98FM's breakfast show, wrote to the paper to reject Dunphy's claims. His departure had been more to do with differences over his contract with the station, she suggested, insisting that his comments about O'Brien's interference with the show's content were wrong. 'At no time did Eamon Dunphy ever bring to my attention – or indeed to anyone else in the station – any concerns in this regard. A core objective at Newstalk is to be objective, balanced and fair and to avoid the slandering or libelling of individuals,' she wrote. 'The notion that Eamon Dunphy would find himself in the constant shadow of anyone stretches the imagination, even one as fertile as his.'

Despite his misgivings about working for O'Brien, Dunphy would return to host a show on Newstalk in 2010. He was switching his allegiance to the new media baron.

Others who have worked for O'Brien's radio stations say he continues to embrace the model that worked so successfully from the start at 98FM. He hires very young and inexperienced staff who work extremely hard and take on great responsibility in an environment where they are expected to broadcast with limited resources.

The journalists are expected to attend company events for advertisers and they are always aware of O'Brien's presence at the station. Some say the Communicorp boss regularly make his views known on commentators and guests in fields ranging from business to sport. And he and Lucy Gaffney will always note how visible the stations' branded microphones are at high-profile press events. If they can't see them, the station boss will know about it and his displeasure will be firmly communicated to his staff. Again, there is a high degree of micro-management that suits some people but that others who have worked for the group find oppressive.

According to Michael Foley, formerly media correspondent of the *Irish Times* and now a lecturer in journalism at the Dublin Institute of Technology, O'Reilly and O'Brien have opposing views on the media. Sir Anthony has a great love for the sector, says Foley, and is steeped in the old Fleet Street newspaper tradition that valued journalism. O'Brien by comparison, has no such feelings towards the sector.

And while O'Brien's first business success was in the media, Foley points out, it is interesting to note that he has never selected his top management team from within the ranks of the journalists he has employed. 'Denis has never shown huge affection for journalists in his own media outlets and it was the regulator, the Broadcasting Commission, that forced him to staff up his news operations. People such as Conor Lenihan got on by leaving journalism and Conor had other connections.'

Given O'Brien's total focus on the bottom line, Foley considers the prospect of him becoming the most powerful man in the Irish media with some trepidation. That, however, was exactly what O'Brien intended to do.

20 Clubbing Baby Seals

However the O'Reillys and the fourth estate viewed the aspiring new media king, Denis O'Brien was ready to do battle to win that crown. By now he had spent close to €100 million acquiring almost nine per cent of Independent News and Media and his wallet was still open. No one was quite sure if he had a strategy other than to wrest control of the company from Sir Anthony's grip. But he was prepared to wage his fortune to do it.

'The campaign started in 2007, and I will call it a campaign,' says Gavin O'Reilly, INM's chief executive. 'The unfortunate thing about it was that it didn't start with direct dialogue with the company, but I suppose that was part of the "shock and awe" tactic.'

O'Brien refused to talk publicly about his intentions regarding INM and whether he was preparing to mount an outright bid for the company. In an interview with the *Daily Telegraph*, he suggested his investment was part of his expansion within the media sector: 'I'm in the media business. I normally buy things I understand.'

He needed little prompting to talk about his concerns about Sir Anthony's stewardship of the company he was investing in. He wanted a regime change. The twenty-strong board was, in his view, ridiculous and he objected to the presence of so many O'Reillys. 'It's one of the poor examples of a plc,' he explained. 'It's dominated by one person. What I'm trying to do is force change – put proper governance in. The company can do a lot better with a proper board.'

The time had come, in his view, for Sir Anthony to step down. In O'Brien's parlance, O'Reilly was no longer the man to drive the bus. 'It's time for Tony to step aside, let somebody else lead the board,' he said in interviews in the international press. 'The board is really too old; they don't understand the internet age.'

A company spokesman described O'Brien's attack on Sir Anthony and the board as 'bizarre'. Independent News and Media, he said, 'is one of the top performing media stocks worldwide, as Mr O'Brien is well aware'.

Gavin O'Reilly says he was shocked by O'Brien's highly personalised attacks on his father. 'It was unwarranted. Some people have long careers, my father is one of them and there are good and bad aspects to that. People can be bitchy about Tony O'Reilly, his failings, his successes or whatever, but Denis's attack did seem to be unnecessarily personal. I kept looking at this and saying, What the hell has this got to do with our business?'

As O'Brien mopped up INM shares, he renewed his friendship with Paul Connolly. Paul Meagher, a close friend of both men, had been trying to broker a truce for some time between the two friends and was finally successful. 'I started back in September 2007, the day his fourth child Isobel was born,' says Connolly. 'Denis said "I'm in the *Indo*, I need you to have a look at it," and we started on it.'

Serious disagreements with friends are often down to O'Brien's perception that they have been in some way disloyal to him. Making up with O'Brien depends on the extent of your perceived disloyalty and finding the right intermediary to repair the situation. 'It all depends on where his head is and who is rooting for you,' says Connolly. Some were not so fortunate. But Connolly, despite having reservations about his friend's assault on INM, was firmly back in O'Brien's cabal.

While INM had been trading successfully when O'Brien first appeared as a shareholder, its fortunes were now on the wane. The shares were trading at €3 at the start of 2007, valuing the group at €2.3 billion. INM shares had been a stellar performer for investors, almost doubling over the previous five years. Over the next six months, though, the shares fell by more than twenty-six per cent and seemed poised for further falls amid concerns about the future of newspapers globally.

The collapsing share price meant that O'Brien was nursing a hefty financial loss on his investment. But that didn't stop him from buying even more shares. As the price fell, he poured further millions into the stock, increasing his stake at ever cheaper prices. Observers began to re-evaluate his prospects of mounting a bid for the company.

Connolly says O'Brien would constantly 'give out about' Sir Anthony. 'Hate is not too strong a word to describe it.' The barrage of negative coverage from the O'Reilly-led newspaper group, he says, had deeply hurt his friend and his family: 'He felt it was coming from Tony O'Reilly. Journalists know what keeps the boss happy. They know the way the stable is being run.'

As part of a plan to loosen Sir Anthony's grip on the company he had built over more than three decades, O'Brien commissioned research to support his claim that O'Reilly and the board were surplus to requirements. He asked Dr Stephen Davis of the Yale School of Management and Davis Global Advisors to examine how well the company's boardroom lived up to the guidelines followed by the best companies to ensure the chairman and directors were governing the group effectively.

Davis's report endorsed many of O'Brien's concerns, questioning the close relationships between the majority of the group's nineteen board members and the chief executive. The board's composition was its 'Achilles heel', Davis suggested, and left the organisation at risk of being branded a 'crony' firm that existed to serve Sir Anthony.

O'Reilly was supported in the company and in the boardroom by his three sons, the report noted. Gavin was his second-in-command at INM, acting as chief operating officer, while Tony junior and Cameron were both directors. And almost all of the other board members, Davis stated, had 'close business links' with Sir Anthony. The profile of INM's board members reflected 'a dated style of corporate governance' that appeared out of step with the company's 'changing 21st-century business ambitions'. In Davis's view, INM's corporate governance practices fell well short of those adopted by its peers; unless resolved, these issues could only serve to depress the share price even further.

O'Brien's spokesman, James Morrissey, distributed the report to the Irish and international media, who felt inspired to create headlines like 'Tony's cronies' to sum up its findings. Sir Anthony's camp, which like O'Brien was always quick to dispatch its media handlers to convey its displeasure forcefully about unflattering stories published in media rivals, was angry. It demanded an apology and threatened to issue court proceedings for defamation. The criticism was unwarranted, it insisted. It was a partisan report paid for by a disgruntled shareholder with an unknown agenda.

Over the following months O'Brien, the consummate letter writer, bombarded the company with correspondence, questioning everything from Sir Anthony's expenses to his use of the company jet. He demanded details of O'Reilly's total pay package: 'This should include salary, bonuses, share options, pensions, insurance, transport, expenses, entertainment, i.e. any and all payments under whatever heading, made to him or on his behalf.' Did INM, or any of its subsidiaries or associated companies, pay any staff or other costs, expenses or allowances related to O'Reilly's private residences at Fitzwilliam Square, Dublin; Castlemartin, Co. Kildare; Lyford Cay, Bahamas; and any other private residence owned by the chief executive? O'Brien was also interested in the cost of any corporate events hosted by Sir Anthony and other executives at their various homes and whether these were paid for by the company. These were all 'serious matters', he said.

Gavin O'Reilly dealt with the correspondence personally, drafting each letter of reply to O'Brien himself. Regarding the company jet, just as O'Brien had grown used to private aircraft, Sir Anthony used INM's plane at all times for 'security reasons', the company explained.

But O'Brien had even more queries. In further letters, he called for the sale of some of the group's loss-making ventures, singling out the London-based *Independent* newspaper. In yet another letter, the group's agitated shareholder asked for details on INM's charitable donations in the last five years. To what extent had the media group made donations to buildings named after Sir Anthony or his parents, he enquired. None, the company replied.

It was a highly personal attack, putting Sir Anthony under a degree of scrutiny he had never before endured during his more than thirty years at INM. A company spokesman said it was 'at a loss as to the provenance and nature' of such questions, as all relevant information was disclosed in its accounts.

At the company's annual general meeting Sir Anthony and his fellow directors mounted a strong defence as O'Brien asked shareholders not to support their re-election. He wouldn't be attending those meetings himself, but dispatched his representatives to raise his concerns. But it made no impact on the shareholders. O'Brien's motions received virtually no support. His attack failed to inflict any damage in the boardroom, for now.

Sir Anthony signalled that, as a veteran corporate warrior, he was taking O'Brien's attacks in his stride. 'You have to realise that I was for twenty-five years the president of the H.J. Heinz company and in America the whole issue of dissident shareholders is a constant theme in almost every board that I've ever been on,' he said. 'And I've been on the board of Mobil Oil and Bankers' Trust and the *Washington Post* and the H.J. Heinz company, so I am somewhat a veteran of the wars in terms of dissident shareholders.' He regarded all such shareholders as having a particular agenda of their own. He wasn't sure just what O'Brien had in mind.

Gavin O'Reilly, meanwhile, went on the attack on his father's behalf. 'It's an easy target to look at myself and my two brothers. I find it slightly outrageous that this shareholder would seek to impugn my father who has essentially created this company,' he said. 'He took a small company back in 1973 and turned it into one of the first-class media companies in the world. There isn't anything as far as I'm concerned in Mr O'Brien's history in terms of running media that makes me feel he's well qualified to make those comments.'

The O'Reillys had won the battle so far. O'Brien, however, was still building his stake in the company and publicly criticising its board and management. They knew they should prepare for a hostile bid and Sir Anthony led the offensive to stop O'Brien causing further mayhem.

The company quickly started buying back some of its own shares, spending more than €120 million to keep its enemy at bay. There was even speculation that O'Reilly might lead a bid to delist the company from the Irish stock market and run it as a private company, free from attack from hostile investors.

*

By mid-2008 O'Brien's stake had swelled to twenty-five per cent, just a few per cent below Sir Anthony's twenty-eight. In less than two years he had ploughed more than €500 million into his rival's company.

The sheer scale of this investment, compared with money he was ploughing into Digicel at the time, is astonishing. He had invested less than $400 million in building Digicel's network in Jamaica since the company's launch in 2001. And this was a rapidly expanding sector with huge growth potential. The rationale for pouring a fortune into Independent News and Media, on the other hand, at a time when the newspaper sector in particular was struggling to survive, is unclear – if not to settle a score with Sir Anthony. As everyone watched the battle develop it was clear that the stakes were high, with both sides prepared to risk their fortunes on a victory.

As he was now virtually neck-and-neck with O'Reilly in his shareholding in the company, O'Brien was becoming increasingly powerful. He could legitimately interfere and block initiatives backed by Sir Anthony and his board of directors, and he intended to do that persistently.

Despite his huge financial loss on the investment O'Brien was talkative about it, often joking to friends and acquaintances about the battle. He liked to say he had cornered the market in INM shares, boasting that investors were pledging to sell their shares to him instead of to the O'Reilly camp. Battling with the O'Reillys, he was fond of saying, was 'like clubbing baby seals'. He was clearly enjoying their discomfort. 'He just loves a good scrap,' one associate laughs. 'He'd thrive on that.'

But was it bravado? It was a bleak situation for him. His €500 million was now worth only about €50 million as the share price dropped lower and lower, while he would have to plough even more of the money he was borrowing to fund the investment into the company if he intended to mount an outright takeover bid.

In 2008 the *Sunday Times* Rich List estimated O'Brien's personal fortune at more than €2 billion, well ahead of Sir Anthony's. But he was highly leveraged. While he had the much-publicised $800 million in cash from the Digicel deal, he was personally liable for $1.4 billion of the restructured company's debts. And although Digicel was winning new customers and boosting its revenues, the company had so far invested more than $3 billion rolling out its network across the region, a heavy weight on its bottom line. In October 2008 the Digicel group reported operating profits of $505 million and a net loss of over $74 million for that year, with accumulated losses of €1.2 billion. O'Brien had lost most of his €500 million investment in INM, his radio company was making a loss and a string of other sizeable investments showed mixed results.

Those who know Sir Anthony say he was 'energised' by the conflict and was using his extensive international contacts and guile to guard his prized empire. His lieutenants were regularly summoned to assess their progress and plan their next strike. During late-night discussions at Sir Anthony's elegant homes, his coterie openly wondered just how much money O'Brien actually had or could get his hands on.

The O'Reilly family's own finances had taken a severe battering. Together with his brother-in-law, Greek shipping magnate Peter Goulandris, Sir Anthony and his family had poured hundreds of millions into ailing crystal and chinaware group Waterford Wedgwood, of which they were major shareholders. It was eating up much of the Independent chief's spare resources, and still he had to find the money to fend off his bitter foe. O'Reilly family members have privately described O'Brien as 'the worst' adversary they have ever encountered. It was now a deeply personal conflict.

As part of their fight back, the O'Reillys and their advisers trawled through O'Brien's businesses and investments and drew up a list of eighteen questions that challenged his suitability as the future owner of INM, based on his business credentials. In a one-page document handed to journalists they asked: 'What experience does Mr O'Brien have of ever managing a broad-based and inter-nationally diversified media group with the complexities and sophistication that INM demands? What experience, if any, does Mr O'Brien have in publishing – the core competency of INM?' And could he point to any business with which he had been associated that had delivered sustained shareholder returns at the level enjoyed by INM shareholders in the past thirty years? 'Isn't it a fact that Mr O'Brien has only ever run one public company in his life – Esat Telecom?'

They also highlighted O'Brien's past business failures, mentioning his doomed foray into home shopping television and his more recent decision to dismantle the ePower electricity company, which had spent millions trying to break into Ireland's electricity supply businesses without making any significant inroads. And as for his own media empire, the INM document noted, his radio group, Communicorp, was loss-making. It also attempted to discredit the true value of Digicel, producing market data that showed, it suggested, rapidly declining revenues at O'Brien's Caribbean telecoms company.

Had Digicel's operations ever made a profit, the O'Reilly camp asked. 'Aren't these facts pertinent to INM shareholders, as Mr O'Brien has most recently been extolling the virtue of his investments in locations such as Haiti, while lecturing INM on why it should get rid of its consistently strong performing investments in South Africa and other markets?'

While O'Brien was the most prominent buyer of INM shares, another rich telecoms legend was also taking an interest in the Irish media company. Carlos Slim, the Mexican businessman described by *Forbes* magazine as the world's richest person was also splashing out on the shares. The founder of Mexico's biggest fixed-line phone business, Telmex, and mobile phone operator America Movil, added another dimension to the battle by purchasing one per cent of the Irish-based newspaper group.

Slim's America Movil is a powerful rival for O'Brien's Digicel in the Caribbean and Central America, where they both fight fiercely to control the mobile phone markets. It was an interesting twist in the dispute and left observers wondering whether Slim was providing some support to Sir Anthony against their joint enemy, or whether perhaps he was acquiring a blocking stake that he might trade with O'Brien in the future as part of a deal between their two companies.

O'Brien publicly welcomed Slim to the company and paid generous tribute to his new rival. 'He is probably the world's foremost telecoms entrepreneur and his company adheres to the highest levels of corporate governance,' he said. 'I hope Carlos Slim will support the move for change at Independent News and Media and an improvement in corporate governance.'

Forbes was also focusing on O'Brien. With his plans to continue to expand aggressively from almost thirty to forty-five countries within the next couple of years, he was keen to raise his profile in the United States, where he was eying up opportunities for Digicel to compete. He appeared on the magazine's cover in July 2008 with a special report on his business exploits inside. He was the daring entrepreneur who had made a fortune by investing where others feared to tread. Despite coups, corruption and kidnappings, said the report, the mobile phone maverick kept pouring money into the world's poorest, most violent countries. O'Brien told *Forbes* he has never been asked for a bribe, or ever greased any palms as he built his empire. 'His bet: Give phones to the masses and they'll fight your enemies for you,' wrote its author, Bernard Condon.

The Irish businessman had been steadily adding a new list of prime ministers to his diplomatic tours as he chased new licences and rolled out his business in Central America. The 'silver chicken' regularly touched down in Panama, Honduras, Costa Rica and Nicaragua, where O'Brien quickly established a rapport with President Daniel Ortega. The former Sandinista militant's struggle against the American-backed contras in the 1980s had been supported by O'Brien's mother, Iris, who regularly dragged the family to the American embassy in Dublin to protest against such injustices. Regaling the story to Nicaragua's head of government, O'Brien asked if he would sign a photograph for his mother. Ortega was delighted: 'Greetings to a fellow revolutionary', he wrote.

Digicel launched in El Salvador in 2007. It would be a tough battleground where some of the world's biggest telecoms companies had muscled in. Digicel would be competing with AT&T and Slim's company, America Movil.

So far O'Brien had built his mobile-phone companies, first in Ireland and then across the Caribbean, by going up against the monopoly operator. By becoming the second player in those markets, Digicel had quickly endeared itself to the public and won over five million customers. It was a more lucrative proposition from the start than attempting to launch as the third or fourth mobile phone company in the region, as it would be in Central America.

Within the telecoms industry there were rumours that O'Brien and Carlos Slim had a sort of 'gentleman's agreement' not to encroach on each other's patch. Slim wouldn't compete with Digicel in the Caribbean and O'Brien would steer clear of his Central American fiefdom. Whether this was true or apocryphal, Slim didn't challenge Digicel in the Caribbean for many years.

In 2007 everything changed. O'Brien moved into Slim's playground and a year later Slim brought his mobile phone company to Jamaica. America Movil, the largest mobile-phone group in Latin America and the Caribbean with more than 180 million customers, would be Digicel's fiercest competitor. Slim's deep pockets and equally formidable personality would ensure a hell of a fight. And his arrival at Independent News and Media was a reminder to O'Brien that he was keeping a close eye on his Irish rival.

And Digicel had moved into the South Pacific. That adventure had started just two years earlier, in much the same way as O'Brien's first Caribbean foray. A businessman seeking a partner to bid for the second mobile phone licence in Fiji contacted Digicel to see if O'Brien was interested. And he was.

Ken Mason, Digicel's business development director, opened the email. 'I was sceptical but sent it on to the chairman. It was the quickest response ever. Before I got up from my desk Denis had replied.' His boss was immediately enthusiastic. 'Sounds fantastic, go for it,' came his answer. 'Good markets are where monopolies operate.' So Mason got on a plane to Fiji to begin Digicel's South Pacific rollout.

Within a couple of years, a sister company, Digicel Pacific, was the fastest-growing mobile operator in the region, with a presence in Samoa, Tonga, Vanuatu, Fiji – where it had won the licence – and Papua New Guinea.

This Irishman was still prepared to invest and build a mobile-phone network in places shunned by his rivals. In the Pacific there were few more hostile territories to conquer than Papua New Guinea. Digicel's first reconnaissance team dispatched to the British colony had to travel deep into the jungle to scout out sites for phone masts, striking deals with the local chiefs along the way. When O'Brien visits, he works from an office protected by razor wire and a half-dozen security guards armed with shotguns and pistols. With a population of just under seven million, it is a very poor country, with about a third of the population estimated to be living on less than $1.25 a day. Yet it is the most important market in that region for Digicel in terms of contributing, revenues, cash flows and new customers. O'Brien is the country's biggest investor outside of the mining companies.

In Fiji, Digicel endured huge disruption and uncertainty before it managed to get its network up and running there. It was even forced to abandon its phone masts for a time during a coup. And having taken tea with Tonga's King George Tupou V, Digicel opened for business in what are known as the 'friendly islands' after buying a mobile-phone company from the monarch. O'Brien's team utilised the tried and trusted business plan that had worked so successfully since 2001. Digicel offered cheaper call packages and began to sponsor the most popular sports, rugby and cricket, including Fiji's national rugby squad. It also established the Digicel charitable foundation in Papua New Guinea, mainly to provide educational resources in that impoverished country.

And there were plans to enter Cuba, the Solomon Islands, East Timor, Nicaragua, Costa Rica and Belize, and to venture farther afield into the Middle East and the USA. O'Brien was keen to start selling his mobile phones to the almost twenty per cent of the US population who still didn't use the technology. The opportunity might be to sell cheap handsets activated with codes on prepaid phone cards, similar to the service Digicel provided in some of the world's poorest countries, he said. The customers would just have to figure it out.

O'Brien's ambition for his company was boundless. He had shown he could win new licences and launch businesses in difficult territories.

Back in Ireland he was still sparring with the O'Reillys and his presence was being noted throughout the newspaper group. Some observers noted a shift in the INM group's reporting of O'Brien's problems with the ongoing Tribunal investigation. There was a perception that his travails were being played down somewhat.

Irish Times Tribunal correspondent Colm Keena says there was a marked difference in the *Irish Independent*'s coverage of the inquiry as O'Brien's stake in the company increased. 'The coverage changed. It had assigned a reporter to publish straight reports on it for years. Now sometimes those reports were appearing deep inside the paper and sometimes nothing appeared.'

Sam Smyth, who reported on the investigation for the paper throughout its sittings, nevertheless says his approach to his job was the same before and after O'Brien's stake in the group swelled. 'I've always taken the view that I write it and it's the editor's view whether to publish it or not. It was other people who said it wasn't getting that same prominence, but then again that's how newspapers work. I have never seen any publicly owned newspaper work against its major shareholders. Most people would be very slow to start doing pejorative stories on the person who owns the newspaper and I make no apology for that. It doesn't mean that I have changed my opinion. That is the way the world works. Denis paid almost €200 million for Today FM and he didn't pay that to have it constantly driving down his reputation. And he has paid something like half a billion for Independent.'

The changes being noted by the public, however, were a pale shadow of the bitter hostilities that were rapidly intensifying behind the scenes. While O'Brien had failed to wield sufficient influence to seize control of INM, the group's immense debt was creating huge financial pressure as deadlines loomed for the repayment of a large chunk of its loans. Paul Connolly says that from the day he began dealing with O'Brien's interests in the company, he had harboured grave concerns about its financial future. 'Denis had made the bet and then realised how much was being borrowed to finance share buybacks and dividends.' Both Connolly and O'Brien believed the board had failed to grasp the extent of the company's impending financial crisis, something that would only accelerate in the eye of a global recession.

'I guess that is where fundamentally we and the seventeen directors differed,' says Connolly. 'They can't understand how Denis is so agitated, so difficult, shouting and roaring. They cannot get their heads around that and they see him as a pest and a nuisance.'

INM, he says, was being run like a private family company and, despite its deteriorating finances, was continuing to pay out huge dividends to shareholders, the biggest of whom was Sir Anthony: 'I take the view that the board took the decision for a €140 million share buyback and to pay dividends of over €250 million over the past two years that effectively drained the company of cash.' In Connolly's view, they took their eye off the ball and failed to deal with the loans that were maturing.

Fundamentally, the two warring shareholders hold opposing views on how the company should be managed. 'Those differences remain to this very day,' says Connolly.

By the beginning of 2009 INM's financial woes had worsened. Gavin O'Reilly was forced to warn shareholders that the group's profits would be well below expectations and that it was in crisis meetings with bond-holders who were owed hundreds of millions of euros. Shareholders on both sides were now fearful for the company's survival.

Worried by the unfolding financial disaster, O'Brien told Connolly to open talks with the enemy. Both sides were now under mounting financial pressure and the various banks and bond-holders watching the bitter exchanges were unimpressed by the bitter wrangling.

'I rang Gavin, not off my own bat, after the profit warning and said "I think we should have a coffee," ' Connolly says. The next morning O'Reilly arrived at Connolly's office. Just after 8 a.m., they began to discuss the unthinkable, at least from O'Reilly's perspective – the reorganisation of the board and the removal of its top executive. 'He and I just went back and forth over different things and agreed a truce mark one.'

'We tried a rapprochement in the belief that nobody should be hurling hand grenades at each other,' says Gavin O'Reilly. 'Some of the things we did in response in hindsight you wish you hadn't done. I think you learn from that. Unfortunately I don't think Denis learned very much from it because it was still a very public campaign. It was an attempt to say we shouldn't be having a fight for the sake of all shareholders. We knew the markets were going to be very difficult. We tried in earnest.'

Those difficult discussions continued over the following weeks and by mid-March it had been agreed to radically reduce the size of INM's board of directors. There was also agreement in principle that Sir Anthony – or 'AJ', as they referred to the former Dr A.J.F. O'Reilly – would relinquish control of his prized empire, but this would have to be carefully handled. O'Brien would meet his arch-enemy for the first time to formally ask him to resign.

'The whole thing was set up for AJ and Denis to meet on the morning of the Ireland v. England rugby match in Dublin,' Connolly says. It took a degree of choreography to organise the first face-to-face meeting between the two rival warriors, with Connolly and Gavin O'Reilly among those involved in coordinating the powwow.

'There was a bit of fuss first about where they would meet,' according to Connolly. 'Denis was kind of indifferent as long as it wasn't in Castlemartin [O'Reilly's County Kildare mansion].' Sir Anthony then suggested a meeting on neutral territory, at the home of his fellow former rugby international Ray McLoughlin, who had also forged a friendship with O'Brien over many years, and had been one of his early financial backers. But as McLoughlin had the decorators in, they finally agreed to a 'fireside chat' at Sir Anthony's palatial Dublin town house in Fitzwilliam Square, from where they could both easily make their way afterwards to Croke Park to watch the match.

O'Brien and Connolly tried to prepare the ground ahead of the meeting. They met McLoughlin at the International Rugby Football Union benevolent fund dinner the night before and outlined their position over a few pints. O'Brien spoke about what he wanted to achieve in his chat with Sir Anthony.

Just before lunchtime, O'Brien arrived in Fitzwilliam Square and was shown to the drawing room for an audience with his nemesis. O'Reilly's household staff had taken out the Waterford Crystal and Wedgwood tableware, setting the table for lunch. It was all very congenial.

For the next couple of hours O'Brien and Sir Anthony talked, rehashing the various points on which they vehemently disagreed. O'Brien told Connolly afterwards that 'AJ' seemed bewildered by his aggressive stance towards him and his company. 'They went over old ground and essentially they were trying to work out how they had got to this situation,' says Connolly. 'Denis was saying "Look, I am an

investor in this company and things haven't gone to plan."' They
'agreed to disagree' amicably and O'Brien left to go to the match.
They never got to eat lunch together that day. When he met
Connolly at Croke Park, O'Brien said he didn't know where things
would go next.

The pair were flying to the USA the next day as part of a new
fundraising round for Digicel. Connolly took a call from Gavin
O'Reilly, who was suggesting another meeting. McLoughlin simul-
taneously called O'Brien to persuade him to meet once more with Sir
Anthony. 'It was decided that Denis and Gavin, Ray and AJ would
meet again at Fitzwilliam Square, and at the last minute I was asked
to come along,' Connolly says.

McLoughlin and Gavin were already with Sir Anthony when they
arrived and they exchanged pleasantries before their host asked them
to allow himself and O'Brien a few minutes to talk alone. 'The three
of us were sent downstairs. I could see lunch was set up, the Waterford
glass was out and the bow-tied waiters were busy,' Connolly recalls.

Half an hour later, they were summoned back upstairs where they
joined the two opposing businessmen around a small circular table. For
the next couple of hours they again thrashed out their differences. 'We
were back and forth but it was inconclusive. We were saying, "The game
is up, AJ," but not as directly as that,' says Connolly. Again O'Brien left
O'Reilly's home frustrated. They had achieved nothing and once again
he left without lunch.

According to Gavin O'Reilly, O'Brien was both forceful and
charming during the exchange. 'I don't think Denis is the sort of guy
who is going to tip the hat to anyone, and why should he? I think he
has enough arrogance, and I say that in the positive sense, that he sees
himself in equal measure with the Tony O'Reillys, the Michael
Smurfits or the Peter Sutherlands of this world. 'Denis can be very
charming and so is my father,' he says. 'My father is, through the
good and the bad, probably more consensus-orientated. He is
charming and will be charming to the end and will try to persuade
you of his particular position. He has greater patience. I think Denis,
being a forceful character, will try to do the same, but then becomes
impatient. I think that is the difference between them.'

Sir Anthony's quest to reach a consensus ultimately failed. 'They disagreed on certain points and found a consensus position at a time and we hoped that we would all work towards it. For reasons that are only clear to Denis, that wasn't available,' says Gavin.

Connolly and Gavin continued to talk over the following days and weeks, but it was clear from these conversations that Sir Anthony wasn't budging. 'In early March we made another push. I met up with Gavin in the Citywest Hotel and from that meeting we started putting more shape on it,' Connolly says. 'Over the next few days we did the bones of an alignment or an understanding where there would be a phasing out of directors. The public relations aspect was dealt with. We didn't want the *Killing Fields*.' It would be an orderly transition, with some directors stepping down immediately while others would exit at the next annual general meeting.

Connolly, O'Brien's right-hand man Leslie Buckley and Lucy Gaffney would join the board, while Sir Anthony would yield to the pressure and after thirty-six years relinquish his control of INM. His upcoming seventy-third birthday in May 2009 was chosen as the date to mark his retirement from the group. He would assume the title of president emeritus. There would be little fuss about his departure, he insisted.

Connolly didn't get the impression that Sir Anthony spoke to a lot of people about his retirement, not even his sons. 'I think he came to that realisation himself. Maybe he had talked to Ray,' he suggests.

Gavin O'Reilly concurs, saying his father decided it was time to let go. 'I think my father had made up his own mind. It was just a question of timing. He wanted to step down on his birthday. He thought there was a nice symmetry there.'

It had been a miserable year for Sir Anthony and his family. By now Waterford Wedgwood had collapsed and with it had gone the €400 million he and his brother-in-law had pumped in to try to save it. INM's bond-holders, meanwhile, were demanding huge debt repayments. Now he was exiting the business. 'I think he was more exasperated with bond-holders at that stage than anyone else,' Connolly says. 'It was a case of "Jesus, how did this come to pass?"'

But while he would no longer be INM's chief executive, Sir Anthony ensured that the role would pass to the next generation, with Gavin stepping into his shoes. His two other sons, Cameron and

Tony junior, however, would be leaving the company alongside their father.

There was some surprise at the announcement when it came. It marked a sea change at INM. It was headline news. In a statement, Sir Anthony said it had been a pleasure to have worked with a range of highly talented and hugely committed directors and colleagues at the group. 'My appreciation of them is undiminished by time. Together we have expanded this Irish newspaper group and enshrined a fiercely independent editorial policy that is widely respected across the world.'

O'Brien was quick to praise his rival. 'I welcome the changes to the board and the appointment of Gavin O'Reilly as group CEO,' he said. 'I would like to thank Tony O'Reilly for his long-standing contribution to the company. I welcome Tony as president emeritus and also take the opportunity to wish him well in his retirement.'

Gavin assured the media that these events marked the end of the confrontation between the two factions. 'I'm happy to say it's water under the bridge. We've been working with and talking to Denis and Denis's colleagues for quite some time now. This is a triumph for common sense and in the interest of all shareholders.'

Sir Anthony was still in situ when O'Brien's three representatives attended their first board meeting. These gatherings would be much smaller affairs in the future, with the head count reduced from twenty to ten. Sources say the outgoing chief executive was most gracious to the new arrivals, singling out each of the three for a special welcome. Buckley he had known for many years, having hired him in a previous attempt to restructure Waterford Crystal. He mentioned that he knew Connolly's father from his rugby days. And Gaffney, he said, would bring some glamour to the boardroom.

Connolly was surprised to see that all his conversations with Gavin O'Reilly in the preceding months had been faithfully recorded in the boardroom minutes. 'He has a good recollection,' Connolly says of Gavin. 'It was funny to see it recorded with "P. Connolly said this". It was like something you would see in a rugby programme.' Connolly had also relayed the details of these conversations to O'Brien during constant and lengthy phone calls.

It was a remarkable result for O'Brien but a pyrrhic victory. While he had wrested control from Sir Anthony, and was sending his three loyal lieutenants to do battle in the boardroom, INM was a pale shadow of itself. Over the previous twelve months the group's share price had fallen by more than ninety per cent. A company, which at its peak had been worth more than €2 billion, was now valued at just €143 million and had debts totalling €1.4 billion.

O'Brien could claim to have slain his enemy, but it had cost him more than €500 million to do it, while there was no guarantee either that the company would survive or that he would ever control it.

21 Denis

In April 2008 Denis O'Brien turned fifty and hosted a huge party for his friends and family. His wife Catherine organised the bash at a local rugby club where she re-created his favourite pub — Hartigan's — inside a marquee. To add authenticity, pub owners Evelyn and Alfie Mulligan joined the O'Briens on the rope line as they welcomed more than one hundred guests to a night at his local. The dress code was casual: the men should turn up in jeans, the invitation advised.

It was an opportunity to gather friends from school and university as well as colleagues who had worked with Denis to create his business empire, some of whom had made fortunes themselves from his endeavours. Together they mingled in a relaxed atmosphere — after all, O'Brien was still keen to be seen as 'one of the lads'. Photographers gathered outside found few celebrities to snap apart from Taoiseach Brian Cowen, who stopped by to convey his best wishes. Everyone danced the night away to the sound of Canadian rocker Bryan Adams. And it was a big crew: these were his loyal and trusted friends, who always celebrated his achievements. For the Irish billionaire, this was a happy time and perhaps the pinnacle of his amazing success.

One of the wealthiest Irishmen who had built an international empire, O'Brien had become an international player and was the man renowned for going head-to-head with the world's richest man, telecoms billionaire Carlos Slim. His Digicel group was a rapidly-expanding mobile phone operator valued at over $2 billion. It employed more than five thousand staff with over ten million customers in twenty-three countries, stretching from the Caribbean to the South Pacific. It's a high-growth, high-risk business, the kind O'Brien loves.

'Running a business with a growth rate of three or four per cent is great, but it's fucking boring,' he insists. 'If you are running a business that is growing by twenty-five per cent a year – *hello*, that's exciting!'

In 2009 O'Brien's Digicel group achieved revenues of over $2 billion, by which time the South Pacific operation that began in 2006 was contributing more than $80 million, with almost two million subscribers. In 2010 it was subsumed into the Digicel Caribbean and Central American operations in a deal that valued the Pacific operations at $825 million and allowed O'Brien to take out $500 million in cash. He runs Digicel as a highly leveraged company, loading it up with debts of more than $1 billion so far, for which he himself is personally liable. However, he is able to raise the funds from bond holders eager to back his ambitious expansion plans and this business model allows him access to hundreds of millions in cash to invest in other sectors.

Digicel's success catapulted O'Brien into the world's billionaire club with *Forbes* magazine ranking him at 258 in 2010, with an estimated $3.5 billion (€2.5 billion) fortune. Beyond telecoms he has invested in everything from start-up technology companies, through his venture capital company e-Island, to the PGA European Tour Courses, which runs twelve golf courses in Europe. His Aergo Capital is also involved in the aviation sector, leasing aircraft across the globe. He still retains a blocking stake in Aer Lingus to keep Ryanair at bay – a deal that has been loss-making for him, with estimates that he could be out of pocket by more than €4 million. O'Brien has always dabbled in the property sector, too, building a portfolio of commercial and residential properties that includes at least three substantial homes in South Dublin as well as a three-acre site purchased from his alma mater, University College Dublin.

And of course he is also a media baron. Communicorp, the company that grew out of his first successful venture at Dublin's 98FM radio station in the mid 1990s, is now a significant media group, being one of the largest radio groups in Central and Eastern Europe, with forty-two radio stations across nine countries. And with two nationwide stations as well as a number of local radio operations in Ireland, O'Brien is a powerful member of the fourth estate, who has shown he is prepared to garner ever more influence through his efforts to control the Independent News and Media group.

The $500 million in cash that O'Brien took from the last Digicel refinancing was in fact shy of the €550 million lost in his Independent News and Media investment, yet he was still prepared to invest further millions in the company once controlled by his great rival, Sir Anthony O'Reilly. His relationship with the O'Reilly family was fractious. While the two warring shareholders attempted to put on a united front to appease bond holders and others with a vested interest in the crisis-ridden group, that truce was short-lived. An insight into the level of hostility could be gleaned from reports of a conversation between chief executive Gavin O'Reilly and O'Brien in 2009. The Digicel owner warned that the group's financial crisis was so bad that the Independent stable of newspapers would have to seek court protection from its creditors. This alarming statement could only undermine confidence in the business; it also drew an angry response from O'Reilly and his management team. The *Sunday Times* reported that during one fiery telephone exchange O'Brien told O'Reilly that if he wanted 'a fight', then he would 'destroy both him and his father' and 'go after everything.' Meanwhile, O'Brien's three lieutenants, Paul Connolly, Lucy Gaffney and Leslie Buckley, fought his corner in the company's newly constituted boardroom.

After months of bitter conflict, it was O'Reilly who claimed victory. The majority of the group's shareholders backed the chief executive's rescue plan over O'Brien's. He was outmanoeuvred, for now. Independent News and Media group would re-structure its debts and raise funds by issuing further shares, thereby diluting the stakes held by existing shareholders, including O'Brien. To continue to wield some influence there, he would have to buy more shares.

Initially he walked away, though privately he let it be known that his battle for the Independent was suspended, not abandoned. Within a few months he returned to raise his stake from fourteen to almost nineteen per cent, making him Independent News and Media's single biggest shareholder. It was a serious statement of intent. Most observers believe he will mount a fresh bid to control the group in the future. Some say a victory at the Independent would be O'Brien's 'sweetest' and most satisfying deal of all.

Denis O'Brien has left his mark on the company. Indeed, he could claim a starring role in ousting Sir Anthony O'Reilly from the company that he built and led for over three decades. What's more, the group was forced to adopt some of O'Brien's suggestions to keep afloat. The most high profile of these suggestions came in March 2010 when the loss-making London *Independent* and *Independent on Sunday* newspapers were sold for £1 to Russian billionaire and ex-KGB man Alexander Lebedev. Naturally, this was a difficult and humiliating deal to execute, but the media group needed to cut its losses in the British market.

Gavin O'Reilly hopes the group's shareholders will manage to co-exist more harmoniously in future but is under no illusions about O'Brien's feelings towards him. 'I don't want any tensions going forward,' he says. 'Shareholders should have a board that is not reflective of any one group. We shouldn't be responding to the whims of any shareholder. It's terribly important that we have a truly independent board that is not representing Tony O'Reilly or Denis O'Brien, but is representing everyone.' And he accepts that he will never form part of O'Brien's 'circle of love' – 'I don't think I am ever going to win Denis's love and admiration,' he says.

At heart, Denis O'Brien is fiercely proud of being Irish and will always fly his country's flag in his international business exploits. He readily committed to join the first Global Irish Economic Forum of Irish business figures hosted by the Irish government to chart a means for the country to overcome the enormous economic challenges that it faces in the wake of a sustained property bubble being punctured. O'Brien stood alongside Taoiseach Brian Cowen and his friend Dermot Desmond, Bob Geldof and other lauded patriots to offer a vision for the future.

In fact, he cares deeply about his image in his home country and even though he is one of the most successful Irishmen of his generation, he feels that his achievements have been tarnished by the ongoing investigation into the circumstances surrounding the award of his first mobile phone licence in 1996, the source of his first great fortune. He fears the outcome of the inquiry could damage his reputation and possibly affect his far-flung business empire.

It's more than a decade since his former best friend Barry Maloney sensationally stated under oath that O'Brien told him that he had paid money to the minister awarding the licence. O'Brien doesn't dispute the conversation but claims it was a 'spoof'. During the eleven-year probe there have been many conflicts of evidence, mostly between O'Brien and former minister Michael Lowry and other testifying parties. There are also several events that are either totally coincidental or indeed, suspicious.

The judge overseeing the Inquiry must answer two crucial questions: did O'Brien make a payment to Lowry, and was Ireland's second mobile phone licence awarded unfairly? If he finds the answer to those two questions is yes, then he will have to state whether, in his opinion, the process was corrupted because of any money that O'Brien gave to Lowry. His findings need only be proven on the balance of probability and while this is a lesser burden of proof than necessary in court, the Tribunal report will carry weight, as Judge Michael Moriarty is one of Ireland's most experienced and respected High Court judges.

O'Brien has had plenty of time to brace himself for Moriarty's final report and got a foretaste of its contents in late 2008 when the judge confidentially circulated his preliminary findings to him and other key witnesses. The telecoms boss gasped as he read it. Moriarty found that the licence was issued 'illegally' because of O'Brien's 'corrupt' relationship with former communications minister Michael Lowry, according to O'Brien. The report, based on the extensive evidence and the testimony of more than seventy witnesses, contained seventy-nine findings, sixty of them negative towards O'Brien. 'They've destroyed Lowry and they've destroyed me,' claimed O'Brien. The findings appeared to back the claims of the consortia who lost out to Esat Digifone in the licence competition that the process was flawed and wrongly favoured O'Brien's bid.

Potentially, the consequences of Judge Moriarty eventually publishing these findings are enormous. O'Brien would be associated with bribing a government minister whose department awarded the most lucrative licence in Irish history. The judge could recommend the findings be considered by the Director of Public Prosecutions and other bodies with a view to taking criminal proceedings. And if the judge stated that O'Brien's actions had contributed towards the length of the Inquiry, he might be forced to pick up the Tribunal's immense costs for that specified period. This was an appalling vista that O'Brien wanted to avert at all costs: his competitors would use the damning findings against him, he claimed. It would be a grave injustice.

He is said to be mindful of the damage suffered by his close friend and business associate Dermot Desmond, when in 1993 an Inspector appointed by the Irish High Court issued a report into a land purchase in Dublin that was highly critical of Desmond's role. 'Dermot got minced by the media,' says Paul Meagher of the reporting of those findings angrily refuted by Desmond. 'He [Desmond] has fought a good rearguard action since and Denis has watched this.'

Desmond, who was once a shareholder in Esat Digifone, is himself aggrieved with the Tribunal's investigation that questions his late arrival at the mobile phone company just as it was about to be awarded the licence. Pledging to underwrite O'Brien's share of the consortium as well as his own, he replaced a group of shareholders at the last minute. Desmond has since given evidence at the long-running Inquiry, incurring millions of euros in legal fees as a result. He shares O'Brien's concerns and contempt for the process.

O'Brien is said to sympathise with Michael Lowry, the former minister who awarded the licence and whose reputation is also on the line as he awaits the final report. 'You may say it is misguided but he admires Lowry as someone who brought competition,' says Meagher. 'He fears that he has been victimised and vilified, particularly by [journalist] Sam Smyth, who always refers to him as "the disgraced former minister".'

The telecoms tycoon, Lowry and others whose reputations were slighted by the judge's preliminary findings are challenging those negative findings in a last-ditch attempt to force Moriarty to revise his opinion. O'Brien launched a high-profile campaign to defend himself and discredit the Tribunal that included a newspaper advertisement to embarrass its most senior lawyers, who had been his nemeses for more than a decade.

The Tribunal was one of a number of inquiries established by the Irish government to investigate serious allegations of corruption and other matters of public interest. They were designed to report within a relatively short period of time but proved to be a lengthy and ludicrously expensive means of investigation. Moriarty's Inquiry into the mobile phone licence arose from a probe into payments made to former minister Michael Lowry during his tenure in government and is the longest-running investigation of this type.

Meanwhile, the Irish public has grown jaded with this and other tribunals. They have seen senior barristers become exceedingly rich at their expense, with few prosecutions arising from the findings. With the bill for the Moriarty Tribunal expected to run to about €100 million and likely to be picked up by the Irish taxpayer, the calls to wind it up are loud.

The Inquiry's senior legal team, which included Jerry Healy, John Coughlan and Jacqueline O'Brien, earned up to €2,500 a day and, as the days turned into years, their total fees ran at more than €6 million, in Jacqueline O'Brien's case, while Coughlan and Healy each earned more than €9 million. Healy controversially had advised one of the losing bidders, Persona, following the competition and went on to lead the investigation into that licence award.

When details of their expenses claims were published in the *Sunday Times*, O'Brien found ammunition for his first strike against the Tribunal. Jacqueline O'Brien had successfully submitted an expense claim for some modest items: two Belgian chocolates from a hotel mini-bar costing €6.25 while on official business in 2002. Colleague Jerry Healy claimed for a £1.50 tip while a solicitor submitted a claim that included £7 for a Toblerone and a £4 tip but this was refused.

In mid 2009 O'Brien commissioned an advertisement featuring a picture of two Belgian chocolates with the heading 'Expensive and Filled with Nuts'. Though it contained no reference to him, it was clear that the mobile phone entrepreneur was behind it. Indeed he claims to have received a 'fantastic response' from the public: 'People are saying, "Give us more." These people [the Moriarty lawyers] need

to be made to look ridiculous. It's like they're saying, "We get paid
€5.8m from the State but we're going to charge for chocolates from
room service". God almighty, one of my staff wouldn't do that in a
million years!'

Next, he invited journalists from the Sunday newspapers to his
office to give a series of interviews where he would discuss the judge's
confidential preliminary findings. Some of the press had obtained
leaked copies of parts of this explosive report but were prevented
from publishing the contents by the Tribunal. Meagher says that as
O'Brien believed every journalist in Dublin already had a copy of the
preliminary report, he decided to go ahead and make it public. It was
a bold move, unlikely to impress the judge, but he needed to take
control and get his retaliation in ahead of the final report. 'We won
the licence, fair and square,' he told each journalist. The sixty negative
findings against him were 'all wrong', he continued. He was the
victim of a grave injustice.

The Tribunal was 'out to get a scalp' to justify its enormous cost, he
claimed. 'I want to be clear: my name, my reputation, is at stake here.
I will confront them on this and the ads are just one part of it,' he
insisted. Indeed, there was nothing wrong with the licence
competition except for what he described as 'Mickey Mouse' stuff. 'If
you take any licence competition, will everything be perfect?' asked
O'Brien. 'There are bound to be some human errors but not serious
things.'

Paul Meagher, who had by now joined his friend's legal team at the
Tribunal, advised against making such public statements. O'Brien had
since parted company with his long-standing lawyer, Owen
O'Connell from William Fry, and the senior counsel who defended
him throughout most of the process, Eoin McGonigal. Barrister Jim
O'Callaghan, who had worked with McGonigal for O'Brien, stepped
up to lead the charge. Their client had always been prone to public
outbursts and nobody could dissuade him when he wanted to vent
his frustration.

'You could tell him, don't do the ads and don't do interviews and
keep your counsel to yourself, but nobody tells Denis what to do,'
explained Meagher. 'I know how much he is hurting from the
damage. He doesn't want to be seen as a victim but he doesn't

understand why certain elements in the media have wanted to knock him from the very start. They always wanted to say that the licence wasn't won fairly and this has led on to this monster that is the Moriarty Tribunal.'

O'Brien also launched his own website – www.moriartytribunal.com – in 2009 which claims to 'present the true picture' of the Inquiry and the events being investigated. 'You're paying for it – start judging for yourself!', it says.

He secured a major victory when his legal team and others forced the judge to admit to two significant errors that affected whether it was legal for the Department to have issued the licence to Esat Digifone in light of Dermot Desmond's late arrival as a company shareholder. The Tribunal's legal team admitted that it had privately met with officials from the Attorney General's office in 2002 on this matter, when it was concluded the licence was issued legally, but failed to disclose this fact in the intervening years. It was a significant error that undermined the credibility of the Inquiry to some degree. More importantly, it could force the judge to alter some of his negative findings.

Later, O'Brien convinced Michael Andersen, the Danish independent consultant overseeing the licence competition, to give evidence. In an affidavit sent to the judge in March 2010, Andersen defended the process, insisting Esat Digifone's application was one of the best he had ever seen in any competition and echoing many of O'Brien's concerns about the manner in which the investigation was being conducted. Even at this late stage, his evidence bolstered O'Brien's position. O'Brien believes that given the errors that have been uncovered, Moriarty should now stand aside and an independent judge be appointed to review the evidence. 'If the provisional findings had been issued as a final report it would have been a travesty of justice for me and many others, including seventeen senior and respected civil servants,' O'Brien has claimed.

His fight-back has certainly won him some sympathy but much depends on the judge's final report. Meanwhile, Moriarty refuses to be deterred from his work by the attacks: 'None of these criticisms will interfere with the impartial discharge of my remit, nor will they deflect me from ensuring that fair procedures are adhered to in bringing my work to conclusion, and nor will they inhibit me from reporting without fear or favour.'

Seasoned Tribunal followers suggest the Inquiry's credibility has been damaged but that it could still land a blow on O'Brien. 'If a judge of the High Court of Ireland makes findings suggesting that Denis O'Brien was part of the corruption of the second mobile phone licence and that he paid money to the minister for that licence, how would that go down with the major banks and the large companies he deals with and who invest in his companies?' asks journalist Sam Smyth. 'Will they be asking, can they afford to be hugger-mugger with somebody against whom such grave allegations are made?'

Then there is the disgrace, Smyth adds. 'Denis is justifiably proud of all he has achieved and the fact that he is one of the most gifted businessmen in the country, but if a High Court Judge says he was involved with corruption and if that's his opinion of him, I'd say it would be devastating for Denis. He has been so robust in the past, what is he likely to do if that happens? I'm not sure he has many options.'

Another Tribunal reporter, Colm Keena, says that while it is extremely hard to prove corruption, the judge's report could impact on O'Brien's substantial media business in Ireland and his ambition to control the Independent News and Media group. 'What will the government do if there are negative findings against someone who has such a strong influence over the media here?' he asks. 'A lot will depend on whether the Tribunal thinks he has been straight with it.'

Disappointed bidders will no doubt seek to use any adverse findings in future claims for compensation against the Irish state, should the competition be found to have been flawed. If this came to pass, the State might counter-sue O'Brien to recover any due compensation.

Others suggest he has little to fear. The events being examined happened such a long time ago and O'Brien has long since sold his stake in Esat Digifone and taken his spoils away from Ireland to replicate and build on his success in new territories. Even if the judge concludes there was corruption, there is no history of successful prosecution of so-called 'white-collar crime' in Ireland. When Moriarty finally presents his report, the public is entitled to question whether it was worth it. And if O'Brien is vindicated, he will almost certainly seek restitution.

According to many of his friends, Denis O'Brien's decision to become a tax exile, thus depriving the Irish state issuing the licence of any tax revenues on his €317 million fortune from the sale of Esat Telecom to BT, was a bad one. In terms of his public image in Ireland, it has compounded his difficulties, providing further ammunition for his detractors to paint him in a negative light, they claim. O'Brien's immediate circle also say that he no longer talks about his former best friend, Barry Maloney. Indeed, Paul Meagher insists that he has 'moved on' from all the hurt caused by the allegation: 'He never discusses it and will not engage in any negativity. He would just view it as an irritating topic.'

Maloney used his great fortune from the sale of Esat Digifone to BT in 2000 to build the successful venture capital group, Balderton Capital. He still lives in Dublin and often bumps into some of O'Brien's 'rat pack'.

Beyond his evidence at the Tribunal, Maloney has never spoken publicly about these events. Just why the best friends fell out so spectacularly remains a mystery.

As the waiting game continues, O'Brien's family and friends are apprehensive about when the Tribunal might end. 'I wouldn't rule out the possibility that Denis will challenge it,' Meagher predicts. 'He could take a judicial review in the High Court and he could go to Europe. He said he will fight it street-by-street, and he will.'

Former Esat executive Conor Lenihan, who is now a junior minister in the Fianna Fáil-led government and a close friend of O'Brien's, says he would 'walk through walls or glass to prove a point – that's the type of fella he is.' Another former employee, television presenter Mark Cagney, believes O'Brien should be judged on his achievements: 'When you think of mobile phones and texting, if Motorola or someone else other than Esat Digifone had won, would it be any better or worse?'

O'Brien's father describes the Tribunal as an 'annoyance' but believes his son has nothing to fear. 'He did nothing wrong. It is terrible that he had to go through this bloody thing, particularly after what he created and the employment he gave,' he insists. 'But we are a very strong family, we see a lot of each other. He has a fantastic wife – she is a great support. She stays in the background for the children.'

Just as he claims to have received a private business education from his father, O'Brien's eldest son Jack has attended a few Digicel board meetings, where he witnessed his father hauling staff over the coals. Digicel chief executive Colm Delves says the eleven-year-old eventually reached for his Nintendo, but was getting a feel for the family business.

It is an irritation that his travails with the Tribunal in Ireland follow O'Brien across the globe. Media organisations in the various countries where Digicel operates regularly publish updates on the investigation.

O'Brien has said that he doesn't think about Carlos Slim and his €39 billion fortune every day, but he is always on his radar. Slim, who declined to be interviewed for this book, is known to closely monitor Digicel and keeps an eye on O'Brien's battles, at home and abroad. The Mexican billionaire is likely to remain his toughest competitor and may also be the man to buy Digicel in the future. Digicel's presence in countries where Slim hasn't expanded makes it a potentially attractive acquisition in the longer term. 'Carlos is the man to sell to,' one observer says of Digicel. And while O'Brien insists Digicel is not for sale, his ultimate goal may be to pull off another mega deal with Slim. 'Anything is possible,' admits one of his associates.

In 2010 another of his rivals enjoyed a victory against the Irishman. Cable & Wireless, the Caribbean's oldest mobile phone provider, ceded much ground to Digicel as it struggled to cope with its new competitor in these islands, but it won a court battle that could cost O'Brien more than £25 million.

Digicel claimed its rival relentlessly tried to block its entry into the Caribbean market, where Cable & Wireless had been the monopoly before O'Brien's arrival, but after a trial that lasted seventy-seven days in London, a High Court judge dismissed all but one claim. Disappointingly, in the one area where the judge ruled in Digicel's favour – where he found Cable & Wireless at fault in frustrating its rival's entry into the Turks and Caicos Islands – he awarded derisory damages of just £2. Digicel had sought damages of £300 million. Cable & Wireless chief executive Tony Rice described the outcome as a 'resounding victory' – 'This case has been a pointless waste of time and money. I am delighted we have won and are now free from this unnecessary distraction.'

Digicel's allegations centred on problems it claimed to have experienced in trying to connect to Cable & Wireless's network when it moved into new markets between 2002 and 2006. It also claimed a conspiracy to keep the company out of some Caribbean territories and sought loss of earnings. O'Brien's company claimed its competitor broke the law in Barbados, Cayman, St Lucia, St Vincent and the Grenadines, Grenada and the Turks and Caicos islands. It also made similar claims against the company owned by Cable & Wireless, together with the government of Trinidad and Tobago – TSTT – that had upset Digicel's plans in that market; it was one of the few places where it was forced to close some of its mobile phone shops in the face of the stiff opposition from TSTT. The judge had some sympathy, describing senior TSTT executives and its contractor Nortel as acting, 'contrary to honest practices'. Digicel is seeking a full Inquiry into these actions.

The case may prove to be a setback financially, but by appearing as the underdog, the company that championed competition and brought value to consumers, Digicel endeared itself to millions of mobile phone users. Across the Caribbean, it is the dominant brand – ahead of Coca-Cola and McDonald's – and hopes to emulate that success in Central America and the South Pacific. And O'Brien carries a long list of countries that Digicel is still keen to conquer.

In the short-term, the re-building of Digicel's network in Haiti after the earthquake will be a priority. The group had insurance in place to cover structural damage and any interruption of its business due to a natural disaster. In the months afterwards, it received $20 million of the $40 million claim it was due. Digicel believes Haiti's telecoms market could double in size in five years if a donor-backed reconstruction effort successfully creates jobs and wealth in this impoverished economy.

As Haiti's biggest investor, O'Brien is at the forefront of efforts to alleviate the terrible devastation. He immediately sanctioned a $5 million donation from Digicel and is using his mobile phone network to raise further funds. In acknowledgement of his work, the Haitian government appointed him a goodwill ambassador to Port-au-Prince and he is working closely with former US President Bill Clinton and others on an economic recovery plan. His charitable foundation will also be involved in the rebuild, particularly focusing on the provision of schools and educational requirements.

Whether Digicel is eventually sold or not, everyone who knows Denis O'Brien insists that he will carry on until he drops. Denis senior, who is now in his 70s, still works. His mother Iris remains an activist and travels with her husband while acting as an interpreter to explain Plusvital's horse products to agents in France, Spain and Italy.

The telecoms boss who is such a prominent figure on the world stage describes how he has learned to cope with managing business and family life. He divides his life in two, he says, half of his time to his wife, family and friends and the rest to business. 'I just carve and make sure of it. I am fortunate enough to have the flexibility to change something that I don't like doing and a lot of people don't have that. I can do long spurts – work for two to three weeks really, really hard every day and then take a week off.'

He just loves doing business. According to associates, for him it is all about the 'thrill of the kill' – 'I will never get tired of the business. Entrepreneurs never know when to leave the casino, they always want to start another business. It is part of you,' he has admitted.

Friend and colleague Leslie Buckley hopes that he will take things a bit easier in the years ahead. 'If he keeps at that pace, something must give,' he says. 'It's very hard to pull back, I know, but because the guy has so many strengths he needs to be around for a long time. I don't want to sound patronising but I actually do believe that.'

In the future O'Brien says that he can envisage doing something completely different, maybe in the not-for-profit sector, where he has built a foundation and supported projects throughout the world. His commitment to Haiti is likely to be a lengthy one, too. Clinton believes they will work together long into their old age. Whatever he does, Denis O'Brien's friends know that he will remain an obsessive user of the technology that has made him so wealthy. He'll always be 'on the blower', wheeling and dealing and obsessing about beating his competitors. As he has said: 'Get big fast. [Damn] the cost. Be brave. Go over the cliff. [The competition] doesn't have the balls.'

Interviews

In compiling this book I interviewed more than eighty people, some of whom spoke openly about Denis O'Brien, while others provided background information and are referred to as sources or associates.

O'Brien declined to be interviewed for *A Mobile Fortune*. I have bumped into him in the course of writing this book and have interviewed him on two previous occasions. In 2004 I spoke to him about his time as Tony Ryan's apprentice for my book *Ryanair* where he was quoted about that experience. In 2005 I interviewed him for *The Irish Times* where, in a lengthy piece, he spoke about his life and business career. I have used that material in this book together with other interviews he has given over the years in other media outlets.

His father, Denis O'Brien senior, spoke to me about his son, as did his school friend, Conn Clissmann. Many of his close friends and business acquaintances also gave of their time to discuss O'Brien. They include, Digicel deputy chairman Leslie Buckley, Communicorp chairperson Lucy Gaffney, his friend and business advisor Paul Connolly and one of his closest friends, and his personal lawyer, Paul Meagher.

A number of people spoke about O'Brien's early business exploits, such as renowned theatre producer Fred O'Donovan, who founded Esat with him and television producer David Heffernan who worked on the failed Home Shopping Television Network. Sir Michael Smurfit also discussed his impressions of the young entrepreneur he backed in his first ventures.

TV3 television presenter, Mark Cagney, talked about his early days as a DJ at Classic Hits 98FM and Conor Lenihan TD, the Minister for Science, Technology, Innovation and Natural Resources, recounted his time as the station's political correspondent and as an executive at Esat Digifone. He remains a close friend of his former employer.

His rivals in the radio business in the early years, Mike Hogan and FM 104 former boss, Dermot Hanrahan, spoke about waging war against his radio station. Hogan is now the executive producer of *Rising Stars*, a television talent show in the Caribbean sponsored by Digicel.

PJ Mara, now a director of Digicel, spoke about his early dealings with O'Brien when he was seeking a radio licence in the Czech Republic in the 1990s, his involvement with Esat's application for Ireland's second mobile phone licence in 1995 and his subsequent alliance with him at the international mobile phone group. Public relations executive Eileen Gleeson talked about working with O'Brien at Esat Digifone and Esat Telecom and handling the media for him during the early years of the Tribunal of Investigation's inquiry into the mobile phone licence. Venture capital executive Massimo Prelz Oltramonti recounts Advent's initial investment in O'Brien's Communicorp and its involvement with its bid for Ireland's second mobile phone licence.

Former Communciations Ministers Alan Dukes and Mary O'Rourke TD gave interviews about their impressions and memories of O'Brien's early assault on Ireland's telecom-munications sector. Cathal Magee, a former executive with eircom, the company formerly known as Telecom Eireann, that was the state-owned telecoms provider in Ireland, recalled the arrival of the new entrant into the market, and O'Brien's subsequent attempt to buy it years later in a bidding battle won by Sir Anthony O'Reilly.

Sean Corkery, the head of Dell's operations in Europe, spoke about his days as Esat Telecoms chief operations officer and Greenstar chief executive, Neil Parkinson, recalled his experiences as the company's finance director. Stephen Brewer, the head of Telecom Eireann's mobile subsidiary, Eircell, talks about the rivalry between the two companies in the mid 1990s. He was later hired by Cable & Wireless in the Caribbean to do battle with O'Brien's Digicel. Brewer also worked for Digicel in Trinidad and Tobago. Con Scanlon, the former general secretary of the Communications Workers Union, recalls the battle for eircom.

I travelled to Jamaica in 2009 where I interviewed a wide range of people. At Digicel, I spoke to the group's chief executive, Colm Delves, chief financial officer, Lawrence Hickey, chief operations officer, Kevin White and former Digicel Jamaica boss, David Hall. Hickey, White and Hall all previously worked with O'Brien at Esat Telecom. Other Digicel executives, past and present who spoke to me were Lisa Lewis, Harry Smith, Ken Mason and Mark Linehan.

Some of Digicel's rivals met with me and Paul Aspin, an executive working with Cable & Wireless who was charged with maintaining the telecoms company's sponsorship of the West Indies cricket team, spoke about the row after Digicel snatched the coveted deal. I spoke to a number of journalists as part of my research in Jamaica and to columnist and public-relations consultant Jean Lowrie Chin, who worked with Digicel in the early years. Lisa Bell, an executive at Jamaica Trade and Invest, spoke about Digicel's arrival in Jamaica and former Prime Minister of Jamaica PJ Patterson talked about Digicel's impact there and about O'Brien.

Gavin O'Reilly, chief executive of the Independent News and Media group, recounted his experiences of dealing with its dissident share-holder, O'Brien, and the events surrounding Sir Anthony's departure from the company's board in 2009. Media lecturer Michael Foley comments on O'Brien's increasing dominance in the Irish media sector.

Mary Davis, the former chief executive of Special Olympics Ireland, and Mary Lawlor, director of FrontLine, spoke about O'Brien's charitable and human-rights interests. Maria Mulcahy, a college friend of O'Brien's who oversees his charitable foundations in Ireland, Jamaica, Haiti and Papua New Guinea talked about this side of O'Brien's life as did Major General Robert Neish, of the Digicel Foundation.

Seasoned Tribunal watchers, *Irish Times* reporter Colm Keena and the *Irish Independent* columnist Sam Smyth, discussed the lengthy inquiry.

A large number of people also spoke to me but did not wish to be quoted. I would like to express my sincere gratitude to everyone for giving their time and assistance to me in writing this book. I would also like to thank my family and my many valued friends for their support and encouragement.

Index